AF606059

About the Cover Artwork

This work speaks to the joining hands relationships practiced by 15M citizens as together they exemplify democracy here and now. Inspired by the works of Remedios Varo, a Catalan-born surrealist painter who fought in the Spanish Civil War, this painting represents the continuous journey of those who keep alive democratic practices in a contemporary setting. With packaging materials symbolizing systems, structures and the limits and margins they delineate, the interaction between them and living entities brings renewed life to what would otherwise be a linear static environment.

The practices of 15M citizens once gathered in squares continue to exist in less perceptible ways today. Following from this, the painting depicts "*La Pasionaria*,"* engaging in the transformative activities of 15M participants. The tensions of human relationships in their interconnectivity, allow us to imagine and create spaces of renewed transformation and life with each other, our ecosystem and established structures.

La Pasionaria by Karen Yen
Size: 97 x 130 cm
Medium: Acrylic and graphite

This artwork brings together painting and drawing through a digital collage. The hands were separately drawn and placed digitally on the scanned painting and the "threads" were drawn digitally. The process of combining the human hand and the digital is to show the presence of technology in the democratic practices of 15M citizens.

* Name of the van with which Pablo travelled, also the nickname of the Civil War Republican politician Dolores Ibárruri, and the common name of the flower depicted on the centre-bottom of the painting (Bluecrown Passionflower/Passiflora caerulea).

Democracy Here and Now

The Exemplary Case of Spain

PABLO OUZIEL

UNIVERSITY OF TORONTO PRESS
Toronto Buffalo London

Toronto Buffalo London
utorontopress.com
Printed in the U.S.A.

ISBN 978-1-4875-4317-4 (cloth)
ISBN 978-1-4875-4318-1 (EPUB)
ISBN 978-1-4875-4319-8 (PDF)

Library and Archives Canada Cataloguing in Publication

Title: Democracy here and now : the exemplary case of Spain / Pablo Ouziel.
Names: Ouziel, Pablo, author.
Description: Includes bibliographical references and index.
Identifiers: Canadiana (print) 20210382252 | Canadiana (ebook) 20210382317 | ISBN 9781487543174 (cloth) | ISBN 9781487543181 (EPUB) | ISBN 9781487543198 (PDF)
Subjects: LCSH: 15-M (Organization) | LCSH: Democratization – Spain – History – 21st century. | LCSH: Social movements – Spain – History – 21st century. | LCSH: Protest movements – Spain – History – 21st century. | LCSH: Political participation – Spain – History – 21st century. | LCSH: Spain – Social conditions – 21st century.
Classification: LCC HN583.5.O99 2022 | DDC 306.0946–dc23

We wish to acknowledge the land on which the University of Toronto Press operates. This land is the traditional territory of the Wendat, the Anishnaabeg, the Haudenosaunee, the Métis, and the Mississaugas of the Credit First Nation.

University of Toronto Press acknowledges the financial support of the Government of Canada and the Ontario Arts Council, an agency of the Government of Ontario, for its publishing activities.

Canada Council for the Arts
Conseil des Arts du Canada

Canada

To Karen

Contents

Acknowledgments

I would like to thank all the individuals who while being 15M agreed to enter with me into dialogues of reciprocal elucidation. I would also like to thank two people who made possible my returning to the university after a ten-year absence. First, Ricardo Vargas, who has always critically supported my intellectual and practical explorations. He was the first person who exemplified for me what it means to have the ability to change one's point of view. Second, Noam Chomsky, who by supporting my application to the University of Victoria (UVic) opened up this space that is now my academic home. This little act is an example of the generosity with which he has always approached the study of politics.

With*in* UVic, the following people have played important roles helping me think through challenging questions: Matt James, Feng Xu, Jamie Lawson, Michelle Bonner, Colin Bennett, Jeremy Webber, Alex Robb, Adam Molnar, Christopher Parsons, Tim Smith, Paul Goertzen, Ana María Peredo, Benjamin Perrier, Peyman Vahabzadeh, Kadi Diallo, Petter Christian Ness, Sam-Alexander Rodriguez, and Denver Willson-Rymer.

The support I have received from the Department of Political Science at UVic throughout my MA, PhD, and post-doctoral fellowships has been instrumental. In particular, the help provided by Avigail Eisenberg, Scott Watson, Joanne Denton, and Rosemary Barlow.

I am also grateful to the Centre for Global Studies (CFGS) at UVic, which has offered me a home from which to put some of my ideas to the test. Here, I am indebted to Jodie Walsh and Oliver Schmidtke for inviting me to join the wonderful community that is CFGS.

The EUCAnet initiative housed at the CFGS with Beate Schmidtke leading the way has presented me with a vision of how to have one foot inside and one outside of the academic institution. I am appreciative of the bond we are building and the weaving of networks we have achieved.

The COVIDA Collective was developed by a group of UVic undergraduate students, Keith Cherry, and I as a response to the COVID-19 pandemic. Since the project was initiated we have experimented with horizontality, democratization, and non-violent conflict resolution. Working with Alina Sobolik, Javier Dichupa, Ethan Connor Quilty, Noah Hathaway, Svetlin Dimitriev, and Keith as we try to weave into our work new understandings of democracy and democratization practices is a worthwhile adventure. Javier deserves a special mention in relation to this book for contributing its index.

The Cedar Trees Institute (CTI) represents the kind of academic community I am passionate about. Initiating and building the institute together with its first fellows has been an amazing experience. Over the past two years, Rebeca Macias Gimenez, Rebeccah Nelems, Keith Cherry, Ryan Beaton, Oliver Schmidtke, Beate Schmidtke, Karen Yu Ping Yen, David Owen, Josh Nichols, James (Jim) Tully, and I have experimented with what democracy here and now is all about. Following from this, I understand this book as a CTI publication.

Outside of UVic, Nilüfer Göle with the NOMIS PublicDemoS Project has supported my work and opened a door to great friendships. PublicDemoS has wonderful people doing important work. Thinking along with Warda Hadjab, Zeynep Uğur, Gokce Tuncel, Tom Junes, Boyan Znepolski, Buket Turkmen, Umut Özkirimli, and Nilüfer has added tremendously to my research.

Stemming from an Institute for Human Sciences (IWM) summer school in Burg Feistritz, Austria, a group of us initiated an international working group on direct action. We have been meeting regularly online and aim to meet for a retreat in Can Poeti, Catalonia, as soon as it is safe to travel again in a manner in which everyone feels comfortable. I am grateful to Elena Rodina, Julia Fierman, Valeria Korablyova, Matyáš Křížkovský, Juho Korhonen, and Aaron Jacobs for this dialogical community we are co-constructing.

In different ways and at different times the following people have also contributed to this study: Law Siak Hong, Francisco Colom González, Francis Dupuis-Déri, Darius Rejali, Anthony Laden, Charles Taylor, Dilip P. Gaonkar, Chantal Mouffe, Michael Temelini, Mathias Thaler, Nikolas Kompridis, Fonna Forman, Peter Kraus, Robin Celikates, Charles Yen, Kru Sngob, Raquel Cohen, Barbara Powers, León Ouziel, Vicente Manzano Arrondo, and Celia Pedró. I am grateful to all of them.

It is important for me to acknowledge the incredible support that Daniel Quinlan at the University of Toronto Press (UTP) has provided during the editing and subsequent publishing of this book. Daniel's professionalism is worthy of mention. Nevertheless, it is his humane and engaged approach throughout the whole process that has made the experience of turning the manuscript into a publishable work a memorable experience. I look forward to working with him and UTP with future texts.

Related to UTP, I also want to highlight the helpful suggestions Reader A-1 and Reader A-2 provided following their review of the original manuscript. In their reviews, both invited me to bring the text into conversation with other traditions. I am grateful for their suggestions because together they helped me better describe the contribution of this book to current debates on democracy and democratization practices.

I must emphasize the value of Reader A-2's encouragement to dig deeper into anarchist literature. It has helped me identify family resemblances between their work and the work I have been experimenting with over the last few years. There are many strands of thought and practice that surfaced in my engagement with this literature and I have now braided them into the broader discussion of the book. Although the major aim of this work is to bring the participatory democracy of 15M into the mainstream of political science and political theory by engaging with mainstream ways of analysing political movements, there are key anarchist thinkers that have walked the walk of 15M and whose voices I consider a part of the permaculture of 15M and expressions of its mode of being.

Regarding the publication of the final manuscript, I must thank Josh Nichols for using his hard-earned position in the Canadian university community to help me overcome some of the hurdles associated with publishing a book with a Canadian academic press while not being a Canadian citizen or a permanent residence holder. Without Josh's support, I doubt this book would have seen the light of day.

Most importantly, however, dialogues with Jim Tully over the past ten years have had a deep influence on my scholarship. Our conversations have contributed to many of the ideas and concepts that shape this study. Working with Jim has proved a humanizing experience. His fearless yet cautious scholarship has been an inspiration. Our ongoing dialogues nurtured the seed that is now this text. They are exemplary of the kind of dialogical public philosophy that I am practising.

The idea that citizens are co-subjects and co-authors in the relationships of power; distinctions between different modes of citizenship (civic and civil engagement); understandings of violence and non-violence; experiments with power-with / power-over / power-under ways of being; engagement with the concept of joining hands; the idea of learning through examples; the multiplicity of overlapping ways in which governance happens in our democratic societies; the need to de-universalize political thought; and understandings of how to build relationships of trust through reciprocal support and enlightenment have all developed in a dialogical manner with Jim as a primary dialogue partner.

His engagement with these ideas can be explored further in the following of his texts:

"Reciprocal Elucidation," in *Civic Freedom in an Age of Diversity: The Public Philosophy of James Tully*, ed. Dimitrios Karmis and Jocelyn Maclure (Montreal and Kingston: McGill-Queen's University Press, forthcoming 2022).

"Reconciliation Here on Earth," in *Resurgence and Reconciliation: Indigenous–Settler Relations and Earth Teachings*, ed. Michael Asch, John Borrows, and James Tully (Toronto: University of Toronto Press, 2018).

"Responses," in *Freedom and Democracy in an Imperial Context: Dialogues with James Tully*, ed. Robert Nichols and Jakeet Singh (London: Routledge, 2014).

"The Crisis of Global Citizenship: Civil and Civic Responses," 84–100, and "On Global Citizenship: Reply to Interlocutors," 269–328, in *On Global Citizenship: James Tully in Dialogue* (London: Bloomsbury Academic, 2014).

"Global Order and Disorder in the History of Political Thought," lecture at Senate House, University of London, 3–4 June 2013.

Public Philosophy in a New Key: Democracy and Civic Freedom, vol. 1 (Cambridge: Cambridge University Press, 2008).

Public Philosophy in a New Key: Democracy and Civic Freedom, vol. 2: *Imperialism and Civic Freedom* (Cambridge: Cambridge University Press, 2008).

These are key texts for anyone interested in deepening their understanding of how this volume engages with Tully's work.

Foreword

The 15M movement in Spain is one of the important participatory democracies of the early twenty-first century. In the nineteenth century Karl Marx said of another exemplary participatory democracy, the Paris Commune, that it is "the people acting for itself, by itself." Democrats have experimented with and learned from a growing multiplicity of forms of participatory democracy around the world ever since. In *Democracy Here and Now*, by means of his participatory mode of research, Pablo Ouziel presents a fascinating and detailed account of the new form of participatory democracy enacted by 15M. Going beyond the "self-determination" or "itself" model of the Paris Commune, 15M is "the peoples (*demoi*) acting for the well-being of 'all affected' (human and non-human), by themselves, yet always in 'joining hands' relations with others." As he notes, this deeply relational, intersectional, and ecosocial mode of "here and now" democracy of 15M is exemplary of similar grass roots movements around the world.

At the heart of this form of community-based democracy are two features. The first is the commitment to the non-violent, democratic form of power relations among free and equal, co-organizing and co-governing citizens (power-with rather than power-over). The second is to always try to extend this kind of relationship to all affected by non-violent means (joining hands). That is, this twenty-first-century mode of "being democratic" builds on the twentieth-century experiments with non-violent forms of organization and social change of the Gandhian movements in India, the beloved community movements associated with Jo Ann Gibson Robinson, Ella Baker, Martin Luther King Jr, and John Lewis in the United States, and similar movements throughout the world. As we read in chapter 2, the touchstone for 15M is the long, courageous and enduring Spanish tradition of participatory democracy against unbelievable odds. Moreover, 15M and other community-based democracies join with recent ecological movements. They include within the "all affected" the well-being of plants, animals, ecosystems, and biodiversity on which all life depends. A democratic relationship among fellow citizens is thus seen as enacting biophilia: friendship among all forms of life.

This is a revolutionary transformation in the way citizens think about and enact democracy. They are finding their feet, learning through trial and error apprenticeship, and sharing practical knowledge through sophisticated local and global networks. 15M is exemplary in this regard as well. They continue to learn and move forward today in "less perceptible ways" than their spectacular initiation in 2011. Pablo Ouziel contributes to this learning process by enabling all of us to learn from the experiences of 15M and adapt this knowledge to our own situations.

One of the many important features of *Democracy Here and Now* is Pablo Ouziel's methodology. He entered into and engaged with 15M citizens in what he calls participatory relationships of reciprocal elucidation. This participatory method is a major contribution to the field of community-engaged research. Moreover, as we see as we read the text, this dialogical way of research enables him to discover, participate in, and co-articulate the most original feature of 15M. This is the six types of intersubjective, joining-hands relationships that 15M brings into being and works to carry on in creative ways.

The basic, joining-hands dimension of 15M is an attempt to overcome the dominant, us/them relationships of power-over that earlier participatory democracies shared with their opponents, built on premises of independence rather than interdependence. In contrast, 15M citizens always offer to enter into trustful democratic and potentially transformative relationships of negotiation with representative democrats and opponents who are not participants, yet who affect and are affected by participatory democracies. This, as he argues, is a revolutionary change in the way we think about and enact social change, yet a necessary one if we are to bring about democracy, peace, equality, and sustainability.

James Tully
Emeritus Professor
University of Victoria
Winter 2020
Songhees traditional territory

Visiting 15M Locales across Spain

In May of 2013, two years after participating in my first general assembly at the 15M encampment in Barcelona's Plaça Catalunya, I set out on a road trip around Spain with La Pasionaria (the VW Westfalia van in which I travelled). The objective of the trip was to learn about what 15M meant to different actors seeing themselves as being 15M and working from within different autonomous communities in the country. The accompanying map shows the route I took and the places I visited.*

* My choice of places to visit was determined along the way, based on recommendations from different interviewees. Interviewees often suggested particular cities to visit, based on the exemplary work of 15Ms in those localities. At the same time, I consciously selected the interviewees to be representative of the general geographic and demographic diversity of 15M. Unfortunately, the map replicates the "España vacía" (empty Spain) dynamic that refers to the fact that large areas of Spain are suffering from depopulation and are often absent from the political conversation regarding the present and future of the country.

Six Distinct Types of Joining Hands Relationships

In this book, I describe six distinct types of joining hands relationships that I have identified as being practised within Spain's 15M community. The way I use "joining hands" is *not* as a theory, but as a *language of description* that tries to bring to light what 15M citizens are doing when they engage with others. It isn't a prescription but an attempt at showing a mode of relating to one's adversaries that is completely different from the us/them modes of communism and fugitivism, and which I am trying to articulate inspired by the tradition of Gandhi–Gregg–King–Deming and their many followers today. In this light, joining hands is a dynamic process rather than a steady state through which communities of practice relate with supporters and potential supporters outside of their particular community of practice.

The six distinct types of joining hands relationships 15M is engaged are presented in the table below.

JH1	civic citizens joining hands with each other
JH2	civil citizens joining hands with each other
JH3	civic and civil citizens joining hands
JH4	civic citizens work with representative governments
JH5	civil citizens work with representative governments
JH6	civic-civil citizens are joining hands with each other in order to influence governments

DEMOCRACY HERE AND NOW

Studying Democracies – Learning via Examples and Exemplarity

If these resurgence-and-reconciliation relationships and cycles continue to grow and flourish, they will gradually reach a tipping point that will transform the vicious global systems that are currently bringing about the sixth mass extinction of millions of species of life on earth into virtuous ecosocial systems and nonviolent modes of conflict resolution and conciliation: that is, reconciliation with and of all forms and ways of life.

James Tully

How did we arrive at a place where the power-with, horizontal, inclusionary, and wall-breaking 15M has been overshadowed by the power-over, vertical, exclusionary, wall-building of nationalist elites in both Spain and Catalonia?[1] Somehow the base has become atomized so as to offer fertile ground for right-wing populism to flourish. If we are to reverse this

1 Although 15M refers to a specific movement that occupied public squares across Spain in 2011, throughout this text I refer to it as a mode of being that persists to this day in less perceptible ways. In this sense, I understand the square occupations as merely one way of being 15M among many that continue apace. As will become clear in this book, in response to the austerity measures enacted by the Spanish government after the 2008 global economic crisis, a demonstration took place on 15 May 2011. An online call made by a platform calling itself DRY (Democracia Real Ya!, Real Democracy Now!) mobilized thousands of citizens across Spain under the slogan "Real democracy now! We are not merchandise for bankers and politicians." Following the 15 May demonstration, in the early hours of 16 May, in Madrid's Puerta del Sol, forty people decided spontaneously to camp. Riot police dispersed them. The following day, 10,000 people took to the streets and encampments were set up in squares across the country in solidarity with the encampment in Madrid. On 12 June 2011, the Madrid general assembly decided to dismantle the encampment at Puerta del Sol. The rest of encampments were soon dismantled as well. Even so, a distinct mode of "being 15M" persists in Spain.

dangerous slide, we must learn about 15M and what has happened to it. Through 15M, we can learn about both the resilience and the fragility of the civic sphere, the similarities and differences between participatory and representative traditions of democracy, and the ways in which these modes of democracy criss-cross and overlap in a multitude of ways. This is valuable knowledge to hold at a time when humanity faces a multitude of crises, all of which seem to be calling for a broadening of democratic imaginaries and a deepened commitment to democratization practices.

This book tells the story of a mode of being democratic and a temporality that in Spain is best exemplified by the social movement known as 15M. In 2011, for a few months, 15M occupied public squares across Spain. Having since been dispersed, and despite the huge transformations and challenges it has faced, a 15M mode of being has persisted in less perceptible ways. Since the first square occupations, Spain has had to confront important challenges: new political parties on the left and the right have gained prominence, the regional conflict with Catalonia has intensified, a powerful feminist movement has arisen throughout the country, and the population is grappling with the COVID-19 pandemic and its consequences. Throughout this period, in many of the actions launched by social movements and political parties, 15M modes of being have proliferated.[2] In this book I will be attempting to bring to life the 15M phenomenon and the 15M way of being, in a manner that invites you to consider the transformative and democratizing possibilities opened up by 15M.[3] The approach I take will focus on identifying and describing democratization practices as they play out on the ground of struggle.[4]

I am writing this book during a time of multiple global crises in which representative democracies are facing multiple threats and being

2 The party/movement Podemos often calls for activities to be carried out in the spirit of 15M. During the International Women's Day march of 8 March 2020, 15M's calls for inclusivity and horizontalism were prominent; see, for example, J. Gallego, "El 8M es el nuevo 15M," *Eldiario.es*, 14 May 2018, https://www.eldiario.es/carnecruda/lo-llevamos-crudo/nuevo_6_771382889.html. In chapter 5, I present some examples of 15M practices in response to the Catalan conflict (see pages 41–4).

3 For important scholarship on the origins/roots of 15M and its transformative practices, the reader can explore some of the following texts: Flesher Fominaya (2020); Romanos (2018, a430); Iglesias and Monedero (2011); Errejón Galván (2011); Taibo (2011); Petit (2012); Garcés (2019); Rivas et al. (2011); Velasco (2011); and Pereira-Zazo and Torres (2019).

4 This approach is in alignment with the one proposed by Ali *Aslam*, David *McIvor*, and Joel Alden *Schlosser* (2019), in which the authors write: "Rather than describing the generic difficulties of democracy, theorizing outside the fray like a detached philosopher, democratic theorists must identify the particular moments of democratic flourishing past and amplify these to encourage stronger and more robust democratic experimentation in the present."

challenged in both democratizing and non-democratizing ways. 15M crystallizes for me a virtuous democratic response to the crises we are facing as a consequence of four decades of neoliberal hegemony.[5]

Since the late 1970s, the world's elites have been reshaping the global economy guided by a neoliberal ideology. By signing free trade agreements and establishing international institutions with the cooperation of national governments, these elites have increasingly enclosed much of what could once have been viewed as the global commons. This process intensified in 2008 when, amid rampant deregulation and trade liberalization, the US financial sector collapsed. This led to large bank bailouts around the world and to the bursting of real estate bubbles across entire continents. The European Union (EU) found itself in crisis, and in most member-states, households fell ever deeper into debt. Governments almost everywhere, at least in the Western world, insisted that austerity was the only solution. The same call had been heard during the Latin American debt crisis of the 1980s.[6]

The EU, reflecting its technocratic and oligarchic nature, behaved in a non-democratic manner, in the process casting light on its disruptive relationships with financial and global governance powers operating in the background.[7] It adopted a series of measures that alienated its

5 Like modern liberalism (welfare liberalism), neoliberalism finds its roots in the nineteenth-century idea of the right of individuals to be protected from overly powerful government. However, welfare liberalism – stemming from a social-liberal tradition – focused on combining development with social protection through direct state intervention (a welfare state), whereas proponents of neoliberalism have posited economic growth as the means to achieve human progress. Since the 1970s, the neoliberals' doctrine of minimal state intervention in economic and social affairs and their commitment to freedom of trade and capital have dominated our imaginary. This has led to the dismantlement, downsizing, contracting out, or devolvement to private/public and private organizations of a number of hard-won regimes of governance. Through this redistribution of decision-making and enactment powers, the principle of democracy as a condition of legitimacy has been eliminated, which in turn has severely restricted democratic citizenship.

6 According to Kevin Farnsworth and Zoë Irving (2018), the responses of the European Union and its member-states to the 2008 economic crisis crystallized the following: *first*, the shrinking of the social welfare state and the deregulation of labour markets, both of which were priorities; *second*, an emphasis on private markets as the drivers of growth; and *third*, the reconfiguring of the interests of capital, peoples' needs, and the role of the state.

7 Judging from the kinds of moves made by global governance powers, it is unsurprising that scholars like John Holloway speak of these economic crises as chronic conditions that intensify from time to time. For Holloway (2018a), "crisis as a chronic inadequacy" has merged with "modern capitalism into the periodic disruption, so that the term 'the current crisis of capitalism' comes (at least since the mid-1970s) to refer to a chronic condition punctuated by intensifications" (36).

citizens by weakening their ability to govern themselves both politically and economically.[8]

Clearly, the EU is part of an international trend: governing powers, more and more aggressively, are supporting corporate interests at the expense of the common good.[9] This power asymmetry between the governors and governed is something that John Holloway views as "all-important," for it points to the fact that the struggle for transformation is not against a particular group of people but against a way of organizing the world.[10]

All of this has facilitated a pattern of corporate greed – to which governments have acquiesced – that since 2008 has increasingly been replicated around the world. It has led to a dramatic rise in right-wing populism and nationalism of the most xenophobic and totalitarian kind. In 2008, a wave of mobilization began that, among many other events worth noting, catapulted Donald Trump to the presidency of the United States; provided Turkey's president, Recep Tayyip Erdoğan, with a platform for implementing his most radical reforms; contributed to the meteoric rise of Marie Le Pen as a serious contender for French president; substantially strengthened the discourse of the far-right populism driving Brexit; brought into the German parliament for the first time since the Second World War an extreme right-wing party; saw a coalition government being formed between a right-wing party and the far right in Austria; and, in Italy, led to the strengthening of the far right.[11]

Spain, for its part, has seen a clash between fervent, elite-led right-wing nationalisms of the Catalan and Spanish kind.[12] This has distracted

---

8 In Spain, this was clearly visible in the modification of Article 135 of the constitution on 27 September 2011. This change, which stemmed from EU pressure, gave the greatest priority to the repayment of the country's debt. See BOE Boletin Oficial del Estado (Official State Bulletin), https://www.boe.es/diario_boe/txt.php?id=BOE-A-2011-15210, which clearly reveals how citizens' ability to self-govern both politically and economically was attacked.

9 For Barbara Epstein, this aggressive support of corporate interests goes hand in hand with the spread of a world view in which business is perceived as the only honourable occupation. This is neoliberalism as she understands it, and according to her, it rapidly broadens the gap between the wealthy and the rest, disregards regulations that have been put in place to protect citizens/workers, and heightens corporate power while rapidly degrading the environment. See Epstein (2017a, 179).

10 See Holloway (2018b).

11 On 3 November 2020, Joe Biden defeated Donald Trump in the US presidential elections; he was sworn into office on 20 January 2021.

12 When I claim that Spain is currently experiencing a clash between fervent, elite-led right-wing nationalisms of the Catalan and Spanish kind, I am not lumping together

the population from the corruption scandals affecting the governing parties, which have continued to hollow out Spain's democracy. It has also fomented an institutional crisis that is threatening the security and well-being of Spaniards and Catalonians.

In 2011, in what is commonly referred to as 15M or Indignados (The Outraged), people flooded public squares throughout Spain and Catalonia to highlight the deep crisis of representation confronting the country. It is important to point out, as many in the squares did at the time, that it was the media that coined the term Indignados – those being 15M rejected it. Those who flocked to the squares emphasized that their struggle stemmed "from" dignity and was a struggle "for" dignity – this was not a struggle about indignation.[13]

Having spent time with people in the squares, and having learned from the Zapatistas through the work of Holloway and others, I now understand that the emphasis on dignity implied that 15M was starting from a place in which the agent existed against and beyond her objectification. This self-understanding of what it meant to be 15M instead of being an Indignado moved those being 15M toward a politics of dialogue rather than monologue.[14] What was evolving in 15M squares

right-wing populism with the Catalan struggle for republican self-rule. I am, though, presenting Catalan nationalism in terms of two contested representations: a republican self-government one, for which there exists huge empirical evidence (but which is beyond the scope of this study); and an elite-driven Catalan nationalism that has hijacked the normative force of recognition of republican self-rule in order to legitimate itself. From the ground of struggle, it seems evident that "innovating ideologists" in Catalonia have hijacked the vocabulary of a republican self-government grounded in historical truths. By turning Catalan independence into an "empty signifier," pro-independence right-wing populists have symbolically structured the political environment of Catalonia. They speak only about independence, all the while approving a neoliberal budget and implementing the harshest austerity measures the region has seen since Spain's transition from dictatorship to democracy. For an explanation of innovating ideologists, see Temelini (2015, 137–64). For an explanation of empty signifiers, see Laclau (1996, 36–46).

13 Through my dialogues of reciprocal elucidation within 15M, it became clear that many being 15M aligned with Holloway's understanding of dignity as "the affirmation that we are not victims. We are exploited, humiliated, repressed, tortured: but we are not victims" (2018b, 389). Holloway also reminds us that the Zapatistas during their uprisings emphasized that it was dignity that made them revolt (2019, 2).

14 Holloway speaks of this politics of dialogue as a politics "of listening not of talking, a politics not of parties and hierarchical structures but of assemblies or councils, forms of organization that seek to articulate equally all the voices of dignity in revolt, a politics that seeks not to win the power-over symbolised by the state but to strengthen the power-to-do that comes from below" (2018b, 389). Here, we can appreciate the family resemblance and complementarity between Holloway's power-to-do and 15M's power-with.

was part of a dialogical exercise involving an experiment with gift/ reciprocity relationships between people co-contesting norms while co-constructing alternatives.

Yet a few years after the square occupations, the same political parties that had been denounced in 2011 are now driving the country's constitutional crisis. It is fair to say that the pro-independence narrative, which is highly critical of the Spanish state, would largely hold up under scrutiny. Nevertheless, the approaches to the Catalan crisis taken by the pro-independence parties and the pro-Monarchic Spain unity parties have left the two sides sniping at each other from the trenches while a large proportion of Catalans and Spaniards have found themselves caught in the no man's land between the two sides. This tectonic shift in the political climate reveals how a vicious cycle of elite development, alienation, and populist reaction is gaining strength.[15]

In response to these right-wing populist developments, I argue in this book that there are ways to reverse such a slide and that these can be found in the ways in which people around the world occupied public squares in 2011, thus setting in motion a way of being democratic that continues to grow today. To that end, I undertake here an in-depth study of how 15M citizens in Spain occupied public squares. I show first how 15M's way of being (power-with) and temporality (one step at a time) present a way of being democratic that has persisted in Spain since the square occupations.[16] I then present 15M as an alternative to right-wing populist solutions such as the repression of a people's right to decide, unilateral declarations of independence, suspensions of regional autonomy, imprisonment of pro-independence politicians and civil society leaders, and the imposition of early elections. Today's representative institutional arenas in Spain and Catalonia have witnessed all of those.

In *No Is Not Enough*, Naomi Klein begins by telling her readers that Donald Trump, who embodies most of the worse trends of the past half century, "is less an aberration than a logical conclusion."[17] His

---

15 For scholarship on the Catalan crisis, I recommend reading Kraus and Vergés Gifra (2017); Cuadras-Morató (2015); and Requejo and Sanjaume-Calvet (2019).

16 Although the distinction between "power-with" and "power-over" that I use in this book derives from my engagement with James Tully's work, it is important to mention that in "On Violence" (1972), Hannah Arendt also tried hard to get theorists to see beyond the ruler/ruled assumption or world view. Arendt presents the distinction most fundamentally in "Socrates," in *The Promise of Politics* (2005). For further analysis on these two concepts and their connection with Arendt's thought, see Tully (2014a). Tully has also traced this distinction between "power-with" and "power-over" to Mary Parker Follett (1924) and Richard Gregg (2018).

17 Klein (2017, 9).

election was the natural outcome of a free-market ideological project embraced by centrist and conservative parties alike, one that is waging war on all that is public and that is casting corporate CEOs as humanity's saviours.[18] Klein suggests that even if the rising tide of right-wing populism could be turned back, the political conditions that enabled Trump's rise would not come to an end.[19]

Hence the title of her book. The slogan "No is not enough," which amounts to a guide to confronting these crises, reveals Klein to me as a fellow traveller. Ultimately, the two of us concur that in order to confront the multiple civilizational crises we are facing, those working on change from *outside* institutions (indeed, *without* institutions) need to join hands with those working with*in* them.[20] Through this kind of collaboration we will be able to co-construct virtuous and conciliatory communities that can resolve without violence conflicts like the Catalan struggle for recognition.[21]

---

18 Klein (2017, 10).

19 When thinking about the conditions that need to be transformed now that Trump is gone if we are to enter a virtuous period of deepening democratization, the work of Pierre Dardot and Christian Laval is helpful. According to Dardot and Laval, society has become an enterprise composed of enterprises and the neoliberal subject is "the correlate of an apparatus of performance and pleasure." "Man enterprise," the neoliberal subject, is immersed in global competition. The objective, then, is not to govern this individual by training their body and shaping their mind into submission; rather, it is to move the individual into a space in which their subjectivity can be fully involved in the activity they are required to perform. See Dardot and Laval (2013, 283, 284, 288).

20 According to Tully, joining hands requires that all citizens involved in a given relationship understand their tradition as one out of many possible alternatives. Adopting such an "aspectival" understanding of themselves within community allows these citizens to enter into genuine dialogues of reciprocal elucidation. Within these dialogues, everyone listens to the others while acknowledging the others' self-understandings and ways of being. When this deep listening and deep sharing is practised, a just, critical, and comparative dialogue is conducted non-violently. This dialogue of honest reciprocal elucidation is what Tully refers to as joining hands. For Tully's best account of "dialogue" of joining hands see: Tully, J. (2016). The second edition of the same journal provides four responses to Tully's ideas: visit https://scholarworks.iu.edu/iupjournals/index.php/jwp/issue/view/21. See also Tully (2019a).

21 The Catalan independence struggle led from above (referred to by its leaders as *el Procès*), which I am writing about in this introduction, is a good example of violence by other means being masked by a discourse of non-violence. Those in the pro-independence movement will continue to construct their non-violent imaginary, but violence is about more than police batons. Non-violence in the Gandhian tradition is based on uncoerced and interdependent relationships of cooperation. These are power-with relationships with friends and foes and are different in kind from power-over spaces, which are guided by an ethos of separation. Practitioners

James Tully vividly describes our present as caught between and within "interlocking vicious systems of capitalism, colonialism, war, power-over forms of rule, and globalization; and the vicious systems that arise in counter-aggression to them."[22] Melissa Williams contends that our democratic institutions are not equipped to face the collective challenges posed by this scenario.[23] In a recent piece, Charles Taylor comes to a similar conclusion: Western democracies are immersed in a phase of regression of great danger for the West and for the whole world. For Taylor, what is most worrisome is that the *telos* (of democracy) is receding in a self-perpetuating decline that seems difficult to reverse. As he puts it, the fiction of democracy is being contradicted by its reality; as it hollows out, it is becoming unbelievable.[24] He tells us that we must reverse this slide. But how are we to do that if, as Wendy Brown suggests, thee slide is "undoing" democratic practices and even democratic imaginaries?[25] In this book I will be arguing that the six distinct types of joining-hands relationships that constitute the mode of being that is 15M together present a democratizing response to the hollowing out of democracy.

1. Joining Hands

When we as citizens try to address the crises of democracy we are currently immersed in, and do so within existing institutional frames, we quickly realize the limits such frames impose. It becomes apparent that we need to go beyond institutional reforms and learn with, and from, those who have been operating outside or beyond such institutionality. In actual fact, the clear failure of institutional reform is what invites us to discover the multitude of ways in which citizens around the globe are practising mutual aid, or cooperative citizenship, in a manner that goes beyond the institutional frame of representative democracy.

---

of non-violence do not seek victory over their opponents through non-violent means. Instead they aspire to promote conflict resolution through a transformation and replacement of the social system in which the struggle takes place. Tully refers to this as "nonviolent agonistics."

22 Tully (2019b), 31.

23 Williams (2012).

24 Taylor (2019), 20. Here Taylor explains how there is an ever-present element of fiction when we think about equal citizenship. Yet, as he puts it, this as a self-realizing fiction that helps us partly realize some aspects of the fiction. For Taylor, the problem arises when the fiction is too strongly contradicted by the reality, which is what he is observing today in most of the Western world.

25 W. Brown, "The Demos Undone: Neoliberalism, Democracy, Citizenship," Lansdowne Lecture, University of Victoria, 15 January 2014.

According to Boaventura de Sousa Santos, when we engage with the activities of these citizens, we are engaging with a multiplicity of spaces in an arena that promotes cross-fertilization among diverse "counter-publics."[26] This space, as Jeffrey Juris describes it, is in effect a multiplicity of self-organized and self-managed spaces.[27] With*in* those spaces, divisions are addressed and people find new and better ways of working together.[28] In fact, this is where, as researchers, we are clearly able to see the difference between two distinct modes of democracy: representative and participatory. We are also able to see the multiplicity of ways in which these modes of democracy relate to and with one another.[29]

When we broaden our vision so that it incorporates the cooperative activities in which citizens are engaging into our analysis of current affairs, we open up a whole different ecosystem of thought and practice. This ecosystem reveals alternatives from which we can learn and with which we can cooperate. These are practices that for centuries have sustained human life on earth.[30] Thousands of books have been written about this cooperative spirit and the mode of being that guides it – about its horizontality, its participatory approach to democracy, and how it differs from the kind of citizenship we are accustomed to when, as moderns, we ponder how democratic citizens should behave.[31] Similarly, we have plenty of examples of how modern citizenship operates and of the many ways in which modern-day citizens can contribute to the transformation of their societies. What we *lack* are examples of how these two modes of citizenship are complementary and thus able to coordinate with each other in ways that might change the world. As this book will make clear, in Spain on 15 May 2011, we witnessed such

26 See Juris (2008), 366. Here, Juris is quoting from Santos in reference to the World Social Forum. Nevertheless, I think this understanding of the space of conviviality shares a family resemblance with the space of 15M's square occupations. See Sousa Santos (2006).

27 See Juris (2005; 2008, 370).

28 See Juris (2005, 270).

29 For helpful scholarship on horizontality/participatory democracy and prefiguration, I recommend works by Sitrin (2006, 2018); Zibechi (2005); and Nunes (2005a, 2005b, 2014, 2018). For works on participatory and direct democracy, texts by Pateman (2004, 2012), Benjamin Barber, Peruzzotti (2008), and Wampler (2018) are valuable. For a classic study on these issues, see Epstein (1993).

30 This position is strongly defended by Peter Kropotkin. See Kropotkin (2006).

31 When speaking of horizontality, I am referring to a practice popularized by grassroots autonomous movements in Argentina. Horizontality is becoming widespread and is characterized by "nonhierarchical relations, decentralized coordination, direct democracy, and the striving for consensus" (Juris 2008, 354). See also Sitrin (2006).

a coming together of these two modes of citizenship. The bond they forged revealed the transformative possibilities of that joining.[32]

15M enacted a horizontal, dialogical, non-violent mode of being. But one can also find, with*in* 15M, manifestations of leadership, vanguards, and representation. According to Rodrigo Nunes, these are not "'residues' of a representative politics to be overcome" but part of the permaculture of practices that those being 15M have at their disposal and are putting to good use to advance their transformative programs.[33] What we must figure out together is how to steer tendencies "towards openness or horizontality, closure or verticalization," in a virtuoso manner that adapts to the specific conditions required by the specific conjuncture in which those being 15M find themselves.[34]

In the squares, citizens being 15M crystallized, for all those who engaged with them, examples of a virtuous relationality between participation and representation.[35]

---

32 Enrique Peruzzotti argues that participation and representation, rather than being opposites, are actually complementary. For him, the challenge arises in the exploration and the development of the relations between the two processes. It is there that we must overcome, on the one hand, the limited conception of democracy presented by minimalist theories of democracy, and, on the other, the anti-representation stance taken by many of the proponents of participation. This complementarity that Peruzzotti speaks of is what 15M exemplifies through its joining hands relationships between civil and civic citizens. See Peruzzotti (2008, 1).

33 See Nunes (2005b, 98).

34 See Nunes (2005b, 112). In that text, Nunes navigates in a fruitful manner the tension that exists between openness/horizontality and closure/verticalization. In a different text, Nunes makes the case for distributed leadership as the actual *modus operandi* of 15M, Occupy, and others. Nunes does not see these movements as leaderless but rather as "leaderful." According to him, leadership is present in a layered manner, with many different kinds of leaderships and scales of leadership operating at any given time. The space of leadership in principle can be held by anyone. This understanding of distributed leadership resonates with understandings of leadership held by certain groups being 15M. It certainly speaks to some aspects of what I have learned in dialogue with 15M. Nevertheless, I see important nuances that I think this book crystallizes. Having said this, it is important to note that Nunes's view of these movements as "leaderful" rather that leaderless has important implications for the summer protests of 2020 globally and in the United States led by Black Lives Matter against police killings. These protests are often characterized in the press and elsewhere as "leaderful," revealing how Nunes's approach is helpful in understanding present-day movements. For a deeper examination of Nunes's ideas on distributed leadership, see Nunes (2014), 34.

35 According to Holloway, in current movements of rebellion these two strands of citizenship are often intertwined. His work on the pro-Zapatista movement, and on movements against neoliberalism more generally, shows how those trying to conquer state power are often allies joining hands with those rejecting the state as a form of organization. See Holloway (2019, 236).

The effects of such a reunion are still being felt in Spanish society. The propositions that citizens made from their square occupations and the mode of being they practised offer responses to the crises Spain continues to face several years after the events themselves.

The terms for describing these two different modes of citizenship vary. I find useful the distinction made between cooperative citizenship, which is horizontal in orientation, and modern citizenship, which is vertical. Horizontality highlights that relationships in the cooperative mode operate in a power-with manner, whereas verticality clearly describes the power-over way in which relationships are constructed in the modern citizenship sense.

Some scholars who have studied movements like 15M, inspired by Deleuze and Guattari, think of these two modalities of citizenship as "rhizomatic" and "arborescent."[36] From this perspective, rhizomatic is understood as being open, mutable, horizontal, and spontaneously organized, while arborescent, is closed, fixed, vertical, and structured.[37] Personally, while I am sympathetic to this perspective and its theoretical underpinnings, which are useful, I find it even more useful to think of these two modes of citizenship as *civil* and *civic*. Civil citizenship refers to the modern type of citizenship that is tied to representative democracy and its associated public sphere, while civic citizenship points to the kind of cooperative citizenship that can operate beyond the institutional limits of modern democracies.

Throughout this book, I will usually refer to these two distinct types of citizenship as civil and civic. This is because, as a graduate student, Tully's work convinced me of the value of using these descriptive terms to highlight the distinctiveness of each of these modes of citizenship. This distinction, and the ethnography presented by Tully when speaking of practices of civic engagement, I find particularly illuminating when thinking about and with public square movements with*in* the *glocal* cycle of struggles of 2011.[38] I am referring here to the cycle of

---

36 For an introduction to 15M scholarship in this tradition, see Nunes (2005); Oikonomakis and Roos (2014); and Toret Medina (2015).

37 For valuable insights on this distinction, see Nunes (2005, 97). It is useful to point out here that when Nunes is thinking of democracy he understands that one can never speak of a full democracy but only of more or less democracy. Therefore, it is in weaving together rhizomatic and arborescent strands that we attain more or less democracy (107).

38 Some people refer to glocality as a confederalism that allows for the locality of participation and the centrality of power-over to come together agonistically. See Saward (2009, 232). Personally, in the context of this text, I am thinking of "glocality" in the sense of people on the ground of struggle acting locally but thinking globally.

struggles that, inspired by the Arab Spring of 2010, saw public squares in democratic countries around the globe occupied by citizens joining hands and demanding (as well as enacting) what they referred to as "real" democracy. These networks of citizens were civic and "glocal" in the sense that they were accountable to local civic nodes but also engaged in civic relationships that developed and extended a whole infrastructure of citizen-with-citizen self-governance. I see 15M in Spain as contributing to this glocal cycle of protest and feel that much can be learned from both its strengths and its shortcomings.

When speaking about practices of civic engagement, Tully makes a clear distinction between these practices and civil citizenship practices. Later in this introduction I will discuss their similarities, dissimilarities, and interconnections, but at this point, it is important to understand that this book is in part a language experiment – that is, an attempt to test these concepts by using them to describe a real-life example of citizens contesting and constructing alternatives by joining hands. What does the language capture? What are the limitations of this language of description? What can we learn from how this language is used to describe a set of citizenship practices in Spain that could extend or enrich Tully's original conception? I ask myself these questions as I work with and through this language of description to explain what I have learned, and continue to learn, with and from 15M.

When one is in the space of contestation and co-construction generated by citizens in public squares, it is not hard to understand what is happening.[39] The difficulty is in trying to explain it. I find Tully's fresh description of citizenship useful as a point of departure for describing what I am learning with 15M. I find it helpful because it broadens our understanding of the field of practice. It reveals how citizens are together resolving conflicts non-violently and horizontally while constructing community and confronting unequal power relations vis-à-vis the individuals and institutions that govern them. Speaking of what transpired in the squares as practices of civic engagement is valuable in this sense because it helps us understand the similarities and dissimilarities between agents within the square occupations. It is also useful because it reveals the similarities and dissimilarities between those within the square occupations and the broader society (other citizens, representative institutions, security forces, etc.). It is a language that

39 Antje Wiener (2014) defines contestation as "a norm-generative social practice, which – pending on the environment – entails four different modes (arbitration, deliberation, contention and justification)" (1).

reveals different modes of being and the agonisms that exist within and between them.[40]

I use this language in dialogue with citizens who describe their activities using other languages that stem from different traditions. The point is not to get caught up in the language of description and the concepts I propose, but rather to focus on the citizenship practices being exemplified by the agents who are being studied. No language can encapsulate the multiplicity of practices presented in this text. Instead, what this language can do is contribute to a sketch of the field of practices being enacted in Spain's 2011 square occupations.

I speak of a sketch because a broadened and more detailed picture of what citizens being 15M have been doing can only crystallize through further dialogues with other traditions. It is these continuing dialogues of reciprocal elucidation that expand our understanding of these modes of citizenship and their complementarity. Nevertheless, whatever descriptive terms are being used, what is clear is that the types of citizenship being discussed throughout this book present their own vernacular meanings and paths toward both the construction of community and its transformation. In the case of 15M, this reveals citizens who want to reform institutions from within, working with those who are organizing from outside these institutions. This is the moment of joining hands, when the complementarity of these two ways of engaging in society as citizens becomes visible in a unique way.[41]

I will be expanding on this in the following chapters. But I would mention here that in the course of this study of 15M in Spain I have identified six types of joining-hands relationships – that is, six different yet "family resemblance" ways of joining hands, cooperating, and contesting non-violently, with differently situated others. These six constitute

---

40 I am using the term "agonism" in the sense that Foucault used it when drawing from Nietzsche. This is how Foucault describes it: 'Rather than speaking of an essential freedom, it would be better to speak of an 'agonism' – of a relationship which is at the same time reciprocal incitation and struggle; less of a face-to-face confrontation which paralyses both sides than a permanent provocation." See Foucault (1982a, 790).

41 In the preface to the fourth edition of *Change the World without Taking Power: The Meaning of Revolution Today*, Holloway emphasizes three things that we need to take into account when thinking about social transformation. *First*, that we need to change the world radically; *second*, that we cannot do so through the state; and *third*, that doing so without taking state power will be a difficult task. Following my engagement with 15M, I am confident that the joining hands relationships of 15M, its permaculture, ecosystem, and mode of being, present a virtuous and hopeful response to the three challenges Holloway identifies. See Holloway (2019, viii).

the "mode of being" 15M.[42] In this introduction, for simplicity's sake, I describe them generically as cooperative and contestatory. As the book progresses, though, six distinct types of joining-hands relationships in which 15M is engaged will crystallize: civic citizens joining hands with one another (JH1); civil citizens joining hands with one another (JH2); civic and civil citizens joining hands (JH3); the ways civic citizens work with representative governments (JH4); the ways civil citizens work with representative governments (JH5); and the ways civic–civil citizens join hands with one another to influence governments (JH6).

What the concept of "joining hands" attempts to do is, first, show that these citizens are not opposed to one another. Civil citizens have not been co-opted, and civic citizens are not marginal, as they often criticize one another as being. Second, the concept of joining hands is an attempt to reveal how civil democracies (representative democracies), in order to be healthy, must be grounded in citizens who are already democratic in their thoughts and actions. In other words, representative democracy depends on civic citizens (participatory citizens). Reciprocally, healthy civic citizens need the support of representative institutions so that they are not crushed or marginalized by the dominant institutions. Indeed, the concept of joining hands reminds us that when coordination between civil and civic citizens fails, representative institutions are reduced to elite institutions with nominal representation, at which point the "people" either support these institutions reluctantly or adopt what strikes them as the only available alternative – pugnacious right-wing populism. Without a doubt, this is the biggest problem we are facing in representative democracies today – and the six types of joining-hands relationships that constitute the mode of being that is 15M are, I argue, the solution. That is the mega-hypothesis of this study.

Civil citizens tend to think that being good citizens simply requires voting thoughtfully. However, the condition of voting thoughtfully presupposes the ability to think about more than one's (individual or collective) separate self. Thoughtful voting requires being able to "think with and for the other," where the *other* refers to all interdependent beings affected by the situation. The problem is that this way of thinking with and for one another can only be cultivated by engaging and working with and for one another – that is, through civic citizenship in constructive programs of various kinds that help develop the being-with

42 By this I mean that it is useful to see these six ways of joining hands in the Wittgensteinian sense as a complex network of overlapping and criss-crossing similarities and dissimilarities. For a brilliant explanation of Wittgenstein's use of the idea of family resemblances, see Temelini (2017, 295).

ethos of thinking and acting with and for one another no matter how diverse the others happen to be. This being-with ethos (horizontality) strives to be non-reactionary and to create in a non-hierarchical and anti-authoritarian manner.[43]

Marina Sitrin's studies in Argentina describe movements working-with in a horizontal manner as breaking with vertical modes of organization and relationality. According to Sitrin, in their rejection of situations in which people have power over others, such movements are attempting to create "power-with" relationships.[44]

Jeffrey Juris points to horizontality as a civic citizenship practice that builds collective processes while addressing internal struggles in a co-ordinated yet decentralized manner.[45] It is because of horizontality's coordinated yet decentralized nature that there can be many kinds of horizontalities. In "being-with" movements we find diverse organizational forms operating simultaneously.[46]

Yet it is important to highlight that this being-with ethos remains permanently open to future possibilities and possible differences. Rodrigo Nunes, writes that saying what democracy is like closes the door to what might come after. The key, then, is to keep our imaginary of democracy open, which is what people who practise horizontality are trying to do.[47] This resonates with the work of Anthony Laden, who contrasts two pictures of democracy: a first that depicts it as closed, and second that depicts it as open.[48] As Laden points out, in the picture of democracy as open, democracy is described as a social form within which the rules agreed upon for living together are worked out in concert.[49]

Collective presences like 15M are responding to the binary scheme that distances these two modes of being democratic from each other.

43 See Sitrin (2007).

44 Sitrin (2007). According to Sitrin, it is through these changing practices that ideas flow, new relations are built, and movements enter into a process of constant growth and continuous creation. It is important to highlight here that horizontality for Sitrin is not an ideology or a political program but a dynamic social relationship based in affective politics. See Sitrin (2018, 314).

45 See Juris (2005, 256).

46 Juris (2005, 256). Rodrigo Nunes points out that in order to avoid universalizing certain ideas regarding horizontality, we must avoid abstracting them from their material contexts. This is point is worth considering when engaging with this study on 15M modes of being. See Nunes (2018, 40).

47 Nunes (2018, 46). According to Nunes, what we need is an ethos of "becoming open" (47).

48 See Laden (2020).

49 Laden (2020).

Through their joining-hands relationships, those being 15M are opening up the space between representation and participation so as to expand existing mixed practices and develop new and imaginative hybrid modes of being. As I see it, 15M is doing exactly what Nunes suggests could help democratize our democracies. According to him, through this process the discussion becomes about balancing "openness and closure, dispersion and unity, strategic action and process and so forth."[50]

2. Going Glocal[51]

In 2010, mass protests erupted in Tunisia. These were followed quickly by protests in Egypt, Yemen, and Syria. This is what is commonly referred to as the Arab Spring. By 2011, these protests had spread to Europe and North America. Many scholars have lumped these events together and treated them as part of the same cycle of protest.[52] The whirlwind of activity of 2010–11 has given rise to a rich body of literature,[53] but that literature has seldom paid close attention to what is happening on the ground.[54] There are now many books that describe democratic practices and suggest what these mobilizations signify, but few of them, if any, approach the subject through reciprocal elucidation. That particular research method will be described in detail later in this introduction, but, briefly, employing reciprocal elucidation makes

50 See Nunes (2014, 13–14).

51 Once we enter the space of contestation as participant-observers, we can clearly see the dual aspect of their way of thinking and acting. Their praxis reveals the primacy of the local while, at the same time, showing the global dimension of their activities. In the square occupations, we see citizens attuned to the global context in which they are making claims and constructing glocal alternatives.

52 See, for example, the work of Nunes, who like numerous others sees this cycle beginning on 17 December 2010, with street vendor Tarek el-Tayeb Mohamed Bouazizi setting himself on fire in the small Tunisian town of Sidi Bouzid. Nunes (2014, 8). For Nunes, in this cycle events have the following similarities: *first*, participants share a distrust of representative politics and representation in general; *second*, they reject formal organizations and are inclined toward networked organizing; *third*, they develop creative extra-parliamentary forms of action; *fourth*, they practise a kind of tactical diversity of tactics; and *fifth*, they use the internet for many aspects of their organizing, mobilizing, and disseminating (9).

53 For an introduction to the breadth and reach of the literature, see Byrne (2012); Rebick (2012); Shiffman et al. (2012); Chomsky (2012); López Petit et al. (2012); Schiffrin (2012); Mason (2013); Werbner (2014); della Porta and Mattoni (2014); Castells (2015); Ancelovici et al. (2016); Hardt and Negri (2017); and Sourice (2017).

54 For a defence of this claim, see della Porta and Rucht (2013, 2).

one more cautious about understanding the Arab Spring and the subsequent uprisings of 2011 as part of the same cycle of struggle. It does, however, suggest it is appropriate to think of the events of 2011 as a glocal cycle of struggles for "real democracy."

When we observe and participate in these movements, we are reminded of similar practices in the libertarian movements of 1930s Spain. We also note how those practices resonate with those of the decentralized communities of socialist humanists in the late 1950s and early 1960s.[55] We see family resemblances with the movements of the 1960s and 1970s that advanced more participatory modes of democracy around the world. The practices we see resonate with those exemplary practices of the Zapatistas that became world-renowned in the 1990s. Furthermore, they take us back to the neighbourhood assemblies that rebuilt communities in response to the 2001 crisis in Argentina. These movements and many others have exemplified what it means to be political for millions of citizens around the world. This has been possible because of a "healthy movement ecology" that preserves this memory (and lifeway) over time.[56] So it is a simple matter for us to study new movements by comparing them to and contrasting them with these exemplars. This ecology of societies in movement provides us with clues and lessons on how to navigate current struggles.

The events of 2011 are already part of the collective imaginary of possibility. I mean this in the sense that 15M is not simply a living memory; rather, it is a mode of being that exists in the present in a less perceptible way than it did during in the occupations, which, after all, were only one way of being 15M among many that continue apace. I do point out, however, that cartographers have presented a map of the field of activity that is misleading. Academics, the media, political parties, trade unions, and governments would all describe the events of 2011 to us as examples of civil citizenship interspersed with acts of civil disobedience. Yet that collective description conceals the thinking, acting, and working together found within local fields of practice – what Clifford Geertz would call "local knowledge."[57] As with any kind of knowledge, it cannot be understood by translating it into a dominant language and making sense of it from a pre-established set of constraints. When we

55 See Epstein (2017b, 20). According to Epstein, socialist humanism opposed forms of socialism that "set social solidarity against freedom of expression and the right to dissent" (20). In addition, they were deeply committed to creating conditions for individual creativity to flourish (20).

56 Engler and Engler (2016, 284).

57 Geertz (1983).

avoid such a move and instead think *with* these movements by spending time with them – "deep hanging out" is Geertz's term for it – the field of practice is revealed in a different manner.[58]

In this sense, I feel that what I have experienced – and continue to experience – in public squares by hanging out with both civil and civic citizens is best described as examples of civic activities and exemplars of civic citizenship. These citizens are slowly but steadily reinterpreting the very ideas around which power in modern societies has been constructed. They have learned to organize themselves in order to free themselves from governance systems that have shrunk their opportunities and that do not adequately represent them.[59] They want to join hands with others who also want to confront vicious systems of domination by co-constructing virtuous democratic communities of interconnected beings. In reclaiming and co-creating public squares as inclusive community spaces of and for resistance, through practices of civic engagement, they are co-generating ideal spaces within which citizens are able to join hands and experiment with alternatives.

Thus, by studying 15M we are able to learn from this power-with exemplar what works and does not work. We can be inspired by 15M and supportive of 15M yet maintain a critical stance toward aspects of 15M. We can learn from both its exemplarity and its shortcomings. We can learn what keeps people in 15M from turning to violence despite the disproportionate use of force by Spanish police. At the same time, we can reflect on the fact that when left-wing populist Podemos appeared on the scene, it was able to take advantage of 15M. Furthermore, we can learn from the fact that, despite the inspiration provided by 15M, right-wing populism seems to have captured the space of political contestation in Spain and Catalonia. This trend is threatening representative democracies everywhere.

3. Practices of Civic Engagement

This book, then, is about a practice-based citizen enactment of governance, democracy, and citizenship. Throughout, I investigate three dimensions of 15M practices of civic freedom through dialogues of reciprocal elucidation. First, how do those being 15M enact a response to the question of how we govern ourselves? Second, how are they

58 Geertz (1998, 69). What deep hanging out means to Geertz, is that anthropologists must spend extended periods in numerous informal sessions with those whose understandings they are trying to grasp.

59 Bollier and Helfrich (2012, 18).

practising democracy? And third, what kind of citizenship is this? Finally, the book evaluates what we can learn from 15M that will help us reverse the slide toward right-wing populism in our hollowed-out representative democracies.

i) How Do We Govern Ourselves?

Both Michel Foucault and James Tully remind us that it was the consolidation of the modern nation-state that brought varied relationships of governance under the state's direct or indirect supervision. This restricted government and the governed to a constrained field of practice constituted by formal institutions of representative government and their associated official public spheres. As a consequence, modern political science and theory came to restrict its focus to these institutions and neglected to investigate other relations of governance. This has led to a kind of blindness to ways of governing ourselves when those ways do not align with this understanding of governmentality. However, events on the ground over the past few decades have inspired different understandings of governance, thus heightening awareness of the many overlapping ways in which governance happens in our democratic societies. Those same events have also revealed myriad governance practices that coexist with, without always passing through, legal and political institutions.

But despite these advances in the field of governance studies, it does seem as if understandings of governance born in sixteenth-century Europe continue to dominate our societies' collective imaginaries. Foucault wrote that the sixteenth century was strongly marked by a debate about how we should govern ourselves: that is, how we could govern and be governed, by whom we should be governed, and how we could become good governors.[60] This debate led to doctrines of reason of state in Europe that marked the starting point of modern governmentality. This form of power, by fostering both control and dependence, both subjugates individuals and leaves them subject to the state.[61] Throughout his later writings, Foucault presented a useful genealogy of these types of power-over relations, with the result that many of us today understand "government" as the "conduct of conduct" and the many forms of resistance and attempts at dissociation as "counter-conducts."[62] This interwoven relationship between the "conduct of

60 Foucault (1991, 87).
61 Foucault (1982a, 781).
62 Foucault (2007, 75).

conduct" and dissenting "counter-conducts" Foucault refers to as the "strategic reversibility" of power relations. As citizens, we engage in hegemon/subaltern games, in a power-over field, within which we are in a permanent state of contestation. Hence, for Foucault the relationship between citizens and government is one in which the citizen works with the government inasmuch as there is consensus. Yet the citizen remains ever restive, avoiding subjection and refusing absolute acceptance.[63] There is always a contested space in which the displacement of boundaries defines the field of the possible.

Both Tully and Foucault view citizens and governors as partners – not adversaries – in free and agonistic power relations. Yet Foucault collapses all forms of citizenship into "being governed" in one way or another by governors, who by definition are elites. Tully highlights five distinct types of joining-hands relationships between citizens, and these help us understand power configurations in a different light. First, citizens join hands to try and reform institutions of participation from within. Second, citizens join hands to reappropriate democratic capabilities that previously had been delegated to legislatures and courts in order to negotiate directly with those they believe are responsible for their problems. Third, citizens join hands and reappropriate, to exercise in common, their capacities for social and economic organization. Fourth, citizens join hands and develop responsible and healthy ways to relate to the ecosystem on which they depend, refusing to contribute to its commodification. And fifth, citizens join hands and "become the change" they wish to see and argue for that change in the public sphere. Within these kinds of relationships, all partners exercise power equally without subjection or a governor/governed division.[64]

These kinds of power-with experiences in our human societies constitute the space within which citizens are able to build, support, and co-construct the commons.[65] What facilitates these experiences is the willingness to strengthen or reconstruct communitarian bonds.[66] This is where community is transformed. Through power-with practices, the community renegotiates and reshapes the agreed-upon conditions for

63 Foucault (1982b).

64 For a better understanding of these five distinct types of joining hands relationships, see Tully (2008b, 267–300). In agonism with Foucault's understanding of power and Tully's joining hands relationships between citizens, Holloway opens up the category of power and presents power-over as the antagonistic form of power-to. However, Holloway is missing the power-with of joining hands that Tully is describing. See Holloway (2019, 21).

65 For a good survey of examples of this kind of "communing," see Parker (2017).

66 See Zibechi (2005, 19).

coexistence. Following from this, when we investigate the square occupations of 2011, we are looking at power-with spaces in which a permanent constituent process is taking place. Collective bodies are forming and are being interrogated; at the same time, limits and inequalities are being challenged.[67] Within the power-with moments in public squares, we observe citizens unbound by the limits imposed by representative government. We see these citizens going beyond representation and struggling within a much broader field of government practices.[68]

This is how I perceive the reality on the ground of the struggle as I witness it in Spain. These citizens practising civic freedoms are not categorically rejecting representation; instead, they are deuniversalizing it. They are bringing to the fore of the public forum their broadened understanding of governance, one that introduces power-with practices of freedom to the field of possibility. By joining hands in a power-with manner, citizens are able to work together without subsuming their differences. The space allows those who seek reform of representative institutions to work together with those who seek to go beyond representation. Citizens co-create a civic space within which revolutionaries and reformists, people of the left and of the right, can work together. What makes this possible is their exemplary commitment to dialogue, horizontality, and non-violent modes of conflict resolution.

This power-with acts as a deeply relational "power-to-do-together." It is not the anti-power that anarchists strive toward. There are no attempts to dissolve power, yet it isn't that people are afraid to step off the edge of reality, as Holloway suggests.[69] Citizens practising civic freedom in Spain are not holding on to the force of their "no" to power as their only protection against elites. Instead, they are practising a double-movement, a non-violent agonistics of contesting and constructing. They say "no" to a particular injustice and present a constructive program that says "yes" to constructing alternatives together. Although power-to and power-with are equally social (the result of doing with others), the key difference between power-to and power-with is that the latter always remains open to deep dialogue/negotiation with opponents. It carves agonistic relationships of contestation rather than

67 See Parker (2017, 33).

68 Leydet (2019, 12).

69 In his discussion of spaces of anti-power, Holloway writes: "all our assumptions about what is reality, or what is politics or economics or even where we live, are so permeated by power that just to say 'no!' to power precipitates us into a vertiginous world in which there are no fixed reference points to hold on to other than the force of our own 'no!'" (2019, 3).

antagonistic relations of "othering." This is 15M's way of transforming and reconstituting their power relations: saying "yes" to power-with and "no" to power-over/power-under configurations of power.[70]

For Holloway, when collective presences come together, their shouting indicates that they are struggling to liberate power-to from power-over. I see this happening in 15M squares to a certain extent, but I think we are missing here the power-with that has been present in the squares since the first encampments and that does not need liberation. This power-with affirms itself relationally, and through that process, power relations are automatically transformed.[71] If power-over is the form of power-to that denies substance, power-with is the reminder that power is a "multiplicity of force relations" in which everyone affected must have a say.[72] If power-to is committed to a politics of "talking/listening" *to* one another, power-with crystallizes an ethos of gift/reciprocity *with* one another and, whenever possible, *with* opponents.[73]

ii) How Are They Practising Democracy?

There are two modes of democracy in the modern world: participatory and representative. But it is representative democracy that receives the most attention. The people I am thinking about in this study are civic and civil citizens practising participatory democracy and joining hands. Participatory democracy does not exclude representation. Yet citizens under this modality of democracy delegate and withhold their powers to elected representatives instead of behaving like atomized voters. This grants those working from within this mode of democracy much tighter control over their representatives. More importantly, it frees participatory democrats from representative-only world views of politics.[74]

---

70 In this paragraph, I am trying to make an important distinction between power-with as I understand it and the power-to that Holloway presents as the antidote to power-over. For his discussion of power, see Holloway (2019, 9–16).

71 Holloway (2019, 16).

72 Although Holloway acknowledges Foucault's move of not thinking of power in terms of a binary antagonism, in his articulation of power-to I fail to see how he avoids this binary. See Holloway (2019, 18–19).

73 For Holloway's conception of a politics of talking/listening, see Holloway (2019, 226).

74 Carole Pateman explains how deliberation, discussion, and debate are key to all modes of democracy. Yet for her it is clear that these are not enough for participatory democracy, which is a far more thorough and ongoing dialogical process. See Pateman (2012, 8).

Instead of "demoarchy," the Greeks chose the term "democracy" to signal that what they envisioned was not a form of rule (*arche*). Protagoras, Pericles, and Meletus described democracy as a non-elite telic mode of governance in which all citizens were equal and exercised power-with instead of power-over. Everyone's will was expressed in the assembly (*agora*), and through consensus a "democratic people" (*demos*) moved forward. People organized, brought into being, and practised self-government together by all having a say and hand in the decisions and actions of the community.[75] Until the eighteenth century this was the primary understanding of the term democracy.[76]

Between 1780 and 1860, this primary mode of democracy was displaced by a state-centric conception emanating from Europe and North America. The definition of "democracy" became formalized as the exercise of power over a governed electorate by an elected representative government, with elites envisioning a common will that had to be represented.[77] Benjamin Constant's 1819 lecture "The Liberty of the Ancients Compared with That of the Moderns" marked a turning point where the distinction between the primary and modern forms of democracy became central to democratic theory. Constant vehemently defended the idea that the freedom of the ancients in their Greek city-state belonged to an earlier stage of development, one without any connection to the modern state.[78]

By 1850, the idea of democracy had become so intertwined with that of representation that the Russian philosopher Peter Kropotkin stopped using the term democracy altogether and began to speak instead of mutual aid, self-government, or anarchy.[79] Despite this appropriation of

75 For further analysis of Greek conceptions of democracy, see Tully (2019b, 9). Tully here is redescribing Arendt's definition of democracy in *The Promise of Politics*.

76 In fact, even in eighteenth-century Europe, many considered the idea of representatives as non-democratic. For example, during the French Revolution those who considered themselves democrats thought of representatives as a new kind of aristocracy. Furthermore, even James Madison, Founding Father of the United States of America, understood representative systems to be non-democratic. For valuable insights into eighteenth-century conceptions of democracy, see Parker (2017, 9).

77 The following texts are helpful in order to understand the distinction between state-centric representative democracy and ancient direct democracy: Manin (1997); Wolin (1993); and Ober (2008).

78 Anyone defending such democratic practice was, according to Constant, suffering from a "maladie infantile." For Constant, the modern state requires a type of liberty that can only be provided by a representative government. See B. Constant, (1819) "The Liberty of the Ancients Compared with that of the Moderns," lecture given at the Athénée Royal of Paris. Constant's essay is available online at the Online Library of Liberty (oll.libertyfund.org).

79 See Dupuis-Déri (2013).

the meaning of democracy by the state, however, it would be naive to assume that the governed embraced the redefinition.

In fact, it wasn't until the expansion of the middle classes in the twentieth century that people began to have faith that elected officials might finally represent the community.[80] By the second half of the twentieth century, the primary form of democracy began to be described using terms and concepts like "deep democracy," "prefigurative democracy," "direct democracy," "radical democracy," or "earth democracy." This was a necessary step taken by citizens themselves to differentiate their practices from the dominant representative mode of democracy through which we are presently ruled.[81]

In the West today, these two distinct types of democracy seem to be following separate paths, with occasional interactions that have both positive and negative consequences. Elites continue to defend the idea that representative democracy is the universal standard by which democratic achievement can be measured.[82] In the meantime, citizens are responding by persistently enacting participatory democracy, viewing this as the primary mode of being democratic. In 2011, 15M in Spain exemplified this primary sense of "democracy," thus crystallizing a lifeway (a mode of being and a temporality) that has persisted.

A deeper understanding of the 15M mode of being can help us expand our current conception of democracy. When we look closely at 15M, we begin to understand democracy as a space within which multiple heterodoxies enter into dialogue and negotiate ways to coexist peacefully and constructively without being subsumed. Most importantly, grasping 15M's "democracy here and now" approach will help us broaden our thinking, which heretofore has trained us as civil citizens to understand power as monolithic, as flowing down from on high. We will then be able to see representative democracy as a set of governance practices, which though regulative are not in any sense constitutive of

---

80 Parker (2017, 10).

81 For some useful literature on alter-democratic pathways, see the following: Aslam (2017); Gibson-Graham (2006); Malleson (2014); Polletta (2004); and Aslam, McIvor, and Schlosser (2019, 34).

82 For Joseph Schumpeter, modern representative democracies have little to do with government of and by the people. The only thing people are allowed to do is select who governs them; se Schumpeter (2003). For Bernard Manin, representative government gives no institutional role to the people; see Manin (1997). For Sheldon Wolin, the institutionalization of democracy can mark its attenuation as much as its realization; see Wolin (1994). For a useful discussion of these thinkers' ideas about the relationship between participation and representation, see Peruzzotti (2008).

democracy.[83] Furthermore, this will crystallize how citizens are able to transform elite democracies into non-elite democracies, by reclaiming the power of Leviathan through speaking and acting otherwise.

Democracy here and now entails moments of representation. Nevertheless, a key difference between a "democracy here and now" mode of being and representative democracy as it is understood in the modern sense, is that in representative democracy representatives generally strive to guarantee their own political continuity, whereas in the "democracy here and now" mode of being democratic anyone representing most often strives to their own overcoming.

iii) What Kind of Citizenship Is This?

Our inherited field of citizenship encompasses many of the most important and long-lasting struggles in the history of our political systems. For the most part, these struggles have been fought over what it means to be a citizen and the types of practices and institutions that make citizenship possible.[84] Since ancient Greek times, every age has understood citizenship as the basis of politics. In this sense, in Western memory and experience we have vivid images of warrior-citizens, patrician-citizens, merchant-citizens, and bourgeois-citizens.[85] This is the genealogy of citizenship in the Western world as dominant groups have narrated it. This narration of the historical process of citizenship has allowed those defending this line of thought to constitute themselves as inheritors and torch-bearers of the citizenship tradition.

The outcome of this process has been the consolidation of a mode of modern citizenship with a civil character. This mode of citizenship presents a set of restrictive democratic practices linked to a pre-established set of institutions. We refer to these practices as constitutional representative democracy. This form of rule originated in the West and was imposed on the non-West over the course of centuries of imperialism and violent dispossession. As a mode of citizenship, it rose to dominance as representative nation-states and their capitalist economies centralized and consolidated. The nationalization of citizenship went hand-in-hand with the subalternizing of local and regional customs, laws, modes of governance, and types of citizenship that existed prior to the rise of the nation-state. In the mind of the modern citizen, the

83 Leydet (2019, 10, 21).
84 Tully (2008b, 243).
85 Isin (2002, 1) 1.

violence of this process and the myriad civic rebellions and resistances to it are necessary to modernization.[86]

Two features of modern citizenship have taken hold since the eighteenth century: the "universal institutional form" and the "universal set of historical processes." These have made it possible for the West to spread modern citizenship to non-Western countries. Under this modality of citizenship, those who are subject to the state are bound to a formal and institutionalized rule of law; yet at the same time, the rule of law is independent of the citizenry. In this sense, to speak of citizenship in terms of the modern conception is to speak of the juridical rights of subjects operating within the parameters of a set of constituent institutions. The idea that these are necessary and universal allows little space for self-critical analysis. So it is hard for moderns to acquire a critical view of citizenship, for this would require suspending the imposition of the modern representation of citizenship onto the field of citizenship proper. Such a move would require us to "deuniversalize" this mode of citizenship in order to reveal its unjustified authority.

Tully's work on citizenship is useful for approaching this deuniversalization. He comes at the issue in two ways. First, he sets out a broadened definition of citizenship that sees citizens as both subjects and agents – that is, citizens are engaged agents in the field of governance who are, simultaneously, governed subjects. Second, he follows this move by differentiating between two particular modes of citizenship: "civil" and "civic." He uses these terms because they reflect etymologically the complex histories endured by these two modalities of citizenship: civil gives expression to the mode of "restrictive," "institution-based," "modular" modern citizenship, whereas civic reveals a "practice-based" non-restrictive mode of citizenship that is grounded in freedom.

In the civil tradition, conflict and coercion are taken to be the basis of politics and of all governance relationships. In this sense, our

86 In *Public Philosophy in a New* Key, vol. 1, Tully broadens our understanding of citizenship; see Tully (2008a). In vol. 2, he then surveys the genealogy of modern citizenship, its constituent features, and its boundaries and institutions; see Tully (2008b, 255, 247, 268, 285). Then, in "Reciprocal Elucidation," he distinguishes clearly between civil and civic citizenship, explaining that "civic," because of its "philological genealogy," is useful as "a family resemblance concept that is neither closed by a rigid frontier nor under the auspices of representative governments and states, but relatively open to the creative uses of the *demoi*." See Tully (2019b, 5, 19, 20–2, 28).

governance structures are modified and determined by those who win the political game. In the civic tradition, by contrast, politics is something different – it entails bonds of practice-generated reciprocal trust and support that are nurtured through citizen-to-citizen self-government relationships. From a civic perspective, representation is always practised in a non-alienated manner. It is not so much that the practices of civic citizenship are different from those of civil citizenship, but that they are "different in kind." The civil tradition claims a particular "Western" lineage of universal institutions and historical processes, while civic citizenship refers to the multitude of ways in which citizens in both the West and non-West act in concert as they negotiate relations of power.

There has been persistent mistrust between those practising the distinct yet overlapping modes of civil and civic citizenship. Yet in 2011, in Spanish public squares, the civic sphere crystallized in a significant way. In these trust-generating spaces, civil and civic citizens were able to bridge their differences and find ways to overlap by engaging in practice-based discussions about ways of joining hands. As an outcome, they were able to enact two types of citizen partnerships. The first partnership is one in which citizens organize to negotiate citizen/government relationships. The second consists of citizens "citizenizing" (i.e., democratizing) their activities by organizing and running citizen-to-citizen initiatives with no intention of entering into negotiations with the government.[87] Individuals being 15M are contesting while constructing alternatives and, in this way, since the square occupations, have been showing the exemplarity of their six joining-hands relationships in a multiplicity of ways.

Theories of modern citizenship mock the idea of an exemplary civic ethic, which is always presented as a pre-modern idea that, at most, reveals an ethics of care rather than a mode of being political that is appropriate for a modern society.[88] Contrary to this view, civil and civic citizens in 15M are collectively enacting "non-heroic extensions" of the everyday practices of negotiation present (and

87 In *Public Philosophy in a New* Key, vol. 2, Tully discusses different kinds of citizen partnerships, misunderstandings that exist around the idea of a civic ethic, and the expanded field of practice in which civic citizens operate; see Tully (2008b, 256, 284, 291, 294).

88 Nevertheless, when scholars encounter this civic ethic they describe a radically different sensibility, exemplary mutual respect, cooperation, and horizontal decision-making. Such traits seem appropriate for any society that aims to be virtuous rather than vicious. See, for example, Graeber (2009, 30).

necessary) in the field of practice of civic engagement. By renegotiating and reinterpreting the terms of their society's social contract, 15M citizens are enacting civic freedom. That is, because they understand themselves as free to think and act otherwise, they decide together when and how to respond to particular governmental actions; they determine whether to ignore their governors or particular norms; they decide when and how to negotiate and even whether they *want* to negotiate; and, finally, they decide when they will conform to a particular social convention.[89] In this manner, instead of presenting yet another way of governing others, 15M reveals a modality of self-governance within dominant governance. It offers an exemplar – not an example – of practices of governed resisters acting otherwise.[90]

The Salt March of 1930 in colonial India, initiated by Mohandas Gandhi to produce salt from seawater in the coastal village of Dandi, is remembered as an exemplary non-cooperation campaign. This march was exemplary because it combined obstruction and non-cooperation (contestation) with a constructive program designed to build alternatives.[91] Thousands of books have been written about this march. In this book, I argue that what has happened in Spain since 15 May 2011, when 15M made its first political appearance, is of equal significance. I contend that 15M is best understood as an exemplar of civic freedom. I make that claim because of how 15M has tied contestation to a constructive program. Civil and civic citizens are joining hands to carry out this dual process, and there is much we can learn from and with 15M as crises of democracy intensify across the globe.

---

89 Ivison (2019, 19).

90 I speak of *example* when describing a thing that is characteristic of its kind; I refer to *exemplar* when wanting to highlight something that merits imitation. This distinction is well articulated in Owen (2019, 21).

91 Richard Gregg describes the Indian Nationalist movement of the 1930s: "The widespread manufacture of salt in opposition to the government salt monopoly, the refusal to pay taxes, the picketing of liquor and opium shops, the combination of making homespun cloth and picketing shops selling foreign cloth are specific instances. These activities were nonviolent. They aimed at replacing a pre-existing order by a new order. They were intended to put an end, among the masses, to the pre-existing fear of the government, and to stimulate courage, self-reliance, self-respect and political unity. They actually had that effect in large measure." See Gregg (2018, 71). For a brilliant article on the topic, see M. Enger and P. Enger, "How Did Gandhi Win? Lessons from the Salt March," in *Dissent*, 10 October 2014, https://www.dissentmagazine.org/blog/gandhi-win-lessons-salt-march-social-movements.

4. Method of Reciprocal Elucidation[92]

In a conversation between Gilles Deleuze and Michel Foucault published in 1972, Foucault tries to explain how he thinks the role of the intellectual changed following the events of May 1968. For him, prior to 1968, the intellectual spoke truth to power in the name of those who could not speak. The intellectual was the voice of the people and their consciousness.[93] Following the "upheaval" (his term for the events of May 1968), the intellectual discovered that the masses no longer needed intellectuals to gain knowledge. People knew exactly what they wanted and why they wanted it, and they were capable of speaking with their own voice.

In *What Is an Author?*, Foucault goes on to imagine a society in which authorship disappears and ideas circulate anonymously.[94] In such a society, the sheer "indignity of speaking for others" can be avoided. I recognized this idea during my time spent with 15M, and it can still be seen today in the everyday activities of engaged citizens. Thinking along with Foucault, two years after the encampments, in 2013, I considered the best and most meaningful way to approach 15M practices of civic engagement and arrived at the idea of public philosophy.[95] Myriad participant methods can shed light on the practices of citizens in particular situated struggles. There are also many kinds of public philosophies that are useful in this regard. Nevertheless, I was particularly drawn to the kind of public philosophy that studies practices of civic engagement by means of "dialogues of reciprocal elucidation."[96]

Inspired by Tully's public philosophy, I devised my own method of reciprocal elucidation, one that is best understood as a family member of this philosophical tradition. Distinguished members of the family

---

92 Although the methodology and timing of the research will crystallize as the book progresses, the following are worth noting: in 2011, I attended square occupations in Barcelona as a participant; in 2013, I set out on a research trip in an old VW camper van, travelling to twenty-five different cities in Spain; in the space of nine months, I engaged in "deep hanging out" practices with 15M citizens across the country (see page 147 of this book).

93 Foucault (1977b, 207–9).

94 Foucault (1977a, 138).

95 David Owen writes that "public philosophy is, and understands itself to be, a practice structured by commitment to the ideal of civic freedom; it is not concerned to found a theoretical school but rather to enable the formation of a community of practitioners who exemplify the change that they seek to bring about" (2019, 21).

96 This is the public philosophy I was introduced to by James Tully and with which I find myself in dialogue as I develop my own particular mode of philosophy. See Tully (2016, 51–74).

include Ludwig Wittgenstein, Quentin Skinner, Tully, David Owen, and Michael Temelini. I have learned from this tradition that one can study these forms of organization as an empirical social scientist without disqualifying them in the process. The researcher can observe and grow with forms of organization that have their own vernacular, shared language, and activities, and thereby can better understand their habitus and ethos. One can engage with 15M and see, through the speech acts one encounters, how the activities of those being 15M are tightly interwoven. These dialogues of reciprocal elucidation with citizens being 15M can help us understand what it is we are referring to when we speak of 15M.[97]

In contrast to monologue, the intersubjective practice of dialogue allows us to see things "aspectivally."[98] Dialogue does not subscribe to the idea that there is only one way of explaining the essential features of a particular phenomenon.[99] Instead, dialogue offers explanations to phenomena that help us understand but that are always open to revision. As epistemically interdependent beings, we are able to gain an understanding of activities in which we are involved by dialoguing with one another. It is in the dialogic space that we are able to exchange points of view and discover partial truths in our understandings. As humans, we can only see alternative sides to a phenomenon if we engage in the freedom of speaking with one another.[100] By listening to

---

97 While in conversation with those who are being 15M, throughout this text I also engage with a range of authors around James Tully and his approach to public philosophy: Ludwig Wittgenstein, Michael Temelini, David Owen, Peter Kropotkin, Chantal Mouffe, Joe Parker, and others. Temelini argues that this is the best approach out there, and I have found it very useful while conducting this study. Clayton Chin, in *The Practice of Political Theory: Rorty and Continental Thought*, argues that Tully has inherited the best features of Rorty's political philosophy, the most influential political philosophy of the late twentieth century, and the way forward.

98 Temelini (2017, 297–8).

99 When speaking of dialogue, I think it is important to mention Mikhail Bakhtin's contrast between the dialogic and the monologic work of literature. It is also useful to acknowledge his contribution to dialogical language and thought. According to him, all language is a relational process engaged in permanent redescription; see Bakhtin (1981). In this study, I draw on different sources to speak about dialogue. In particular, I enter into conversation with David Bohm and others, who are linking dialogue to the exercise of power-with or joining hands. Nevertheless, it is important to highlight Bakhtin's contribution to the dialogic method as a divergence from normative Eurocentric objectivist social science methodologies. For a Bakhtin-inspired analysis of social movements, see Meek and Simonian (2017).

100 Arendt (2005, 165).

the voices of those being 15M in their own terms, we can overcome our partial understanding of their activities and avoid any underlying universal presumptions in our analysis.[101]

Mikhail Bakhtin writes that the "living utterance" becomes active in social dialogue by taking its meaning and shape through the weaving of a multiplicity of "living dialogic threads." This utterance arises through dialogue, as both its "continuation" and its "rejoinder." The utterance never enters a dialogue from the sidelines – there is always a "tension-filled interaction" between the utterance and the alien word, a "dialogic inter-orientation." One's own word and the word of another "dialogically interanimate each other." The living utterance is not a "single-voiced vehicle for expression" but a far more complex, dynamic, and dialogical living expression. Each utterance crystallizes a particular view of the world, and with every utterance there is a constant interaction between meanings. The utterance is always co-authored. The dialogical relationship between self and other is always one of simultaneity.[102]

Bakhtin's dialogical conception of being helps us understand that reality is always experienced from a particular position and is not simply perceived; multiplicity is inextricably linked to human perception.[103] This is why, through dialogue with others, we are able to broaden and illuminate our parochial understandings of modes of being, of events and their multiple meanings.[104]

This is also why I think a dialogical ethics is needed if we are to better understand what those being 15M are doing. In order to reveal 15M's field of practice and excavate the histories of those practices, we need to listen carefully to the multiplicity of voices within 15M. We need to critically think through 15M's analyses of the past and the present as well as 15M's suggestions for moving forward. Most importantly, we need to establish the kind of ongoing open dialogue with those being 15M that will allow us to modify our understandings as the conversation

101 By conducting research in dialogue with those who are in sympathy with 15M, I am practising what Dána-Ain Davis has characterized as being "between objectivity and subjectivity"; see Davis (2006, 8). In essence, I am trying to generate what Jafari Sinclaire Allen, describes as "a radical shift away from 'traditional' authority and legitimacy, toward the margins"; see Allen (2008, 371).

102 For an in-depth understanding of Bakhtin's ideas on the dialogical, see his *The Dialogical Imagination* (2008, 276–7, 279, 293, 354–5, 426); see also Holquist (2002, 13, 19).

103 Holquist (2002, 21, 22).

104 Holquist (2002, 40).

progresses. In doing so, we as researchers will be cooperating with citizens, learning with them but also advancing a mutual understanding through our own descriptions and examples. This will make the relationship one of reciprocal support and enlightenment.[105]

Jeffrey Juris argues for a kind of practically engaged research that does not separate observation from participation;[106] Katia Valenzuela-Fuentes invites researchers studying movements that practise horizontality to join the movements' quest for horizontality through the horizontalization of their knowledge production;[107] Bertie Russell opposes the idea that the researcher must maintain a critical distance from the "object" of the research;[108] and Donna Haraway reminds us of our situated and partial understandings of phenomena.[109]

On an equally useful note, Patricia Maguirre asks researchers to develop relationships of reciprocity and mutual empowerment with those they are looking to learn with;[110] María Isabel Casas-Cortés, Michal Osterweil, and Dana Powell encourage researchers to remember that people being studied are "knowledge-producers in their own right";[111] and

---

105 Tully speaks about the important relationship between academic researchers and the citizens with whom they are in dialogue; see Tully (2016, 51–74).

106 This is what Juris calls "militant ethnography" in the context of his engagement with alter-globalization and anti-authoritarian networks. It builds from what Nancy Scheper-Hughes referred to as "enraged" anthropology and invites people to do research from within rather that outside social movements; see Juris (2005, 255).

107 See Valenzuela-Fuentes (2019, 719), who brilliantly articulates the rich history of militant ethnography. It is important to mention it here because, although it stems from different traditions, it has a family resemblance to my method of reciprocal elucidation. Valenzuela-Fuentes traces the roots of militant ethnography to the tradition of militant research started by Marx with his *Workers' Inquiry* in the 1880s; she then extends that tradition to *Socialisme ou Barbarie* in the 1950s, Italian workerism in the 1960s, the Latin American participatory action research (PAR) tradition of the 1960s and 1970s, and the work of contemporary scholars like Hannah Hale, Jeffry Juris, María Isabel Casas-Cortes, David Graeber, Theresa Petray, Miguel Ángel Martínez, Elísabeth Lorenzi, Alexander Khasnabish, Bertie Russell, and Nicholas Apoifis; see Valenzuela-Fuentes (2019, 720–1).

108 See Russell (2015, 222–9). For Russell, the researcher contributes to movements by attempting to move them through a critique of their own activities. This differs slightly from what I am doing in this study: I am equally interested in contributing politically, but for the purpose of this work I am mainly interested in understanding what those who are being 15M are doing. Thus, I listen to their self-descriptions and respond to them with my own understandings following our dialogues of reciprocal elucidation.

109 See Haraway (1988).

110 See Maguirre (2001).

111 See Casas-Cortés, Osterweil, and Powell (2008).

Sarah Motta describes the politics of dialogue, what she understands as a prefigurative epistemology – a means by which the researcher and the person being researched break disempowering and vanguard-oriented, hierarchical understandings of knowledge.[112]

I see all of the above as approaches whereby I join hands and wherefrom I learn as I attempt to engage with 15M. I also bring to my study a feminist ethics of care, through which I hold a deep awareness about the interconnected and interdependent relationship between responsibility and practices of care in researcher/researched relationships.[113] Because of this ethos of care, just as Valenzuela-Fuentes explains in regard to her own research, my role as a reflective observer and participant shifts and overlaps repeatedly throughout dialogues of reciprocal elucidation in which I participate with*in* 15M.[114] This is partly to do with the fact that 15M is enacting a dialogical and engaged mode of being through which the distinction between "being" and "being political" is blurred.

15M's 2011 uprising caught both elites and most Spaniards/Catalonians by surprise: millions of people had begun to practise a mode of citizenship that, I argue, is different in kind from what moderns in representative democracies are used to. To better understand 15M practices of civic engagement, I travelled in an old van across the many territories that comprise what is today recognized as Spain. I immersed myself with*in* what looked and felt like a complex and non-violent, mutating and dialogic, collective and cooperative, agonistic and transformative "climate" that many referred to as *el clima 15M* (15M climate).[115]

My travels lasted from May to November 2013. I interviewed 213 people being 15M in eight of the country's autonomous communities, in twenty-five different cities and in many smaller towns and villages. I engaged in ongoing conversations alongside and sometimes in the course of visits to assemblies, cooperatives, liberated social spaces, community-run recuperated social housing estates, union headquarters, factories, offices, universities, parliamentary buildings, farms, public squares, virtual meeting rooms, and secured military-level encrypted video conferencing spaces (for cases where people were in hiding), as well as in people's homes.[116]

---

112 See Motta (2011).

113 See Evans (2016, 214).

114 See Valenzuela-Fuentes (2019, 727).

115 A term coined by Spanish philosopher Amador Fernández-Savater.

116 As I stated on page xvi, my choice of places to visit was determined along the way, based on recommendations from different interviewees, who often suggested particular cities to visit, based on the exemplary work of 15Ms in these localities. At the same time, I consciously selected interviewees who would reflect

As I engaged 15M through dialogues of reciprocal elucidation – "Caminamos preguntando" (walking we ask questions), as the Zapatista saying goes – the way of being of those being 15M revealed itself. Within cities, I walked across the urban landscape from meeting to meeting. The slowness of walking – often walking with those I was interviewing – stretched time and deepened space. This slow approach made me familiar with the landscape within which the struggles I was attempting to understand were taking place. It was not so much that I was drawing nearer to a given destination; it was more that 15M was becoming more insistent in my body. Following Henry David Thoreau's advice, I took experience to be my only solid foundation; thus, I only sat down to write "in the aftermath of those solidly marked, hammered paces."[117]

In this manner, I engaged those being 15M through participation rather than abstraction. This allowed a "participatory consciousness" to grow between us.[118] I discussed 15M with many people who preferred to remain anonymous. Interviewees included town mayors, politicians of numerous political parties, union leaders, hackers, lawyers; public intellectuals, philosophers, artists, school and university teachers, journalists, squatters, and public administrators. The people I interviewed

---

the geographic and demographic diversity of 15M. A set of questions guided the dialogues I maintained with 15M individuals. However, conversations quickly evolved into free-flowing spaces in which interviewees and I interrupted, facilitated, and translated one another in order to deepen our co-understanding of 15M. I conducted the interviews mostly in Spanish; however, some were conducted in Catalan, French, or English. In a few of the interviews I conducted in Galicia, I asked the questions in Spanish and the interviewees responded in Galician. After finishing the interviewing, I transcribed the 213 one-hour interviews and then translated them into English in their entirety. I anonymized the interviews by randomly allocating a number between 1 and 213 to each interviewee, which means I can now cite each interviewee within the text as AI + Number (AI 173, and so on). Throughout the trip I made field notes, recorded assemblies, and collected materials that participants provided. I have written this book as a response to these dialogues of reciprocal elucidation. The interviewees ranged in age between seventeen and eighty and were mainly white, non-immigrant, and of the middle class. Men and women were equally represented. The demographics of my sample seem to align with 15M as I perceived it.

117 This is Gros (2014, 98) quoting Thoreau. In the same text, Gros describes the stretching of time through walking and how things become insistent on one's body through the process (37–8). On a related note, Rául Zibechi reminds us of the Zapatista saying *caminar los caminos* (walking the walk). According to him, it is in the walking that we see elements of a new society; see Zibechi (2005, 24).

118 I am inspired by the work of David Bohm in this regard. See Bohm (2004, xiii).

all identified themselves as active participants in 15M or as having collaborated with or felt closely aligned to 15M.

As I progressed in my dialogues, travelling from locality to locality across Spain, it became clear to me that dialoguing with those "being" in public squares in 2011 was indispensable in order to grasp the kind of citizenship they were practising. This relational approach allowed me to interpret 15M through a process of constructing mutual understandings.[119] I came to realize that the 213 individuals I spoke with were in fact the co-writers of this book. Through our dialogues of reciprocal elucidation, they helped me better understand what it means to be "being 15M." I was able to actively experience how 15M practises self-government, democracy, and citizenship. Researching on the road like this was an academic and sociopolitically transformative experience. It was a way of enriching my academically trained philosophy by entering into a philosophy of shared experience with fellow citizens.

5. 15M as an Exemplar

In treating 15M as exemplary of civic freedom, my objective is not to develop a theory of practices of civic engagement. Nor is my aim to construct an ideal type out of the examples of civic practices enacted by 15M and presented throughout this book. I am not trying to reveal to people what they ought to do or who they should be. I am simply presenting what it means to be 15M by redescribing the ways of doing and modes of being of civil and civic citizens joining hands in public squares. This is how theory can learn from practice.[120] We can learn from 15M in a twofold manner: from their examples in practice, and from the example their practice sets.[121] 15M does not simply show us that another world is possible, it reveals how another world is actual.[122]

It does this through an exemplary performance of a multitude of practices of civic engagement. Mastering their non-violent, horizontal, and dialogical conduct, individuals being 15M become exemplars of the civic ideal, an ideal that cannot be specified through principles but

119 For a useful explanation of how parties move through dialogue from a unilaterally constructed "prior theory" to a "passing theory" of interpretation, see Davidson (1986).

120 See Celikates (2019, 2).

121 Here I am drawing from Michael Temelini, who discusses how Wittgenstein in his *Philosophical Investigations* thinks about examples; see Temelini (2017, 288).

122 As Holloway puts it, there is a real weaving of different worlds going on; see Holloway (2018a, 34).

is exemplified through performance.[123] This is why I believe that the uprisings that began on 15 May 2011 represent the most important political and social event in Spain since the end of the dictatorship.[124]

15M came into being, organized, and exercised power simultaneously. Besides displaying great resilience in a challenging struggle against state violence, 15M has been effective in all sorts of horizontal short- and long-term ways. 15M individuals were able to occupy squares across the country for months. After the decision was made in the general assembly of each of the encampments to move the encampments, 15M individuals moved their activities to neighbourhoods and expanded from new spaces. Some 15M individuals joined other projects; others helped bring different projects together; still others have offered spaces from which to extend the struggle to individuals without prior activist involvement.

"Vamos lentos porque vamos lejos" (We go ever so slowly because we are going on forever) was one of the most prominent mantras when 15M occupied city squares.[125] This mantra eventually moved citizens away from old conceptions of revolution and the violent agonistics of

---

123 Owen (2019, 4, 5, 7, 17).

124 I acknowledge both the historical significance and the political importance of Catalonia's recent unilateral declaration of independence. I do understand that the independence movement ranks as one of the most important developments in Spain since the end of the dictatorship. Nevertheless, the transformation of the political imaginary brought about by 15M is redefining what it means to be political in Spain in a unique manner.

125 *Vamos lentos porque vamos lejos* seems to be in alignment with a number of similar articulations from different traditions and places. They all seem to be telling us that it is a mistake to take big steps, because you will end up being captured by power politics. Once that happens, either you become subalternized or you "win" the race and turn into the new hegemon. For example, Bill Reid says about his famous sculpture *The Spirit of Haida Gwaii*: "the canoe goes on forever in the same place." Vandana Shiva suggests that we take small steps because they are more powerful, since everyone can take these small steps in their everyday life. Among the new neuroscientists and philosophers working in this post-Cartesian area of re-embedding the mind back into life, the mantra is "humans lay down the path in walking." We "bring forth the world to consciousness in the very way we enact it in every step we take." This derives from the Santiago Theory of Cognition, which posits that every sentient form of life brings forth a world in living. For those who are being 15M, *vamos lentos porque vamos lejos* is a reminder that they have to be the change they want to see and that things done quickly risk reproducing the very structures and injustices they are trying to alter. I am grateful to James Tully for coining what in my opinion is the best translation into English of the Spanish phrase *Vamos lentos porque vamos lejos*. The English phrase being: We go ever so slowly because we are going on forever.

our history.[126] It allowed these citizens to blaze a path toward a non-violent agonistics of mutual aid. Following from this, regarding the question of how we govern ourselves, 15M responded by joining hands and making sure that means and ends aligned.[127] This has been their virtuous answer to vicious social systems that are trying to devour them.

By the time of my research trip, the encampments were being remembered as a moment of transformation when self-governing people enacted a new world and presented alternatives. In the encampments, people learned the importance of generating dialogical power-with relations among those striving for change. The encampments made visible and accessible to a large proportion of the Spanish population a powerful way of being together as citizens, one based on "being the change." By that I mean that they engaged in practices that tried to build the egalitarian and deeply democratic world they wished to see. In this way, their presence challenged the government and other formal and/or informal, vertically orientated, power-over governance structures through their mode of being in the world together.

By being ethical (practising freedom informed by reflection), 15M citizens are transforming what Gandhi referred to as a "nominal" democracy into what he described as complete or integral democracy (*purna swaraj*).[128] In the kind of democracy practised by 15M, citizens are co-subjects and co-authors in relationships of power. Through their civic practices, civil and civic citizens working from within 15M reveal their ability to be free within and against their society's rules of governance. It is true that the slow pace of 15M's "means and ends in alignment" approach to social transformation discourages many political actors, but this is more the result of a lack of understanding of the process than it is a marker of that process's inefficiency.[129]

While commentators point to the inefficiency of the ways of being of 15M, those being 15M are continuing to enact a powerful kind of "conviviality" that reveals the following as the core ethical virtues of their joining-hands relations: seeking truth by speaking truthfully to others; mutual care; courage to speak truth to power; openness to the

126 The 15M mantra "we go ever so slowly because we are going on forever" is reminiscent of the Zapatista saying "walking at the pace of the slowest." See Zibechi (2005, 19).

127 As Marina Sitrin has also spotted in her own work, these horizontal joining hands relationships are both the means and ends of the struggle; see Sitrin (2018, 316).

128 See Pantham (1983, 165). This theme runs through Gandhi's writings; in *Hind Swaraj* it is ever present. Through this lens he sees governors as being governed by the citizens. For a good overview of Gandhi's thought, see Gandhi (2008).

129 See Gregg (2018, 144).

views of others; humility about the perspectival character of one's own views; reciprocating non-violently rather than retaliating; cooperating; sharing power; and a slow temporality. These virtues constitute the 15M relationships of joining hands because of the autotelic relation between means and ends. They describe the 15M mode of being in specific relationships.[130]

Many hard-earned lessons can be learned from spending time with 15M. Yet many people think that 15M and various other mobilizations around the world in 2011 achieved nothing. This claim is made and defended largely on the basis that these movements did not present a political party with a specific political project. Yet 15M's unmediated contestation, however momentary its expression in public squares, has launched a permanent transition movement. It has changed the conversation in Spanish society by introducing a culture of care to sociopolitical transformation. It has also marked the end of a particular mode of state in the country and thereby generated a series of potential tipping points.[131] A first potential tipping point was the abdication of the Spanish king in favour of his son. This came about largely after 15M denounced corruption involving the king himself and the royal household overall. A second has been the rise of Podemos in Spain's mainstream politics. Notwithstanding the agonisms between those being 15M and party movements such as Podemos, it has become abundantly clear that 15M made possible the birth of Podemos.[132] The institutionality brought about by the country's transition from dictatorship to democracy is, for the first time, being seriously challenged from within the country's parliament.

The same can be said in regard to local government. Since 15M, mayoralty races in Madrid, Barcelona, Valencia, and many other cities and towns have been won by candidates who are deeply rooted in social

---

130 This way of relating to one another, enacted by 15M, was not only present in the first ever self-organizing human community, but is also found in the mutual aid networks that constitute the largest informal, symbiotic fellowship of engaged citizens in the world today. For a thorough study of the global dimension of these struggles, see Hawken (2007). For further explication of the idea of "conviviality" see Tully (2008, 143).

131 This is important in the context of Spain, because here the state often resembles that vision of it painted by Bertrand Russell of "a stupid elderly man accustomed to flattery, ossified in his prejudices, and wholly unaware of all that is vital in the thought of his time." See Russell (2004, 200).

132 During 2011, public square occupation movements sharing family resemblances with 15M occupied squares in numerous countries. These occupations made possible parties and initiatives that resonated with the experience of Podemos in Spain. I am thinking for example of SYRIZA in Greece, Jeremy Corbyn and Momentum in the United Kingdom, and Bernie Sanders in the United States.

movements and who participated in 15M. These municipal governments have already introduced concrete measures to welcome refugees, reduce homelessness, fight speculation and aggressive tourism, and tackle local pollution. More importantly, the relationships between these municipalities and grassroots social movements such as 15M have often been exemplary. The shifts we are seeing in the municipal sphere have been made possible by 15M, and they mark a third potential tipping point, in that citizens in these localities have recovered powers of self-government previously usurped by elites.

6. The Persistence of 15M's Lifeway

In 2017, Spain faced yet another potential tipping point in its power configurations following an attempt at secession by Catalonia's pro-independence leaders.[133] This secession attempt did not reveal a 15M way of being; that said, it was 15M that first raised the need for a deconstituent process in 2011. The aim was to deconstitute the regime born in 1978 out of the transition from dictatorship to democracy so that a different regime could be formed in a collective manner. In this sense, although the Catalonia secession attempt differs in kind from 15M – it is an elite-led process, launched from a previously constituted body – the fact is that the process presented yet another potential tipping point for the constitutional order that 15M has been challenging.[134]

133 On 1 October 2017, a referendum was held in Catalonia with no institutional guarantees, in which fewer than half of Catalan voters participated. This referendum was violently repressed by Spain's security forces. In response, the Catalan parliament declared unilateral independence, and the Spanish government applied Article 155 of the constitution, which – dubiously interpreted – allowed for a suspension of the Catalan government and early elections. Numerous Catalan parliamentarians together with civil society leaders have been imprisoned pending trial for secession. Other parliamentarians, including the ousted Catalan president, Carles Puigdemont, have self-exiled in Belgium. (Puigdemont was arrested in Germany on 25 March 2017 but was eventually released.) Elections were held on 21 December 2017, and together the pro-independence parties retained a majority in parliament. Nevertheless, the party that received the most votes (1.1 million, thus 37 seats) was *Ciutadans*, a right-wing populist party that has been an ardent defender of Spanish unity.

134 Spain is a multi-nation state with a multiplicity of authentic sub-state minority nationalisms, one of them being Catalan. As one of the many examples of constitutional movements in the modern age, Catalan sub-state nationalism presents itself as a historical identity with historical demands. It has a long history that can be traced back to at least the eighteenth century. In this sense, Catalan national identity is as legitimate and sincere as Spanish national identity. Catalonia has been and remains a powerful and heartfelt locus of political allegiance, stemming from a venerable and long-standing language of politics – republican self-rule. It

In addition, as the Catalan crisis intensified, we saw 15M-inspired responses to it. For example, on 4 October 2017 a group of social scientists at various universities (together with other citizens in Spain and abroad) put out an exemplary call raising a collective voice against abuses of democracy by the Catalan *and* Spanish governments.[135] A few days later, on 8 October, while nationalist demonstrations were being encouraged on both sides, thousands of Spanish and Catalan citizens came out in cities across both Spain and Catalonia demanding that the two sides begin a dialogue that I would characterize as reciprocal elucidation. Symbolically, people came out on the streets wearing white clothes, carrying white flags, and raising their hands in a characteristic 15M gesture that showed they were unarmed. Among their numerous chants, one could hear the following: "less hate and more conversation"; "less flags and more dialogue."[136]

This whole way of thinking about democratic change shows the persistence of a way of thinking and acting embodied in being 15M. It reveals how 15M is a living exemplar. What these people seem to be saying is that the *way* (the means) determines the *ends*. We must be peaceful, democratic, and negotiating-with if we are to get to where we want to go in Spain. A 15M-inspired process of reconciliation could well lead to multinational federalism through constitutional negotiations, whereby Catalonia would be recognized as a nation within a Spanish federation. This kind of reconciliation process, and this end result, would simply

---

is important not to dismiss it as an obvious example of minority nationalism; we must not risk overlooking its legitimate demands for self-government. Yet it is also important to keep in mind that, with its nationalistic agenda, the political right in both Spain and Catalonia is capitalizing on the deep social crisis stemming from the 2008–9 economic collapse. In contrast, the issues brought to public attention by 15M in 2011 – corruption, the crisis of representation, the consequences of the economic crisis, and the failures of the political establishment that was born out of the transition to democracy of 1978 – have been largely silenced by these elite debates. This has hijacked the transformative path that was opened up by 15M in 2011, as well as its drive toward a cooperative federation of nations on Spanish territory, and its cooperative relationships with republican self-rule movements in Catalonia and other nations *within* Spain. That is why in this book these two elite-driven nationalisms – Spanish and Catalan – are understood as local articulations of the kind of pugnacious right-wing populism currently spreading around the globe.

135 "Call to the democratic Left on the events in Catalonia," *Opendemocracy.net*, 4 October 2017, "Call to the democratic Left on the events in Catalonia," https://www.opendemocracy.net/can-europe-make-it/group-of-social-scientists-working-at-various-universities-and-citizens-in-barcel.

136 J. Marcos, "Miles de ciudadanos reclaman diálogo en varias ciudades de España," *El País*, 8 October 2017, https://politica.elpais.com/politica/2017/10/07/actualidad/1507376592_202279.html.

be the application of 15M's call for "peoples" to join hands (each with the right of self-determination, and exercising it with one another). This is 15M's understanding of relational self-determination.

Such a process would surely need to have two central features: first, the elites who negotiate the multinational constitutionalism would have to be delegated by the people in some way; and second, those elites would need to present the resulting agreement to both the Spanish and Catalonian peoples in the form of a referendum.[137] This would align with the tradition of democratic nationalism, with the tradition of 15M, and with the expressed wishes of many opinion leaders in Spain and Catalonia, as well as with post-Westphalian trends in modern constitutionalism.

The Catalan conflict reveals the ongoing relevance of 15M ways of thinking and acting. It underscores why this book asks those who question the value of collective enactments of civic freedom – such as those practised by 15M – to suspend their judgment and engage in a genuine dialogue with those being 15M. Through dialogue, 15M's continuing importance and legacies are revealed. As stated at the beginning of this introduction, it seems clear that to confront today's multiple civilizational crises, we who are working for change from outside of institutions need to join hands with those working with*in* them. In doing so, we will be able to co-construct virtuous and conciliatory communities that can resolve conflicts non-violently. Through this process, a more democratic form of representation can come into being – one that is both accountable to and revocable by the base.[138] For this to happen, though, civic and civil organizations need to be understood as complementary so that together they can disrupt the iron law of oligarchy and confront the multiple crises of democracy our societies are currently facing.[139] In this regard, 15M's exemplarity and shortcomings offer

137 It is probable that through such a process, some of the key demands made by 15M, which have been silenced by today's elite-led right-wing nationalist populism, could become part of the constitutional agreement.

138 Arendt suggests in "On Violence" that there could be room for a democratic form of representation that embodies power-with to a sufficient extent. Gandhi also sees this as a possibility, although (he writes) for this to happen, government would have to be different: "Life will not be a pyramid with the apex sustained by the bottom. But it will be an oceanic circle whose centre will be the individual always ready to perish for the village, the latter ready to perish for the circle of villages, till at last the whole becomes one life composed of individuals, never aggressive in their arrogance but ever humble – sharing the majesty of the oceanic circle of which they are integral units." See Gandhi (1942, 73–4).

139 For insight on Robert Michels's "iron law of oligarchy," see Saward (2009, 235).

valuable lessons and steps that we, as citizens, might learn-with as we continue to take positive steps to transform our societies.

7. Chapter Organization

To present my findings about 15M practice and what we can learn with 15M citizens, I begin with a "thick description" of 15M. Chapter 1 discusses how 15M practices come into being and what motivates people to engage with them. It then explores the six joining-hands relationships in which 15M is immersed, thus revealing the distinctive 15M climate with its various agonisms, differences, convergences, temporalities, traditions, and languages, as well as shortcomings. This will enable us to better understand how citizens self-organize democratically, exercise self-government together, reason with one another as equals, and commit themselves to non-violent dispute resolution. We hear various individuals being 15M explain what brought them to the squares. We also watch them create encampments and expand those encampments into neighbourhoods, so as to glean how their six distinct joining-hands relationships have continued since the 15M occupations. Participants' self-descriptions reveal what matters most to those being 15M. Clearly, 15M is not a fad, rather it is a way of being in the world that is being ever more broadly embraced.

In chapter 2, I continue to work toward an approximation of 15M knowledges using a dialogical approach. Through dialogue, one begins to see and appreciate the truly multifarious nature of 15M. I do this by genealogically working through some of the traditions that those being 15M whom I interviewed recognize as having contributed to the construction of what we refer to as 15M. In this regard, the chapter excavates events and ways of being that have inspired and/or marked individuals being 15M. In this way, the origins and antecedents of 15M are revealed. These are important because they show that 15M did not arise out of thin air or with the advent of social media. 15M has deep roots in more than a century of collective practices of dissent that together offer an alternative history of our present day. This history of the present uncovers a cooperative spirit that has animated generations of engaged citizens.

Understanding the origins and history of 15M is important for two reasons: (1) it helps clarify the relationship between means and ends, and (2) it helps us appreciate the transformative, intergenerational change of which 15M is an integral part. The chapter shows how 15M counter-modernity grew out of knowledge of previous growths and the six types of roots and routes of Spain's counter-modernity – that is, the Kropotkinian virtuous social systems that 15M ancestors cultivated and that provided 15M with foundational social ecologies that enabled it to grow further and in new directions. This counter-modern social change helps explain 15M and the strength it derives from its history.

As the chapter reveals, 15M's roots include both constructive programs (*swaraj*) and modes of non-violent contestation (*satyagraha*) on the basis of which 15M was empowered. Given the relationship between means and ends, this is the only way a healthy, virtuous counter-modernity can emerge in the interstices of the vicious social systems of modernity, in Spain and elsewhere. In this sense, chapter 2 elucidates the necessary social ecology of 15M once we understand the nature of virtuous social systems and social change.

Chapter 3 sets out various future visions of Spain as they were presented in dialogues with individuals being 15M. During the interviews, I encouraged participants to predict the future. However, in presenting these futures I am not by inference extolling the predictive gifts of people being 15M. Rather, I am providing glimpses into the future that individuals being 15M are trying to construct by being the future they want to see. To our phenomenology of 15M, this contributes valuable insights into 15M's long-term thinking, besides showing its deep understanding of the challenges and opportunities faced by Spanish citizens today. The chapter reveals the multiple and intricate ways in which individuals being 15M are thinking through the reconstruction or reconstitution of the Spanish state, always in terms of making current social, political, and economic structures and norms more inclusive, horizontal, non-violent, and democratic. Hearing what futures 15M envisions is important because such collective presences are often dismissed for not providing an alternative to the capitalist state and representative democracy. Those being 15M are often criticized in the media for not providing alternatives. In fact, they do, and here, I present the futures and alternatives they see.

Chapter 4 sets out to interrupt modern conceptions of democracy and to critique the central place given to representative institutions. This is necessary if we are to recover the infrastructure of power-with organizations found with*in* the 15M climate, which state-centric analysis would have us erase. When examined from a state-centric perspective, this infrastructure is seen as at best "discussion groups" – a sort of proto-civil citizenry. Such a mindset restricts possible alternatives by channelling all their energies toward getting into the power-over infrastructure of the state without respecting existing networks of mutual aid. Since the alternative infrastructures are not seen or heard, state-centric theorists see no infrastructural alternative. Yet as the chapter reveals, 15M is not an instrumental "mobilization" intended to gain power-over through a party movement like Podemos. That has been the assumption made by mobilization theorists and political theorists describing 15M. The chapter shows how Podemos violates the means/ends relationships essential to 15M's lifeway in two very specific ways: first, by mistakenly claiming that it can bring about power-with organizations by means of power-over methods, and second, by acting in "crisis time" rather than in the "ever-so-slow" temporality of being the change in each step we take, which has been a key feature of being 15M. This chapter is valuable because it addresses a body of literature on horizontality, commoning, populism, the rise of verticality, and the co-optation of power relations into relationships of subordination.

Chapter 5 closes the book by showing how, where, and why 15M failed to auto-generate the kinds of being-with civic practices that would have allowed it to build strong relations with civil citizens. Presenting a critique *by* 15M *of* 15M, it offers a space within which 15M can learn from itself. The chapter also presents a critique of Podemos *by* Podemos that can help the party listen to its own self-critiques. After this, the chapter offers two hypotheses that crystallize 15M's mode of being and *raison d'être* and that can help avert the contemporary de-democratization of modern societies. The "virtuous *versus* vicious democracies hypothesis" serves as a cautionary note for leaders who employ power-over methods. The "ever-so-slowly hypothesis" suggests that for 15M to enact its mode of democracy, it must take into account both its way of being (power-with) and its temporality (one step at a time). Overall, the chapter shows how 15M is not just a movement or a network, but a mode of being in Spain that can do much to transform constitutional federalism and strengthen democracy. The chapter presents 15M and the book as "experiments in truth" in Gandhi's sense and thus as contributions to a democratic social science for the twenty-first century.[140]

140 Gandhi's word, *sarvodaya*, which means to always act with and for all affected by your thoughts, attitudes, and actions, and for present and future generations, is a fit way to describe what 15M practitioners are doing. By this he means that ethical self-practices are always exercised in relations with others, the earth, animals, and so on. Even if those being 15M do not articulate it in this manner, it is relevant to their way of being and to the kind of social science I am enacting and defending in this text.

Chapter One

Exercising Power Together as Equals

In 2011, Spanish public squares were occupied by a "collective presence" constituted by a "strange multiplicity of culturally diverse voices" shouting "¡Basta ya!" (Enough!).[1] These voices were challenging the political system of representation with the phrase "¡No nos representan!" (They do not represent us!). They demanded "¡democracia real ya!" (Real democracy now!) and shouted "¡no somos mercancia en manos de politicos y banqueros¡" (We are not merchandise in the hands of politicians and bankers).

In the immediate wake of the national DRY (Real Democracy Now!) demonstration of 15 May 2011, in the early hours of 16 May, in Madrid's Puerta del Sol, forty people decided spontaneously to camp: "Many of us did not know each other but being antagonized by police, we quickly established some bonds. Riot police eventually dispersed us and nineteen of us were actually arrested" (IA 106).[2] The following day (17 May), 10,000 people took to the streets and encampments were set up in squares across the country in solidarity with the encampment in Madrid (IA 114).[3] Spanish police quickly evicted around 250 people

1 Tully (1995, 34).

2 "Pervasive anonymity" enacted, as the anonymity of the multitude, is key to 15M counter-discourses. That is why all 213 interviewees agreed to participate in this research on the condition that they remain anonymous. Following from this, all interviewees will be cited in the text as "Interview with Anonymous + Number" (thus, IA 173). In describing this 15M mode of being, I have borrowed the idea of "pervasive anonymity" from Foucault. To learn more about what Foucault means by that term, see Foucault (1977a). There he writes: "We can easily imagine a culture where discourse would circulate without any need for an author. Discourses, whatever their status, form, or value, and regardless of our manner of handling them, would unfold in a pervasive anonymity" (116).

3 At that time, Spanish expats set up solidarity camps in many other countries.

camped in Puerta del Sol. That same afternoon, thousands of people returned to the square and Facebook and Twitter overflowed with messages emphasizing that #acampadasol continued. Across Spain, spontaneously organized encampment general assemblies decided to continue their occupations.[4] Most of them (in more than fifty cities across the country) remained until 12 June 2011, when the Madrid General Assembly decided to dismantle the encampment at Puerta del Sol.

The message coming from the square was clear: "No nos vamos nos expandimos" (We do not disappear, we expand) (IA 94). That same day, popular assemblies were created that together would constitute the Asamblea Popular de Madrid (Madrid Popular Assembly): "When we left Puerta del Sol, there were around 150 assemblies with around 60,000 people, meeting in different neighbourhoods and localities in Madrid; in an interlinked manner" (IA 66). A similar process took place in other cities following the dismantling of encampments across the country.

In May 2013, two years after participating in my first general assembly at the encampment in Barcelona's Plaça Catalunya, I set out on a road trip around Spain with La Pasionaria (a VW Westfalia van). My objective was to learn about what 15M meant to various actors who saw themselves as being 15M and as working from within different autonomous communities in the country.[5] During my travels I visited the autonomous community of Andalucía, the autonomous city of Melilla, the community of Valencia, the community of Madrid, and the autonomous communities of Galicia, Asturias, Catalonia, and the Basque Country.[6]

---

4 Spain has a thriving *okupa* (squatter) movement with a long tradition. Also, internet activism led by self-organizing citizens has been strong in the country since the early twenty-first century. These two factors helped spur occupations in public squares across the country. Although in chapter 2 I describe other roots and routes of 15M besides, these two influences deserve a special call-out.

5 In accordance with the Spanish constitution of 1978 (as part of the country's transition from dictatorship to democracy), autonomous communities were created with the aim of guaranteeing the autonomy of the nationalities and regions that together form the Spanish state. Spain is not a federation; sovereignty resides in the state as a whole and is represented by state-wide or central institutions of government. Spain is instead a highly decentralized unitary state that has devolved power to the communities; these communities exercise their right to self-government within the limits set forth in the constitution. Seventeen autonomous communities and two autonomous cities collectively known as "autonomies" comprise the Spanish state.

6 As mentioned in the Introduction, my choice of places to visit was determined along the way and guided by recommendations from interviewees. Interviewees often suggested particular cities to visit, based on the exemplary work of 15M in these localities.

The multilogue I engaged in during this research trip helped crystallize for me that since 2011, culturally diverse voices across Spain have been debating at length whether to come together to deal responsibly with common problems, and if so, how. Since 15 May 2011, activist circles, university departments, political parties, and unions have been considering whether a confluence of social movements, political parties, and unions can help steer the country toward some form of constituent process, a process by which the idea of what it means to be a person in what is today legally defined as Spain can be radically rethought and transformed.

Since the occupations of May 2011, many people in Spain have endured beatings by police, have been evicted from city squares, and have been arrested. Nevertheless, their actions have spread throughout local communities, and the seeds of social, political, and economic democracy are beginning to flower in the hearts and minds of large swathes of the country's population. Many of the practices employed during these occupations and their associated constructive programs have since become part of the repertoire of practices employed by other popular initiatives. As the political, social, and economic situation has continued to deteriorate and more people have been drawn to the streets, 15M practices have been broadly adopted.

Yet, as this book argues, most commentators have presented a map of the field of activity that is misleading. 15M practices have been described most often as examples of civil citizenship interspersed with acts of civil disobedience. This has blinded us to the fact that 15M shows civic and civil citizens joining hands to practise participatory democracy. This chapter seeks to address this blind spot by explicating these two concepts and their relationality by means of quotations from 15M.

With their examples of civic activities and exemplars of civic citizenship, individuals being 15M are contesting the present situation and simultaneously constructing alternatives to it. In doing so, ever since the square occupations, in a multiplicity of ways, they have been revealing the exemplarity of their six distinct types of joining-hands relationships between citizens. Identifying these six relationships helps us understand power configurations in a different light. This is important since the incremental, non-violent, democratic, horizontal, power-with steps that individuals being 15M take continue to have kaleidoscopic transformative effects that may lead to unpredictable tipping points in Spanish society.[7]

7 Gregg (2018, 140).

Six Joining-Hands Relationships

"Being" with*in* 15M, is much like arriving at Macondo for the first time. I do not know if you are familiar with the novel *One Hundred Years of Solitude* by Colombian writer Gabriel García Márquez. He begins that novel by describing the village of Macondo and setting the time: "the world was so recent, that many things lacked names, and in order to indicate them it was necessary to point."[8] I have often felt that way with*in* 15M while learning practices, sharing ideas, and working on theories and methods.

Over the course of my dialogues with*in* 15M, I have come to view it as something collective as well as personal, global and local, theoretical and practical, revolutionary and reformist; progressive and conservative, civic and civil. I have discovered that 15M has a temporality that encompasses past, present, and future and that works within and outside societal structures of power. It is now clear to me that for those involved in it, 15M is movement, transformation, and hope. 15M is *alive*. It is a multiplicity of ideas and a constant mutation of something that escapes definition.[9] Yet when one is immersed in its climate, it is easily recognizable and can be genealogically explored through its ideas, its relationality, and its actions. 15M is a multiplicity of knowledge(s).[10] 15M is dialogical; it is new and old, wise and ignorant, vanguard and rearguard, mainstream and marginal, migrant and immigrant. 15M is rupture and continuity, destruction and construction. 15M is internal and external, inclusive and exclusive. 15M is utopian and grounded, virtual and real, intuitive and analytical, spontaneous and planned. 15M is legal, illegal, and alter-legal. It is all of these and much more.

Much can be said about 15M, yet as mentioned earlier, one cannot define it clearly. But we can try to understand the phenomenon that calls itself 15M by engaging with its own self-descriptions and studying its practices. Once we do this, 15M's six distinct joining-hands relationships are revealed: civic citizens joining hands with one another (JH1); civil citizens joining hands with one another (JH 2); civic and civil citizens joining hands (JH 3); civic citizens working with representative

---

8 García Márquez ([1967] 2014).

9 No precise statement or description is possible for capturing the full nature, scope, or meaning of 15M.

10 In Spanish, for the plural of the noun *knowledge* in this context, I would use *saberes*, because it clearly speaks to the different types of knowledges inhabiting the same space. For this reason, I am using the plural of knowledge in English –*knowledges* – which, although not common, I have seen used in different spaces.

governments in numerous ways (JH4); civil citizens working with representative governments in numerous ways (JH5); and civic/civil citizens joining hands with one another in myriad ways in order to influence their governments (JH6). These joining-hands relationships have continued to evolve beyond the square occupations of 2011, so improving our grasp of them can help us identify them and thereby better understand the transformations taking place in Spanish democracy today. Furthermore, seeing how these six joining-hands relationships are being enacted in Spain can help us identify family resemblances between them and other relationships now being enacted in multiple contexts and spaces around the globe. This will help us map the field of activity more accurately when, as researchers, we encounter practices of civic engagement.

Before we begin to explore these six distinct joining-hands relationships, it is important to grasp how the criteria for applying these two terms – civic and civil – overlap in practice in complicated ways.[11] A crucial feature of the civic and civil practices I am trying to explicate is that they do overlap: the terms do not rigidly signify two separate modes of citizenship that share no defining criteria. So it is important to note that the use of the terms civic and civil in the sections that follow is often contestable precisely because their criteria overlap. Indeed, this overlap actually helps make "joining hands" possible.

A second feature of joining hands that must be mentioned is that it essentially involves an internal *and* external commitment to power-with relationships. As James Tully points out, *demoi* that practise joining hands must operate in a horizontal manner both internally and in their relations with other *demoi*.[12] This is how the *demoi* of civic and civil citizens unwed themselves from the power-over relationships they are abandoning and/or attempting to transform.

JH1 – Civic Citizens Joining Hands with One Another

When working-with*in* 15M, people co-develop a kind of cooperative citizenship that operates beyond the institutional limits of modern

11 In speaking of "family resemblances," Wittgenstein points out how we "see a complicated network of similarities overlapping and crisscrossing: sometimes overall similarities, sometimes similarities of detail"; see Wittgenstein (2001, §65–7).

12 This insight from James Tully, I draw from an ongoing conversation (2019–20) around the meaning of "joining hands" with a group working within the Cedar Trees Institute, CTI (cedartreesinstitute.org). I align myself with Tully's claim that joining hands is a method of engagement that, while seemingly less radical than violent vanguardism, is in fact far more transformative.

democracies. This mode of being-with one another found within 15M reveals a "practice-based" mode of citizenship grounded in freedom. In dialogue with individuals being 15M, one is presented with a kind of politics that builds from practice-generated reciprocal trust and support bonds, which are nurtured through citizen/citizen self-government relationships. These relationships exemplify the civic tradition of joining hands with one another.

So it is not surprising that months before the square occupations of 2011, the idea of occupying public squares was circulating in the collective imaginary of political activists in Spain. Plenty of people were saying that the country needed its own Tahrir Square: "there was a general feeling of needing to reclaim control of our political future" (IA 188).

By the time of the first encampment, many people in Spain were thinking of previous and existing structures of political organization as obsolete (IA 16). People working from within traditional spaces of contestation were trying to create political parties, but "people did not want a new political party, people wanted 15M" (IA 69). There existed an embracing of "absolute horizontality because of subterranean conflicts between factions" (IA 39). The encampment "had in its biology a clear rejection of leaderships" (IA 108). 15M's intent was not to defend institutions or to inspire people to go and vote in elections. "It was born to remind society of the fact that we cannot just go on voting every four years; and of the fact that our most important task is to collectively empower each other" (IA 176). In this sense, 15M presented an opportunity to reclaim the commons in an extremely transformative manner. "We could create a new world with each other and function perfectly" (IA 39).

On arriving at a 15M encampment, one's typical first response was amazement that people who did not know one another were able to organize collectively. 15M was a new commons in which "nobody managed and everybody knew what to do" (IA 47). It was a laboratory where "one learned to think together; decide together; and act together" (IA 67). Through 15M, people where "building a micro city from zero, while reclaiming common space." (IA 146). There seemed to be a collective awareness of the need to "construct from the local and from the collective. Not from big ideas and meta-thought coming from above" (IA 161).

A grassroots, assembly-based initiative was developing in the squares (IA 62). People were "enacting direct democracy with its beautiful traits and also with the problems that it raised" (IA 166). The three ethical norms that constituted the DNA of 15M were non-violence, non-partisanship, and horizontality (IA 183).[13] Its methodology included "civic non-violence, democracy, and assemblies" (IA 25). People wanted to deeply and radically transform the system through "constructive resistance" (IA 46). To do so, what was needed was "a space from which to think ourselves by ourselves" (IA 42). The squares served that purpose: people approached, listened, contributed, and left when they chose; 15M encampments were "open spaces in constant transformation" (IA 182). From them, 15M proposed "a serious integral reform" (IA 36). It aimed to achieve this by joining hands with existing and newly risen civic initiatives.

As people in the squares advanced their projects, the exemplarity with which 15M was able to join hands with other initiatives contributed to the construction of a power-with infrastructure that in many instances has remained. As I travelled from square to square, I got a sense of the kinds of joining-hands partnerships that those in the squares built with a multitude of civic initiatives beyond the squares. In Barcelona, for example, I experienced the encampment's relationship with Can Mas Deu. This involved the occupation of an abandoned farmhouse in the city's national park, Collserola. Since 2001, Can Mas Deu has been reinforcing a neighbourhood network designed to protect the city's last forest from speculation (IA 206). People from Can Mas Deu provided much valuable logistical and infrastructural support in the early days of Plaça Catalunya's square occupation.[14]

While travelling, I also witnessed virtuous gift/reciprocity relationships between people at encampments and those working at the Cooperativa Integral Catalana (Integral Catalan Cooperative). The Cooperativa Integral Catalana works to expand interlinked, alternative social and economic spaces that are trying to operate outside of existing economic and social norms (IA 202). Cooperating with 15M felt like a natural step for those working in the cooperative, and the know-how they brought to the square was instrumental during the first days of the occupation.

---

13 When we contrast these three features of 15M expressed to me repeatedly during interviews throughout Spain, with the two features of Occupy in the United States highlighted by Marina Sitrin, we begin to see similarities and differences. This is how Sitrin describes Occupy: "The various sites of the Occupy movement have all created the same two features, and ones that must be explored in depth and taken seriously: horizontal spaces and new territories in which to create new social relationships"; see Sitrin (2018, 319).

14 Already in 2005, Jeffrey Juris in the context of the alter-globalization movement highlighted that the notion of building "separate, yet connected" autonomous spaces came quite naturally to many in Barcelona; see Juris (2005, 261).

During the research trip, I learned first-hand how individuals being 15M and those living in the Sant Antoni area of Barcelona set up a neighbourhood resistance network to stop police from evicting an occupied social centre. This happened at the six-year-old, self-managed, occupied social centre of La Carboneria (The Coal Yard). Observing how those being 15M resisted revealed the power-with force of their civic engagement.

Throughout the country, I saw plenty of examples of civic citizens joining hands. These relationships were being enacted by 15M civic citizens in cooperation with one another and with other citizens working within Spain's civic sphere. In the city of Málaga, various groups within the 15M orbit were working to create a popular plenary. These sessions would run parallel to those of the town hall. In the same city, the Banco Bueno (Good Bank) occupied the branch of an old savings bank and created a self-managed canteen offering food to poor families (IA 79). In the city of Granada, La Hortiga (The Nettle), an agro-organic cooperative that predated 15M, had gained a lot of strength since May 2011. La Hortiga's 130 members shared food that was grown collectively (IA 72).[15] In the city of Sevilla, the Corralas that had emerged from 15M were still active (IA 36).[16] "Originally the project came out of the inter-commission on housing of 15M. From the Corralas project, 400 individual occupations to serve homeless families had developed" (IA 36). In the city of Córdoba, YoNoPago (I Do Not Pay) had conducted actions of not paying public transportation while wearing masks with faces of local corrupt politicians (IA 50). Also in Córdoba, Stop Desahucios (Stop Evictions) regularly occupied bank branches, demanding that mortgage-related issues be resolved. Individuals across the city identified abandoned houses in preparation for future occupations (IA 48).

By 2013, this kind of civic engagement had become so widespread that the PAH (Plataforma de Afectados por la Hipoteca; Platform of Those Affected by Mortgages), through its program for stopping

15 La Hortiga has vegetable gardens in the town of Durcal, 50 kilometres from Granada. This land had been abandoned and was loaned to them by the community. Members make all their decisions by consensus and are currently working within a space of alegality. The police often harass them.

16 "The *Corrala Utopía* was occupied on the first anniversary of the 15M. Twelve families coming from 15M information points on housing occupied the building. These families worked for three months preparing the occupation. People being 15M with backgrounds in the okupa movement helped them open it up. These activists disconnected alarms; changed locks; and activated water and electricity."

evictions, had become "the ministry of housing of the 15M climate" (IA 110).[17] By the time I finished my interviewing, abandoned buildings were being occupied in all corners of the country. Madrid, for example, found itself with the highest number of occupied social spaces in its history (IA 120).

Within 15M, civic citizens joining hands revealed a way of building relationships based on consent and trust. As Rebeccah Nelems points out, one can take one's hand away at any time, which means that the joining-hands metaphor crystallizes how prior consent does not guarantee future consent.[18] In their "ongoingness" and "aliveness," 15M's civic joining-hands relationships disclose 15M's commitment to a permanent and forward-moving state of negotiation.

JH 2 – Civil Citizens Joining Hands with One Another

Civil citizenship is different from civic citizenship. It claims a particular "Western" lineage of universal institutions and historical processes. Civil citizenship, then, refers to the modern type of citizenship that is tied to representative democracy and its associated public sphere.

With*in* 15M, it became apparent as soon as the occupations began that civic citizens were not alone in the encampments; civil citizens were joining hands with them and with one another. Although most of the activity one sees in the camps and beyond involves civil and civic citizens joining hands, there is also clear engagement by civil citizens with civic ideas. This engagement is then followed by civil citizens joining hands with one another in multiple ways. In later chapters I will be arguing that the civic nature of the encampments generates a kind of virtuous civil citizenship that contributes to the oxygenation of the civil public sphere.

For those steeped in civil traditions and institutions such as political parties or trade unions, the difference in organization and contestation was apparent the first time they entered the encampments. Notwithstanding existing frictions, the early days of the encampments and the demonstrations that were organized "had the magic of offering anyone a space to speak and be listened to. They offered the possibility of getting involved based on individual possibilities" (IA 47). For those more accustomed to activism within political parties or trade unions,

---

17 To learn more about the PAH, visit http://afectadosporlahipoteca.com.

18 This insight from Rebeccah Nelems I draw from an ongoing conversation (2019–20) around the meaning of "joining hands" with a group working *within* the Cedar Trees Institute, CTI (cedartreesinstitute.org).

this space seemed to embrace "existing marginal political and social practices while giving them new meanings and legitimacies" (IA 166). To those not accustomed to the civic sphere, everything seemed different: It was all "so horizontal, so dynamic, and so imaginative that in three hours we were able to organize mass demonstrations" (IA 176).

During the interviews, civil citizens described 15M as "a new form of development through which we relate to each other as equals. (IA 178). For many of 15M's civil citizens, the square appeared as "the first non-mediated public sphere since that short parenthesis of the transition to democracy" (IA 33). In this sense, 15M challenged civil ideals as "discussions about democracy versus dictatorship quickly shifted to conversations about what democracy we wanted to have" (IA 199). The idea that different kinds of democracies existed was new to many, but a large proportion of individuals being 15M rapidly acknowledged that these types of conversations served as a "vaccination against fascism" (IA 25).

As the encampments progressed, people in the occupations separated into working groups. Those who were more comfortable with working on improving representative democracy and its associated public sphere tended to congregate together. Discussions centred on creating new political parties that could act as open forums for citizens (IA 46). Within these groups, individuals were concerned mainly about "electoral laws; labour issues; citizen participation; women's rights; or simply corruption" (IA 66). There was also a clear consensus on "the need to work towards more coordinated collaborations" (IA 178). Ultimately, for civil citizens joining hands with one another in the squares, 15M was "revolutionary through reform" (IA 38). In this sense, much of the activity of civil citizens imbued with the civic climate of 15M was geared toward radical reform of existing institutions.

I found a good example of this kind of civil radicality in the town of Marinaleda.[19] It was there that in 2011, individuals being 15M attempted to write a new constitution for the Spanish state.[20] The aim of

19 Marinaleda has since the 1970s been an inspiration for many of Europe's socialist thinkers, collectivists, cooperativists, and grassroots activists working on and thinking through other possible worlds. As I arrived in this small town in arid Andalucía, a road sign greeted me: "Marinaleda: Una utopia hacia la paz" (Marinaleda: A utopia toward peace).

20 The project for writing a new constitution and beginning a citizen-led constituent process began in the fourth state-wide 15M encounter. That encounter took place in Marinaleda on 26–27 November 2012. See "Los 'indignados' redactarán su propia Constitución," 3 February 2012, http://www.libertaddigital.com/sociedad/2012-01-16/los-indignados-redactaran-su-propia-constitucion-espanola-1276447023.

this initiative was to mobilize people toward demanding a constituent process in the country and spearheading the process through the exemplarity of their civil action.

In the city of Cádiz, I witnessed another example of civil radical reform in the form of a collective of unemployed people working to create an unemployed people's cooperative. This cooperative occupied abandoned land and turned it into parking-by-donation lot while it negotiated with the local authorities for concessions on empty public lands (IA 23). In the same city, Graba tu Pleno (Record Your Plenary Session) was also gaining strength. With this project, citizens organized to fill the town hall plenary sessions with questions from activists. These questions and the subsequent responses from city officials were recorded and later posted online (IA 23).

In the city of Córdoba, the Yayoflautas, the old age pensioners who consider themselves children of 15M, carried out numerous silent actions around the city (IA 49). The aim of these actions was to disrupt public events without breaking the law in order to gain attention for various pressing issues. In the city of Málaga, the Marea Verde (Green Tide), defending public education, and the Marea Blanca (White Tide), defending the country's public health system had gained a lot of strength (IA 75). These tides were sectorial responses to the inaction of trade unions, which many citizens within 15M considered corrupt. Across Spain, the White Tide had been imbued by the 15M climate. For this reason, even though civil citizens believed that representative institutions were necessary, "unions, doctors and nurses had adopted 15M practices" (IA 111).

In February 2013, while I was visiting the city of Valencia, Totes Juntes (All Together), a new confluence of social movements and nongovernmental Organizations (NGOs), organized a demonstration against what they called a *coup d'état* by the financial markets. The demonstration was a huge success, and at the time of my interviews, this self-generated dialogical space remained open as a place where groups could coordinate collective actions (IA 92). By 2013, in the city of A Coruña, some political parties had listened to what was being said by 15M and were attempting to rethink the politics of political parties within a 15M frame (IA 144). In the city of Santiago de Compostela, a broad civil rights movement called Silveiras came into being. The work at Silveiras revolved around "gender violence; violence against immigrants; prison repression; police repression; detentions; violence against homeless people; and evictions of occupied social centres" (IA 132). In the city of Sevilla, debt auditing of local government, which had been gaining traction during 2012–13 was being worked on. In the city of Granada, Stop Represión was providing legal and financial support to those who had been fined or arrested for joining demonstrations and engaging in civil disobedience (IA 66). In Madrid, civil citizens had joined hands with one another to fight against the privatization of water (IA 102). In addition, much civil activity revolved around the struggle against new abortion laws (IA 102).[21] Finally, in the city of Barcelona, civil citizens worked toward making a universal basic income a constitutional right in Spain (IA 190).[22]

As civil citizens joined hands with one another following their encounters in the squares, most saw opposition to the idea of leadership as counterproductive. Nevertheless, engagement with fellow civic citizens in the squares and activities outside the encampments crystallized in the imaginary of many the idea that "leaderships need to be representative, constructed from below, and multiple" (IA 50). Inspired by this premise, through un-co-opted and virtuous civil citizenship practices, these citizens continued joining hands with one another as they attempted to reinvigorate healthy forms of civil democracy.[23]

The way in which civil citizens within 15M joined hands reveals the open-ended nature of their relationships. As Keith Cherry points out, their ongoing activity highlights the potential of a multitude of ways of engaging that together can encourage or facilitate a thorough decentring of state power.[24]

JH3 – Civic and Civil Citizens Joining Hands

From the outside, distinguishing between civil and civic activity among people being 15M is not always straightforward. However, once one

---

21 This bill was finally dropped.

22 Discussions within 15M around the idea of introducing a universal basic income bear a family resemblance to Carole Pateman's focus on basic income as a democratization practice that requires a reinforcement of reciprocity/mutual aid across the whole of society; see Pateman (2004, 103).

23 Rodrigo Nunes argues that movements like 15M are not leaderless but display instead "distributed leadership," by which he means a way of organizing in terms of complementarity. I see something similar. Yet Nunes also says that assemblies and horizontality are not the movement's defining traits. He acknowledges the complexity of the power relations within encampments, and one can certainly see distributed leadership operating at certain moments in certain spaces; even so, I think that he fails to see the transformative nature of the power-with horizontal joining-hands relationships among citizens in the squares. Through these relationships between equals, citizens can always decide to support or reject distributed leadership actions promoted by different citizens within 15M. See Nunes (2005b, 98, 105).

24 This insight from Keith Cherry I draw from an ongoing conversation (2019–20) around the meaning of "joining hands" with a group working within the Cedar Trees Institute, CTI (cedartreesinstitute.org).

enters the space of contestation and construction with*in* 15M, the multiple ways in which civil and civic citizens join hands become apparent.

In early 2011 the Facebook group Plataforma por la movilización ciudadana (Platform for citizen mobilization), which eventually became known as DRY, presented a document in which three main streams of thought converged: "Views from the environmental movement; views on socialism coming from anarchists and communists; and input from advocacy groups dealing with accountability, transparency, and Internet freedoms" (IA 138). This Facebook page led to the creation of a document that listed eight demands, later presented for discussion in 15M encampments across Spain.

During the preparations for the DRY demonstration that culminated in the 15M occupations, it was agreed (through a vote in DRY's online forum) that a demonstration bringing together people without divisions should be organized for 15 May 2011. "The call for the demonstration stated that we should not promote particular groups, so on our banners we just wrote our desires" (IA 4). 15M "carried no flags, it had no frontiers" (IA 201). During the first hours of the occupations, there was a lot of trust, respect, and care towards the other. In the beginning, there was no organization, "people were in the street, sitting, talking, and organizing" (IA 14). As people began to work collectively, there was music in the streets, children were running around, and there was a beautiful atmosphere: "it made one want to be a part of this that was being born" (IA 47).

Once squares had been occupied, a code of ethics was agreed upon. This code stated that people spoke as individuals and not as representatives of organizations: "We did not know what we were co-creating, but we all seemed to feel that it was worthwhile attempting it without representation" (IA 102).[25] This predisposition created space for currents of activism and created a situation in which a variety of people with diverse viewpoints could come together, discuss their respective positions, and negotiate a common ground (IA 204). This collective moment served to remind people that they could change things together (IA 19).

To facilitate such a process, it was decided in assembly that all currents of thought and organizations were legitimate and would be welcomed

25 This current of thought within 15M aligns strongly with John Holloway's critique of representation. For Holloway, representation involves definition, exclusion, and separation. Through elections, he says, we exclude ourselves as subjects until the next election, and meanwhile, political journalists and political scientists teach us the logic of the politicians' "peculiar language" and help us see the world through their blind eyes. See Holloway (2019, 229).

in the squares (IA 13). There were some instinctively agreed upon "fundamental principles of democratic participation and horizontality" (IA 9). People in the squares wanted "a more participatory democracy and more social and economic rights" (IA 3). To that end, it made sense for everyone to treat fellow citizens as agents of change. This allowed for squares to be "filled with right-wing conservatives; congregating with left-wing libertarians; and in between them every other ideology one can imagine" (IA 84). This brought about a conversation in which one "could find a grandmother who would contribute 30 euros for buying food without being politicized, sitting next to a long-time syndicalist on one side and a computer hacker on the other" (IA 26). The square became a *demoplaza* (demosquare): "A space where different ideologies; different generations; and different social classes got together to discuss the future of democracy in the Spanish state" (IA 90).[26] Right from its inception, 15M behaved more like a mass political synchronization than a mass political union (IA 30). As civic and civil citizens joined hands, everyone's ideas became dissolved, nurturing others and in turn being nurtured by them (IA 191).

15M was a "plural utopia, unlike the closed utopias social movements had strived for in the past" (IA 49). Through "its methodology of collective listening, it taught us to get together around projects not ideas" (IA 57). Starting from concrete grievances opened up non-ideological spaces (IA 111). People could "co-create with others without the need for leadership simply by consensus and rotation" (IA 69). That some people were political novices meant that they could adapt and modify their views and priorities based on dialogue with one another (IA 129). Work on the learning of unknown vocabularies was a constant (IA 102). The diffuse nature of 15M meant that "unknown actors had to face each other collectively" (IA 130). By invoking the whole of society and avoiding segmentation, "we were able to construct very friendly relational spaces; positive and cordial despite everyone's differences" (IA 163). There were even assemblies for children in the squares: "Although only in a playful manner, these gave children an introduction to democratic participation" (IA 88).

Some more seasoned activists had a slight aversion to these "theatrical" representations of what an assembly is all about. Yet they were soon reminded by their colleagues that this was their chance to let their ideas be known by broader spectrums of society (IA 85). Spending time

26 Juris's description of networked spaces that overlap and converge resonates with descriptions of the first weeks of the encampments, which were shared with me during my time within 15M. Juris (2005, 255).

with*in* 15M "was a lot of work that required facing agonisms between different interests and ideologies" (IA 85). Yet at the encampments, although "always exhausted, you always had someone to hand you some water, a smile, or a kiss" (IA 101). In addition, the open-ended discussion that was generated in and between squares made people across Spain feel a part of a collective intelligence. A web had developed linking encampments in different cities, so that one "would read what was happening in the city of Murcia, and at the same exact time and without previous coordination the same thing was happening in A Coruña's Praza do Obelisco" (IA 134).

It quickly became evident that people were no longer just debating and playing together; the square was no longer simply a place to think but had acquired a voice of its own (IA 134). At the same time, 15M was revealing how it had "come to be in order to disappear by diluting itself with others" (IA 110). Through the squares, civil and civic citizens created cooperative and collaborative networks "without a clear centre and with numerous aggregation nodes that did the work and coordinated with each other" (IA 82).[27] In practice, this made 15M into "a catalyst of change which could be reformist or revolutionary depending on the specific situation" (IA 126). For example, in its revolutionary imaginary, it rejected trade unions as corrupt, but in the framework of its reformist possibilities this agonism was overcome.

Such was the case in the city of Sevilla, which slowly established links with more combative trade unions like UGT (Unión General de Trabajadores; General Workers Union) and CNT (Confederación Nacional del Trabajo; National Confederation of Work). At first, the unions held their demonstrations on different days than those organized by 15M. "Nevertheless, as time passes, one notices that events begin to converge and everyone starts to demonstrate on the same day and at the same time" (IA 43). On a similar note, in the city of Jerez de la Frontera, through the collective experience of living in the encampment, agonisms that hitherto existed in theory were

27 Nunes attributes the imaginary of horizontality and openness of movements like 15M to a politics of networking. According to him, it is this kind of politics that allows for openness and horizontality to become goals. I do see a politics of networking facilitated by technology and current social habits operating within 15M. At the same time, I think that the self-descriptions of people being 15M and their descriptions of their traditions reveal a means-and-ends approach to openness and horizontality that stems from a multiplicity of exemplars and traditions with which those who are being 15M identify. Chapter 2 of this book offers extensive examples and exemplars that nurture 15M's open and horizontal imaginary. For Nunes's descriptions of a politics of networks, see Nunes (2018, 38–9).

transcended in actual practice. At first, there was a reluctance to use the trade unions' buildings. Faced with bad weather, however, 15M in Jerez began "using the meeting rooms in the union's building whenever the weather required it" (IA 6).

People in the encampments often joined hands with those outside. To take one example, in the city of Málaga, the encampment would not have been possible without the virtuous support of civil citizens living around the square. Those within the encampment needed to join hands with fellow citizens in order to maintain a basic daily existence: "People near the square would let us shower in their homes. One man came to the encampment to donate 1,000 euros" (IA 82). But in the city of Cádiz, when 15M decided to occupy Valcárcel, an abandoned building, for use as a cultural centre, there arose a serious conflict between autonomists (who wanted to turn the space into a squat), and those who wanted to turn it into a friendlier space open to the community (IA 12). Eventually those looking to make the space more inclusive won the struggle: "With Valcárcel we were able to be radical, yet, at the same time remain inclusive" (IA 21).

Civic/civil joining-hands relationships were widespread by 2013. In the city of Granada, for example, in the El Zaidín neighbourhood, the 15M assembly had joined other neighbourhood assemblies and occupied the neighbourhood's library, Las Palomas (The Pigeons). This was done after the government had closed it. Together, this civic/civil network created the Platform against the Closure of Las Palomas: "95% of the people in the platform were women and its constitution spanned three generations of users of the library; grandmothers; mothers and daughters" (IA 61).

In a different instance, in the city of Valencia, in November 2012, the abandoned Faculty of Agriculture at the University of Valencia was occupied in preparation for the country's general strike of 14 November: "The idea was to catalyze the general strike. After the strike, it became a makeshift headquarters for social movements in Valencia; we called it *Calavaga*" (IA 89).[28]

Two years after the first demonstrations, the network of active projects in which civil and civic citizens were joining hands was broad and very effectively interconnected. In the city of Jerez, a critical block had been created, spearheaded by the SAT (Sindicato Andaluz de Trabajadores; Andalucian Workers Union) together with numerous organizations (IA 9).[29]

28 *Calavaga* in Valencian language means "home of the strike."

29 The SAT views its struggle as both active and non-violent. It is a struggle against injustice, unemployment, and government austerity measures.

In the city of Cádiz, the one remaining 15M assembly was being kept alive by "Christian communities and the people from the neighbourhood" (IA 20). In the city of Málaga, the PRC (Plan de Rescate Ciudadano; Citizen Rescue Plan) was created to bring together different struggles from both civil and civic spheres (IA 75). In the city of Valencia, Plataforma por la Libertad y contra la Represión (Platform for Liberty and against Repression) offered support to those who faced police repression or who had been fined for committing acts of civil disobedience (IA 86). In Barcelona, "those who before were hostile towards immigrants for stealing their government subsidies were now fighting side by side with them to protect each other's home[s]" (IA 188). Also, the Front Civic (Civic Front) worked to foster convergence and cooperation among citizens (IA 190). And finally, in the occupied abandoned factory complex of Can Batlló, civil and civic citizens established good relationships among themselves and began to discuss the possible independence of Catalonia and civil/civic responses to the brewing crisis. The network of occupied spaces like Can Batlló played an integral part in supporting and contributing to 15M encampments across the country.

The many joining hands initiatives between civil and civic citizens within 15M point to how actors maintain a deep commitment to their own struggles even while linking their efforts together. As Cherry suggests, this ability of 15M citizens to link efforts while individual actors remain committed to their own forms of struggle presents joining hands as a powerful method for people to engage with one another in a non-instrumental manner.[30]

JH4 – Civic Citizens Working with Representative Governments in Numerous Ways

The relationship between civic citizens and representative governments is an agonistic one. Representative governments tend to think of themselves as central to politics; civic citizens engage representative institutions in a manner that seeks to move political processes outside the space of institutional representation. In the case of 15M, civic citizens have built networks that are both civic and glocal. As described in the introduction, I mean by this that they are accountable to local civic nodes yet at the same time engaged in civic relationships that develop a

30 This insight from Keith Cherry I draw from an ongoing conversation (2019–20) around the meaning of "joining hands" with a group working within the Cedar Trees Institute, CTI (cedartreesinstitute.org).

whole infrastructure of citizen self-governance. It is through this unique infrastructure that civic citizens engage representative governments.

15M civic citizens are neither marginal nor opposed to representation. Yet they also contend that healthy forms of representative democracy must be grounded in citizens who are already democratic in their thoughts and actions. In other words, representative democracy is dependent on civic citizens. At the same time, civic networks within 15M are aware that healthy civic citizens need the support of representative institutions to avoid being crushed or marginalized by society's dominant institutions.

Regarding engagement with representative government, for civic citizens perhaps the main premise is that 15M marks "the end of the transition and beginning of new constituent processes" (IA 129).[31] In other words, these citizens are willing to engage with representative government provided there is a new social contract, the product of negotiations among people as equals. From the earliest days of the encampments, people came together to work toward a minimum consensus: "I was thinking, are we crazy? Do we think we are going to change capitalism from this square in Málaga? Here? Tonight? But then that is it, that is what is Utopia" (IA 77).[32]

15M was "a space of collective aggregation practising a kind of democracy-affirming disobedience" (IA 121). It acted like "a web-system that was behaving as a constituent power" (IA 122). For civic citizens in 15M, this process began with "a destituent rupture" (IA 120).[33] With*in* 15M "transformation was no longer initiated through vanguards, tutelages, or monologues" (IA 124). 15M was a "decolonizer of the collective

---

31 The interviewee is referring to the idea circulating within 15M squares that the transition from dictatorship to democracy in Spain had not been completed until the arrival of 15M.

32 This vision of Utopia painted by the interviewee resonates with the idea of "living utopianism," which David Graeber contrasts with scientific utopianism. Living utopianism creates radical alternatives in the present, whereas scientific utopianism awaits the revolutionary agent that will guide us all through the inevitable march of history; see Graeber (2009, 9).

33 Destituent power and/or destitutent process were terms often used by individuals being 15M whom I interviewed. Giorgio Agamben attributes the idea of destitutent power to Mario Tronti and describes it as a force that by its very constitution deactivates existing unjust government structures: "If revolutions and insurrections correspond to constituent power, that is, a violence that establishes and constitutes the new law, in order to think a destituent power we have to imagine completely other strategies, whose definition is the task of the coming politics"; see Agamben (2014, 70).

imaginary" (IA 123). It created a rupture with old ways of doing politics: "New frames were being created" (IA 133).

Civic citizens generated constituent and destituent moves and created new ad hoc institutions. For them, the future seemed one of ad hoc institutionality (IA 196). They never rejected the possibility that states could become obsolete over time (IA 212). So when engaging with representative institutions, there was no straight path. A map of possibilities was being opened up (IA 67). The search for new ways of being political and engaging representative institutions was constant and not necessarily linear. The ethical position was always one of continuing the search – in line with Mahatma Gandhi's idea of experimenting with truth (IA 29).[34]

During the square occupations and after, 15M's gushing river of traditions continued to rise with the objective of transforming society (IA 190). Civic citizens understood that if a majority interiorized this way of being, current systems of oppression would tumble and things would radically change (IA 90). Inspired by the president of Uruguay, José Mujica, they envisioned the president of Spain governing the country while planting his own tomatoes and living in his old, humble cottage (IA 79). That said, 15M civic citizens viewed constituent assemblies as the only possible means to change the country's dismal state. Indeed, one constituent process would not be enough – a whole set of processes would be required. To preserve the unity of the collective, that collective would have to be able to accommodate plurality and diversity (IA 121). To achieve that, diverse common fronts were being opened in an attempt to accommodate the multiplicity of voices that needed to be heard. These voices might then converge in a common program that would force multiple and federated constituent processes (IA 33). All of this aimed to integrate nationalist and regional narratives with the narrative of the 99 per cent (IA 111).

Regarding interactions with representative institutions, civic citizens suggested that as citizens, we ask ourselves first where the space of that which is constituent resides (IA 134). They then emphasized that the space of that which is constituent might be found in our ability to disobey all unjust laws and rebel against an unjust state (IA 189). From the perspective of civic networks within 15M, it was paramount to avoid the reproduction of old codes by investing time and energy in new spaces of organization; this would allow constituent processes to

34 One cannot see the whole truth, but one can be experimenting with truth and can discover and test new understandings, new truths. For more on what Gandhi is referring to with regard to experimenting with truth see, Gandhi (1957).

develop as the culmination of a revolutionary and democratic transition (IA 82). They saw this transition as necessary to give legal body to all the instituting practices that existed in Spain: occupied social centres; the PAH; grassroots referendums; vegetable gardens on occupied land; and all kinds of autonomous social initiatives exemplary of other ways of living (IA 120).

While engaging existing institutions, 15M civic citizens also took part in creative dialogues about whether an institutionality of the commons could take shape, and if so, how. Yet there was always a sense in the civic sphere that civic activity was misunderstood: "There are some people who do not understand that this path is slow. Slow in the sense that different times mark different rhythms" (IA 141).[35]

Being within 15M means acknowledging this integral view of politics and its temporality. This helps crystallize the way representative government is engaged by civic citizens. A good example of this involves the relationship between 15M citizens and the Participation Council of the Andalusian government. In 2013, when the government of this region in southern Spain was preparing a bill on citizen participation, 15M civic citizens and members of other social organizations and movements acted as advisers (IA 37). Another example of civic citizens working with representative government was the encampment created in Málaga outside a CIE (Centro de Internamiento de Extranjeros; Foreigners Internment Centre). Those in the encampment refused to dismantle it until the government granted asylum to an immigrant who had been detained. After a standoff between the Spanish authorities and those at the encampment, the two sides managed to negotiate a solution and the individual was released (IA 80).[36] Similarly, in the city of Granada, the city's unemployed collective conducted a lock-in while demanding space for a food bank. After negotiations with the local government and the Catholic Church, the city's archbishop loaned 15M a space. At the time I visited the city, the food bank was up and running (IA 71).

When the occupations first began, there was already a clear distinction between how civil citizens chose to work with government

35 This description by the interviewee explains very well the importance of this chapter's title. It reflects very clearly an important "misunderstanding" of the process of social change/transformation, one that is addressed throughout this book.

36 A paramilitary group and the government of his country wanted the person dead. Yet the Spanish government refused to grant him asylum. Finally, his girlfriend (a Spanish citizen) was allowed to enter the CIE to marry him. He was then released. A large movement in Spain has organized to demand the closing of CIEs across the country.

and how civic citizens opted to do so. For example, in the city of Sevilla, civil citizens preferred to continue the square occupation, whereas civic citizens "saw the need to decentralize 15M and move to neighbourhoods in an attempt to get closer to the social dramas" (IA 41). For civil citizens, the priority was to have their demands heard by representative government, and remaining visible in the public square seemed the most appropriate strategy to strengthen the voice of a healthy public sphere. For civic citizens, engagement with government was always secondary. Once representative government had lost its central place, it needed to be engaged through networks of civic citizenship spread across the country's neighbourhoods. For them, leaving the square to disperse into the neighbourhoods made the most sense.

All of that said, the many approaches that civic citizens in 15M take to working with representative governments all emphasize that their joining-hands mode of transformation is fundamentally non-violent. As Cherry puts it, "joining hands is a physical act that is not only non-violent, but makes violence almost physically impossible."[37] According to Cherry, non-violence is integral to the joining-hands method, in that those linked in this manner are unable to turn their hands into fists without unlinking from their comrades.[38]

JH5 – Civil Citizens Working with Representative Governments in Numerous Ways

Among civil citizen networks within 15M, there is broad consensus that 15M has shown that the country's current representative institutions of power have failed. They also sense that without alternative political parties the existing parties (beneficiaries of the pacts of the transition to democracy) will simply alternate in order to keep the country under their control (IA 162). In this sense, the majority of those more inclined to civil citizenship practices tend to align with those more interested in civic activities on a very important point. Predominantly, within the 15M climate, most individuals are seeking a radical transformation of the existing legal, economic, political, and social conception of Spain. That said, civil citizens, whose main focus is on working within official institutions, understand revolution as an escalating process of radical

37 This insight from Keith Cherry I draw from an ongoing conversation (2019–20) around the meaning of "joining hands" with a group working within the Cedar Trees Institute, CTI (cedartreesinstitute.org).

38 As above.

reforms that can be more easily and completely implemented once they attain political power (IA 82).

Within civil citizen networks, there is an idea that a new political party or a number of new parties will have to be created in order to win elections for office and reclaim the institutions from within. This idea is best exemplified by the rise of the party-movement Podemos in national politics and by the victories of citizen-candidates in local elections in major cities in Spain (see chapter 4). For now, what is important to understand is that all of these initiatives set out to attain representative power and, once in power, to return sovereignty to the people through new constituent processes arrived at in coordination with civil and civic initiatives (IA 31). It is the task of organic intellectuals (in the Gramscian sense), when faced with a rejection of existing party structures within the 15M climate, to rechannel the voice of the people by means of a vanguard that attains hegemony and sweeps into power through elections (IA 134). This civil vanguard sees itself as the true representative of the downtrodden majority, the 99 per cent, and wants to reconstruct the state by rebalancing it in favour of the oppressed. The most vocal proponents of this view at the time of my interviews now hold leadership roles in these representative formations. They are slowly winning elections and are now governing in many parts of Spain.

These civil citizens understand that to take state power, a broad progressive front is necessary. In some circles, this broad front is thought about in the context of the nation-state. In others, people think about it in terms of southern Europe (IA 124).[39] Nevertheless, it is almost always thought about as a convergence of social movements, political parties, trade unions, NGOs, citizen-candidacies, and sectorial tides. Down/up initiatives serve as inspiration. Before Podemos was created, many were asking themselves what a Spanish version of SYRIZA might look like (IA 9).[40] The premise behind the plans of those most interested in transforming official institutions from within is that the less you demand from people, the more massive the response will be. In this sense, getting people to vote is much easier than getting them to occupy parliament (IA 11).

---

39 Southern Europe is key in the imaginary of 15M activists, who think geopolitically, in terms of a bloc of Southern European countries that includes Portugal, Spain, Italy, Greece, and sometimes France.

40 SYRIZA was founded in Greece in 2004 as a radical-left coalition. Since 2015, it has been the largest party in the country's parliament. Its chairman, Alexis Tsipras, serves as prime minister.

The main concern of those who favour this approach is that unless there is a broad front, the vote on the left will be fragmented and the right will win the elections. A broad front, then, is an absolute necessity, an emergency response that requires millions of disillusioned Spaniards to trust a new group of representatives. These new representatives only intend to change the rules of the game. They want to carve out a space within representative politics where people can decide their future by collectively deciding how to confront the country's multiple crises (IA 24). Organic intellectuals call on the most mobilized citizens for help in achieving power. This is premised on the idea that while mobilization, self-organization, and mutual aid are important, nothing will change unless they take actual control of the state (IA 26).

While networks of civil citizens throughout Spain work on putting into motion this virtuous civil government, they engage with the existing representative governments in myriad ways geared toward realizing their dream. Basically, they hope to contribute to social change by transforming the "system" from within (IA 128). In this sense, they take firm steps toward "constructing not only different organizations but different attitudes and cultures" (IA 175). They are attempting to inject the ideas arrived at within 15M, and with their fellow civic citizens, into existing institutional structures (IA 177).

It must be emphasized that for civil citizens it is not institutions that are the problem – it is the people who run them. They always show utmost respect for institutionality even when disobeying or demonstrating against certain corrupt practices. This is why, by 2013, in the city of Jerez, the 15M assembly that coordinated with all other movements and was a catalyst for large mobilizations had entered into negotiations with the local government in order to press forward its many demands. It is also why, at the time of the city's occupation, individuals being 15M decided to negotiate with the police (themselves suffering public spending cuts) over issues of public order. The relationship between the encampment and the police was so good for a time that one 15M civil citizen and the police officer who used to arrest him in previous demonstrations had become good friends (IA 8).

In 2013, I travelled with a group of individuals being 15M and members of the SAT from the town of Marinaleda to Las Turquillas estate, owned by the Ministry of Defence. On the day of my visit, the SAT, supported by other organizations and activists, was attempting its sixth occupation of this land. During the occupation, the workers defied armed military and Guardia Civil officers in what they described as an act of civil disobedience. They did this by camping on the property and planting thousands of watermelons and other fruits and vegetables.

This action was aimed at making visible the need for land to produce for the people. Their ultimate goal was to force the Spanish government to negotiate.

By 2013, confluence initiatives were widespread in Spain. Groups like Ciudadanía Activa (Active Citizenry) in Valencia and Espai de Coordinació (Liaison Space) in Barcelona had been created. These initiatives were working on generating confluence toward an electoral platform (IA 88). During the time of my interviews, it was evident that civil citizens were collectively rethinking what leadership meant. Imbued in the 15M climate was "broad support for the idea of soft leaderships. Leaderships more appropriately defined, as numerous facilitators working together from collectively shared leadership spaces" (IA 124).

As the preceding examples above show, 15M civil citizens worked with different state actors and institutions in multiple ways. Most importantly, however, we see that by taking a joining-hands approach, they managed repeatedly to pull these actors and institutions into relationships of non-violence. 15M citizens remained non-violent throughout the struggle. The state, for its part, had one foot in its violent ways while at least partly entering 15M's space of non-violent contestation.[41]

JH6 – Civic/Civil Citizens Joining Hands with One Another in Myriad Ways in Order to Influence Their Governments

On 25 September 2010, months before the first 15M encampment, Spain had its eighth general strike since the country transitioned to democracy. In Barcelona, many spoke of that particular strike as prefiguring what would later be referred to as 15M. A few days before it began, people occupied the abandoned building of the Banco Español de Crédito (Credit Bank of Spain) in Plaça Catalunya (Catalonia Square). The civic citizens who occupied the building wanted to give support to the strike and to their fellow civil citizens working within the country's trade unions: "In the assemblies in the bank, one could already see that not everyone was a militant of a political group. There was a diversity of views being exposed" (IA 155).

A few days before the 15 May 2011 demonstration, DRY coordinated press conferences in each of the cities where the event was being

41 I draw this insight from an ongoing conversation (2019–20) around the meaning of "joining hands" with a group working within the Cedar Trees Institute, CTI (cedartreesinstitute.org). This reflection was contributed by Keith Cherry in response to a reflection from Dennis Dalton.

planned: "From that moment onwards, the media began to pay more attention to us. They had seen our ability to coordinate" (IA 56).

By 16 May, tension was mounting in Spain as encampments across the country began. The central and local governments did not know how to respond. That night, in the city of Málaga, police turned up at the square with a street-cleaning crew. They said that people had to move because the square needed to be cleaned. Those in the square refused to comply, but eventually they were hosed down and spent the whole night walking around the square. The group went around in circles, with all their belongings in their hands, because the police said it was illegal to camp: "The guy with the hose was saying to us: 'I am not going to hose, I am with you guys not with the police.' But he had a police officer telling him he had to do it" (IA 55). This event was indicative of how civic and civil citizens across Spain joined hands. As more and more of these types of relationships were formed, the government could not help but take notice.

On 20 May, the Central Electoral Board determined that the encampments were illegal; the day of reflection prior to the country's municipal elections on 22 May needed to be respected. Yet "by the time of the Electoral Board's decision to ban the gathering, the Internet was already covered with hashtags such as #15M; #spanishrevolution; #democraciarealya; #nonosvamos; and #juntaelectoralfacts" (IA 120). At that point, many people who had never participated in politics decided to sleep in the squares: "I am confident that only one day before they would have thought that laws existed to be obeyed, and here they were disobeying a law from the highest body of the Spanish state" (IA 3).

That same night, in the city of Granada, people were in assembly when the police arrived. Two lawyers among the group were selected by consensus to be spokespeople and informed the police officers that they were in assembly. The police then said that they had to abandon the square, and the spokespeople responded by saying that the decision had to be made in assembly and that the police officers would have to wait. "This same conversation happened four times, intermittently, while the assembly continued" (IA 67). Although they were eventually evicted, the collective behaviour of civil and civic citizens during Granada's 15M occupation on that night showed they were able to think communally.

On 21 May, the day of reflection prior to the municipal elections, the encampment in Valencia organized a funeral for democracy in which they made a coffin, cloaked in black, and walked in procession to the doorsteps of City Hall: "The coffin ended up confiscated and was buried inside the Mayoral building" (IA 89). This demonstration and the many that followed revealed the joining-hands ethos of civil and civic citizens and their power-with force: "Not so much because of the demonstrations, but because when people construct demonstrations they can easily construct other things. There is no longer a need to delegate to a saviour with good intentions" (IA 22).

As long as the encampments were in place, there was an ongoing conversation regarding whether 15M should channel its energy toward the creation of new political parties (IA 29). Numerous collectives were discussing how to enter institutions in order to "change the system from within" (IA 75). In the same manner that the initial DRY demonstration of 15 May 2011 managed to erase the dichotomy between right and left, it was hoped that 15M would expunge "that dichotomy between institution and street; that hierarchical distance" (IA 112).

Many shared a deep conviction that the prefigurative politics of advancing dreams and building on the margins would not be enough to achieve their goals: "We need to also occupy and inhabit institutions of political representation" (IA 134). There was a general consensus in encampments across the country that 15M needed to participate in existing institutions: "then what we need to do is to discuss whether our objective is to destroy them, transform them or disperse them" (IA 148). By 2013, many saw themselves as having come together through the internet, then moved to the squares, then from the squares to the congress, and now they were beginning to start platforms to enter electoral politics and have "a 15M in the institutions" (IAs 183 and 186).[42]

Some people being 15M prefer to work outside of official institutions; others prefer to work within them. Nevertheless, in the 15M that I encountered during the interviewing, most people agreed on the need to combine both work outside and work within official institutions. "One foot inside, one foot outside" was common way to put it. People continued to make requests to institutions while at the same time attempting to change them. This, however, was always combined with the self-constitution of new institutions when deemed necessary. Requests for rights continued to be made to official institutions; whenever those rights were not granted, people claimed them by disobeying (IA 110).[43]

42 The interviewees talked about surrounding congress, in reference to Rodea el Congreso (Surround Congress; 25S). That was a demonstration held on 25 September 2012 during which people surrounded the Spanish Congress in Madrid.

43 This is how the strategy worked; many in the squares referred to it as "one foot in, one foot out." The term was coined at the Strasbourg No Border Camp in July 2002, when activists were debating various proposals for autonomous spaces at the Florence European Social Forum. See Juris (2005, 262).

In 2013, there was broad support from both civil and civic citizens for working within official institutions. This was understood as the best way to influence government. Yet as strategies were being thought and rethought, understood and reunderstood, many concerns were being raised. Some voices from within 15M thought that bureaucracies were too slow and unimaginative: "Working with them often blocks the imagination of those being 15M" (IA 176). Others expressed concern that electoral logics divided that which on the streets was converging – that the multitude of voices working together outside of the electoral arena would be divided once individuals were forced to select particular parties (IA 111). Nevertheless, initiatives like Coordinación Constituyentes de Valencia (Valencia's Constituents Coordination) continued to promote a new constituent process by bringing together new political coalitions (IA 84). Also, following 15M, alternative political groups like the CUPs (Candidaturas d'Unitat Popular; Popular Unity Candidatures) in Catalonia were gaining popularity. The CUPs had existed for twenty-five years, but it was the exemplarity of the joining-hands relationships between 15M civic and civil citizens that made political initiatives like theirs appealing to broader constituencies (IA 195).

During my research trip, those holding power in Spain were adamant that the changes sought by 15M needed to come from established institutions. Many within 15M concurred but also had concerns related to the rigid structures of the current representative system. People were aware that institutional rigidity could suffocate that which was new, vital, and forged outside of existing institutions (IA 195). There was also concern that the collective imaginary regarding elections tended to lead to individuals delegating their responsibilities and decisions to a party structure (IA 5).

Within 15M, individuals expressed the concern that mobilization would self-bureaucratize if the events aligned themselves with the representative calendar. It was feared that alternative practices would be shunted to one side and that without those practices, 15M would be unable to creatively overflow current institutional frames (IA 162). The idea began to take hold that elections could be important and useful if they were approached as mobilizations, that is, as quotidian referendums (IA 2). For 15M civil and civic citizens, power was not something to be taken; rather, it was something to be co-created, constructed through relations (IA 162). Many people feared that the institutional path through the corrupt representative system had become a dead end and that all efforts along the representative front might turn out to be a waste of the transformative energy that 15M had generated (IA 8).

15M civil and civic citizens who had joined hands to influence their governments thought it paramount that means and ends align. Yet they also felt a sense of urgency, having concluded that there was no outside to run to and that institutions therefore needed to be addressed (IA 162). The representative option might not be the most attractive, but lesser evils (hopefully allies) still had to be voted into power to aid in the transition (IA 99). So those who were more comfortable working from the outside needed to join hands with those most comfortable working within (IA 128).[44] From the paradox presented so clearly in the slogan "No nos representan" (They do not represent us), two new questions had arisen: How are we going to be represented in official institutions? And how is the process of representation going to work? (IA 111).

Joining hands captures well the collaborative element of the activities that civic and civil citizens engage in when attempting to influence their governments. As Tully has pointed out, the "space" in which joining hands takes place is the "middle ground."[45] This is the space that pure anarchists reject and that is overlooked by those who advocate for one foot inside and one foot outside of institutions. Meanwhile, 15M civil and civic citizens joining hands try to "bring [that space] into awareness and into being."[46]

Conclusion

This chapter has shown how, two years after 15M encampments, 15M practices were widespread across Spain. 15M had metamorphosed from being a large and very powerful gathering of collective presences in public squares, to thousands of different initiatives addressing all aspects of social, economic, and political life. The label 15M remained the identifier for some groups; in other groups, individuals who identified as 15M were contributing (often spearheading) under different labels.15M had established itself as a term for describing a way of being in the world, of doing and thinking differently than what had been hegemonic in activist circles and in society at large. 15M had bequeathed a climate of collective empowerment rooted in multiple factors: new

44 Civic citizens do not adopt a dichotomous relationship with the state; instead, they utilize a wide range of strategies, working both within and outside the state to advance their aspirations democratically. See Wampler (2018, 721).

45 This insight from James Tully I draw from an ongoing conversation (2019–20) around the meaning of "joining hands" with a group working within the Cedar Trees Institute, CTI (cedartreesinstitute.org).

46 As above.

technologies; historical and current exemplars of struggle and alternative modes of being; solidarity; a sediment of existing practices that, when networked, was able to empower voices not heard; a deep and collective understanding of the power of a dialogical multiplicity; an ethical commitment to the ideal of democracy; and an acknowledgment of non-violence as the only way of being 15M. Not everyone rejected violence, but all whom I interviewed understood that what was violent was not, fundamentally, 15M.

At the time I embarked on my research trip, the encampments were remembered as a moment of transformation when self-governing people organizing together and taking their lives into their own hands enacted a new world and presented alternatives. From the encampments, people learned the importance of generating dialogical power-with relations among those striving for change. The encampments had made visible and accessible to a large proportion of the Spanish population, both inside and outside of the encampments, a powerful way of being together in Spain as citizens, one based on "being the change."

The thick description presented in this chapter enables us to see the six complex and mutually empowering ways of being together that constitute 15M in motion. We have seen how the dynamics of being political have been altered in Spain since 2011: "The mode of being political is no longer what it has traditionally been, at least since the transition to democracy. This new way of being political is given a name, 15M" (IA 5). This chapter has revealed that 15M is a way of being in the world whereby people generate a being-with ethos at the civic level and forge good relations with civil citizens. Through the self-descriptions of participants, we have heard what brought people to the squares. We have also lived with them the creation of the encampments and the expansion of 15M encampments into neighbourhoods. Most importantly, the strange multiplicity found within this collective presence offers us a window onto the six joining-hands relationships in which 15M is immersed. These six distinct relationships have continued since the 15M occupations.

In Spain since 15 May 2011, many people have begun to question the current social, political, and economic system and to subject it to public discussion, negotiation, and transformation. 15M, then, is a manifestation of people taking the initiative to exercise power together and act in concert in order to bring about change by means of complementary methods.

These methods include self-organization; civil disobedience; protesting; discussing; cooperating; negotiating among diverse members and sub-groups; negotiating with government, police forces, and the media; negotiating with various trade unions, political parties, and social organizations; setting up committees; pushing for legal and constitutional reforms; seeking changes to democratic accountability; and building a true social and economic democracy from the ground up in a non-violent manner.

Together, these methods represent a clear example of citizens self-organizing democratically, exercising self-government together, reasoning with one another as equals, and committing themselves to non-violent dispute resolution to try and resolve their differences. All of this in an effort to change the way their societies are governed. By enacting a commons in which different agonisms, differences, convergences, temporalities, traditions, and languages surface, and shortcomings are discussed, 15M has brought about an "abyss of freedom."[47] That is, it has generated a situation within which what it inspires can be neither predicted nor controlled.

15M's six joining-hands relationships crystallize the activities of a multitude of *demoi* coming together to resolve disputes non-violently while transforming unjust behaviours. Within 15M, no group tries to convert others to their way of life. Civic and civil citizens agree to engage with each other, each from their own mode of being. Through their non-violent engagement, they seek all kinds of support from bystanders and people around the world. 15M needs this kind of external joining-hands support in order to undermine the social basis of support of those responsible for the injustices they are protesting against. With one hand, 15M asserts itself truthfully against injustices (political and corporate corruption and social inequality); with the other, it offers an "open hand" as opposed to a closed fist.[48] Through this double-movement, 15M reveals its commitment to non-violent contestation while also offering to join hands (with opponents and bystanders) in negotiations to resolve the specific conflict.

47 See Arendt (1971, 195).

48 James Tully describes the activity of joining hands in this manner in an ongoing conversation (2019–20) around the meaning of "joining hands" with a group working within the Cedar Trees Institute, CTI (cedartreesinstitute.org).

Chapter Two

Roots and Routes of Spain's Counter-Modernity

At its peak, 15M encompassed between 6 and 8.5 million people. They were not merely passive participants. Rather, those who flocked to 15M were actively involved in co-creating the 15M experience.[1] "Intangible, like an atmosphere or an ecosystem," 15M launched an important and ongoing conversation (IA 37). It transformed knowledges by "making old certain behaviours and practices, while rejuvenating others" (IA 162). Appearing as "a multiple, multiform subject carrying multiplicity in its DNA," it attracted those who previously identified with different traditions and invited them to join the conversation (IA 121).

This chapter explores how individuals within 15M interpret certain events in Spanish history. I present a detailed account of various traditions and past events and conflicts, suggesting that these, and the particular ways in which they are remembered, have made 15M what it is today. When asked about their histories, those being 15M responded with the multiplicity of traditions presented here.

The different traditions co-being, co-interpreting, and co-creating within 15M do not constitute a single "tradition of resistance." Rather, they represent what many within 15M claim to be genealogically linked causes with their roots in distant times and places. Unearthing this multiplicity is important, for the metanarratives of people being 15M are not empty dreams but have real effects in practice. In presenting a 15M

1 These numbers come from an Ipsos Public Affairs survey conducted in the early days of the encampments. Other data presented included the following: 0.8 and 1.5 million Spanish citizens participated intensely in 15M initiatives; 76 per cent of Spanish citizens considered the demands and the practices of 15M reasonable and felt that there was a democratic right to fight for them in the way those being 15M were doing. See "Más de seis millones de españoles han participado en el Movimiento 15M," *RTVE*, 5 August 2011, http://www.rtve.es/noticias/20110806/mas-seis-millones-espanoles-han-participado-movimiento-15m/452598.shtml.

historical imaginary, we are excavating those events and ways of being that inspire and/or mark individuals being 15M. Rather than accepting the scholarly consensus on events in Spanish history and counterpoising this with the views of those being 15M, this chapter offers a space within which those being 15M can narrate a 15M history of Spain.[2] By taking this approach, I arrive at the origins and antecedents of 15M, which are important, for they show that it did not appear out of thin air and was not an invention of social media. 15M has deep roots (and routes) in more than a century of collective practices of dissent.

Nineteenth-Century Libertarian and Cooperative Traditions

When thinking about autonomous movements and social mobilization outside of institutionalized structures, those being 15M are immediately "taken back to the country's libertarian traditions and the activities that began towards the end of the nineteenth century" (IA 60). That era witnessed an unprecedented level of social struggle for freedom, much of it carried out under the principles of non-violence, cooperation, and direct democracy. The strength of these traditions was plain to see as early as 1869. One could see it, for example, in the way the First International was created. In stark contrast to the First International in other countries, the Spanish First International was strongly influenced by anarchist thought and adhered to ideas of horizontal collectivism (JH1, JH3).[3] These ideas were apparent in the actions of

2 Through their oral histories, individuals being 15M bring to the surface events and movements that scholarly consensus might have missed. Particular dates are well-known because of their impact on the whole of society, but the ways they are narrated by interviewees do not reflect obvious, dominant, "everyperson" understandings. So in Spain, given that General Franco's dictatorship is still recent, excavating oral histories in such a manner is an important step toward remembrance, reparation, and reconciliation. The literature on Spanish history I engage in throughout this chapter aims to expand on the issues raised by the interviewees. Once they shared their imaginaries of historical events, I identified written narratives and studies supportive of their claims. Howard Zinn made a similar move; see Zinn (2005).

3 In the previous chapter I explored the six distinct types of joining-hands relationships between citizens being enacted within 15M. In this chapter, I identify in brackets different joining hands relationships as they appear within this 15M history of Spain. These will be identified as follows: civic citizens joining hands with one another (JH1); civil citizens joining hands with one another (JH2); civic and civil citizens joining hands (JH3); civic citizens working with representative governments in numerous ways (JH4); civil citizens working with representative governments in numerous ways (JH5); and civic–civil citizens joining hands with one another in myriad ways in order to influence government (JH6).

the organization known in Spain as the Federación Regional Española (Spanish Regional Federation).[4] In 1870, counting 30,000 members, the federation organized its first congress in Barcelona, which ended with agreements on direct action, electoral abstention, and a push for a general strike (JH1, JH3, JH4). These processes were considered means to achieve social and political change.[5]

In 1878, Peter Kropotkin visited Spain, where he stayed with renowned anarchist José García Viñas. Kropotkin had developed a close association with Spanish anarchists and expected "an outbreak of social revolts as a consequence of the country's serious economic crisis."[6] During his visit, Kropotkin was tasked with reconciling groups in Barcelona and Madrid that disagreed on tactics. The groups in Madrid thought primarily in terms of individual and more or less terrorist acts; the Barcelona Internationalists, by contrast, favoured collectivist action. Kropotkin succeeded in his task, and the Spanish Federation remained firmly committed to collectivism (JH1, JH3).[7]

During the interviews, most people referred to Kropotkin as the greatest influence on Spanish anarchism. In the 1970s, Murray Bookchin, the most famous American anarchist, wrote that Kropotkin and Bakunin were the most influential intellectuals in Spain's anarchist movement and that Kropotkin's model of "anarchist communism" held the most sway there in the 1930s.[8]

Well into the 1880s, translations of Kropotkin's works were available in Spain. As a result, when the Anarchist Organization of the Spanish Region was founded in Valencia in 1888, anarchist communism was its preferred approach. This was different to Bakunin's collectivism. Bakunin believed that the means of life individuals received must be tied to the amount of labour they contributed, whereas Kropotkin was adamant that after the revolution each commune should distribute its produce according to need. The principal text of the time seems to have been *The Conquest of Bread* – a thorough cooperativist program.[9]

4 The federation was banned in 1872, but it operated underground until the International was eventually dissolved. See Peirats (2006).

5 Cuevas (2010, 101–10).

6 Cahm (1989, 60).

7 Cahm (1989, 59). At their Barcelona Congress in September 1881, the federation reiterated its firm commitment.

8 See Bookchin (1978, 29, 110, 115–16, 126, 172, 257, 320).

9 See Kropotkin (2002). See also Kropotkin (1913). Finally, a recent biography by Dugatkin (2011) tells an amazing story that places Kropotkin at the heart of what 15M is trying to do in Spain.

Throughout the 1880s and until the end of the century, an intellectual renaissance swept through Spain. It was spurred not just by the Federación Regional Española – horizontal collectivist ideas were being propagated by many other groups, including the Federación de los Trabajadores de la Región Española (Workers Federation of the Spanish Region, 1881–8) and the Pacto de Unión y Solidaridad (Union and Solidarity Pact, 1889–96) (JH1, JH3, JH4).[10] Inspired by libertarian communist ideas, these organizations called for the abolition of the state, private property, and capitalism and favoured common ownership of the means of production, direct democracy, and self-governance. Thanks to writings by people like Kropotkin, Élisée Reclus, Jean Grave, and Errico Malatesta, these ideas were having a significant impact throughout the country by the end of the century.

Between the 1860s and 1900, people in Spain began to enact alternative modes of citizenship on a large scale. Collectivist ideas spread rapidly across the country, and the cooperative movement gained momentum. As one of my interviewees recognized, "we are part of the cooperative tradition which in these territories has been active for over one century" (IA 206). In Spain, a tradition was born in 1856 with the founding of La Proletaria (The Proletarian), a silk cooperative, in the city of Valencia (JH3, JH6). This led to the formation of textile collectives in the town of Mataró in 1864 and, soon after, across Catalonia. Cooperatives were promoted by people like Fernando Garrido, Antonio Vicent, Josep Roca i Galés, and Doménec Perramon. The world-renowned Basque cooperative Mondragon is an often-cited exemplar of the power-with force of this tradition, which has deep roots in Spain (JH3, JH6).

Pre-Civil War Contestation and Constructive Programs

Within 15M, the years 1900 to 1936 are remembered as a time when citizens gradually empowered themselves and became self-governing in many ways. Despite the elites' attempts to silence dissent, contestation continued to increase and constructive programs continued to expand.[11] The first two decades of the twentieth century were marked

10 Peirats (2006). Alternative projects included the following: the satirical newspaper *La Tramuntana* (1881–96), started by collectivist writer José Llunas Pujols; initiatives like the Catalan anarchist publication *Acracia* (1886–8); and the newspaper *El Productor* (1887–93).

11 Although the history of Spanish anarchism here is presented through the imaginary of 15M citizens and focuses on the traits of the anarchism remembered by those in

by solidarity-building, mutual aid initiatives, and numerous worker strikes: "This was the time when the libertarian movement really began to pick up strength." The libertarian movement of the early 1900s resembled 15M in that it put forward "theories and practices that were not in common use but which, once experienced, were hard to abandon" (IA 55). From within 15M, the spirit of anarchism that marked the early decades of the twentieth century is understood as having been largely non-violent from its inception: "It had been working on mutual aid and fighting against oppression" (IA 149). In this sense, the century began where the nineteenth century left off – constructive programs seeded by the country's collectivist, cooperativist, and libertarian traditions expanded rapidly (JH1–JH6).

By 1900, numerous "worker resistance associations" had been established. They included El Provenir del Trabajo (The Future of Work), for construction workers, La Precisa (The Precise), for miners, and El Bien (The Good), for metallurgy workers (JH1, JH3, JH4, JH6).[12] On 13 October 1900, a congress of worker resistance associations was held in Madrid, with 150 associations attending. There, La Federación de Sociedades de Resistencia de la Región Española (Federation of Resistance Associations of the Spanish Region, FSORE) was founded. Its main aim was to build solidarity among workers in different trades (JH1–JH3).[13]

By 1907, anarchism was becoming the most popular option among the working class for organizing unions and federations. That same year, the labour federation Solidaritat Obrera (Worker Solidarity) was founded in Barcelona (JH1–JH3).[14] In 1910, groups coming together through Solidaritat Obrera founded CNT; this confluence significantly expanded anarchist influence in the country (JH1, JH3, JH4, JH6).[15]

By 1915, the political positions of Spanish anarchists were beginning to gel. With the First World War now under way, the International Congress against the War was held in the Galician city of Ferrol. There, Spanish anarchists made plain their antiwar stance. The congress ended with strong declarations in favour of pacifism and against militarism,

---

15M squares, it is important to note that around the turn of the previous century, a great deal of violence was associated with anarchism, in terms of some of its practices as well as how it was suppressed. This violence provides an important historical context to the debates about violence and non-violence in which 15M citizens engage (see page 114–16 for these debates). For more information on the violence associated with anarchism in Spain, see Avilés and Herrerín (2010).

12 Guareña et al. (1999, 239).

13 Iñiguez (2001, 239).

14 Bookchin (1998, 131).

15 To learn more about the CNT, see Liarte (1977).

and with the a statement of support for a revolutionary general strike inspired by the ideas of Ferdinand Domela Nieuwenhuis (JH1, JH3, JH4, JH6).[16]

In 1919, the disconnect between the governors and the governed resulted in a large, non-violent strike in Barcelona that eventually paralysed 70 per cent of Catalan industry (JH3–JH6). The strike lasted forty-four days and became known as La Canadiense (The Canadian).[17] It garnered so much popular support that the government declared a state of war, during which it restricted the movements of ordinary people and crushed the political opposition.[18]

By 1929, the situation had deteriorated so greatly that students were constantly demonstrating in the streets and committing acts of civil disobedience (JH2, JH5). Inspired by the students, workers initiated strikes of their own, including a public transit strike that paralysed the city of Barcelona (JH3, JH6).[19]

By 1930, a transformative collective imaginary had taken hold of Spanish society. Across the country, neighbourhood workers' cultural associations had opened, as well as popular cinemas and cultural centres (JH1–JH3): "People were proud of being workers; there was an affirmation of worker pride" (IA 170). Whereas "15M has appeared at a time when hegemony is in the hands of capitalism, in the 1930s this was not the case" (IA 170). Since 1931, anarchists across Spain had been working to form a National Industrial Federation. These efforts prepared them for the coordination of strikes as social conflict intensified in different parts of the country.

On 14 May 1931, after municipal elections in which Republican candidates won the majority of votes, Spain's Second Republic was

---

16 The anti-militarist and pacifist position of the CNT is also expressed in the libertarian literature of the time, in publications such as *Tierra y Libertad*, *Solidaridad Obrera*, *Acción*, *Acción Fabril*, *La Colmena Obrera*, and *El Vidrio*. In a 1916 issue of *La Colmena Obrera* magazine, we read the following: "We condemn all wars because we consider them barbaric and inhumane" ("Los grandes problemas," *La Colmena Obrera*, 23 September 1916, 3). See also Devesa Pájaro (2008, 7).

17 *La Canadiense* was the company in which the conflict began.

18 On 13 September 1923, General Miguel Primo de Rivera led a military coup that ended with him being appointed prime minister by the king. He suspended the constitution of 1876 and established a dictatorship that lasted seven years. During the interviews, Primo de Rivera was seldom mentioned. Yet as Catalonia struggles with Spain today, it is important to remember the clampdown on Catalan culture that is associated with Rivera's time in power. For useful context on this period and the relationship between the dictatorship and Catalonia, see Smith (2007); Reguillo (1998, 289); and Michonneau (2004).

19 Peirats (2006, 33, 43).

proclaimed and King Alfonso XIII left the country.[20] For many today, the period leading up to this event resonated strongly with the birth of 15M: "At that time there was a regime that was like a corpse waiting to be buried and people were asking for a transition. Today we are asking for a constituent process; a democratic rupture" (IA 144).

On 8 January 1933, anarchists launched an uprising across Spain with the goal of instituting libertarian communism (JH1, JH3, JH4). Three days later, Assault Guards massacred twenty-four peasants in the town of Casas Viejas in the province of Cádiz, one of the most tragic events of the Spanish Second Republic and one often remembered within 15M spaces: "Those of us entering 15M coming from libertarian traditions have had very present our inheritances; all of us here remember what happened in Casas Viejas" (IA 28). As communities became more and more collectivized, the government responded by bringing out the tanks: "People were acting from a position of non-violence, wanting to take charge of their territory and manage it collectively through municipalist collectives" (JH1, JH3, JH4) (IA 67).[21]

By November 1933, the governing Republican and Socialist coalition had collapsed. A national election was held on 19 November. The anarchist uprising and the events at Casas Viejas, and the fact that anarchists favoured abstention from voting, resulted in a strong electoral showing for Spain's right-wing parties, which formed a governing coalition. Alejandro Lerroux became the new president.[22] On 5 October 1934, the UGT called for an Alianza Obrera (Workers Alliance), an insurrectional general strike aimed at achieving socialism by abandoning the parliamentary path (JH1, JH4). This was the time "when Buenaventura Durruti and other key figures of the working-class movement were asking people not to vote" (IA 67). The government's response was to again proclaim a state of war.[23]

20 The new republican period officially lasted from April 1931 to 1 April 1939. That date marks the end to the country's civil war, which gave rise to Franco's dictatorship. Nevertheless, the Second Republic is usually seen as comprising three periods: from 1931 to 1933, Spain was governed by a Republican/ Socialist coalition; from 1933 to 1935, it was governed by a coalition of right-wing parties; finally, from February 1936 until the *coup d'état* of 17–18 July, a coalition of left-wing parties known as the Frente Popular (Popular Front) governed. For an excellent account of this period, see Pla (2006).

21 According to Jerome R. Mintz, the events of Casas Viejas were not non-violent; however, in the imaginary of this interviewee they were. For a description of events at Casas Viejas, see Mintz (1982).

22 These were the first elections in Spanish history in which women could vote. For a useful account of this period, see Jackson (2005).

23 For good explications of events during this period, see: Tamames (1974, 230); Ruiz (1988, 13–14); and Thomas (1976, 162).

In my dialogues with*in* 15M, these years were remembered as "years during which laws that had been passed during the early days of the Republic were annulled and the military and police were used to repress the population" (IA 129). There was often a sense that post–15 May 2011 events resonated with the events leading up to the 1936 elections: the right was in power, autonomy for Catalonia was being discussed, and there was an upsurge of different nationalisms: "People were asking for bread and occupying properties, while repression by the security forces intensified" (JH3, JH6) (IA 56). Those being 15M identified with this complex reality.

Spanish Civil War Mutual Aid and Cooperation

On 18 July 1936, an attempted military coup marked the beginning of the Spanish Civil War. As the coup began, the social revolution was well on its way. Millions of the country's cooperative democrats were deep into their constructive projects of mutual aid and cooperation (JH1, JH3, JH4, JH6). In the countryside, much previously unused land had already been collectivized (JH1, JH3). In the parts of Spain in which the republican government remained in power, social changes were accelerating at unprecedented levels. There were innovations in the domains of economics, politics, social life, culture, education, and sexuality. In areas where the CNT had majority support, another Spain was taking form. A new organization for producing, consuming, and governing the capabilities "of" the *demos* was being put into practice "by" the *demos* (JH1, JH6). The means of production were being collectivized, and self-government was taking root (JH1, JH3). Especially in Catalonia and Aragon, citizens' social reality was undergoing drastic change. The structure of the state was shrinking, and the abolition of a class-based society was becoming a reality through cooperative endeavours (JH1–JH4).[24]

By the time the civil war began, there had already been numerous revolutionary accomplishments. In fact, many workers who had been on strike when the war broke out soon began to reclaim their production capabilities, seizing corporations and organizing themselves into assembly-run collectives (JH1). Even strategic industries such as the oil company CAMPSA were collectivized (JH1, JH2, JH3, JH6). Within a week of the military uprising, various self-organizing *demoi* were running public transportation, the train system, and water and energy sources.[25] Collectivization was often so far-reaching that it encompassed

24 Cuevas (2010, 105).
25 Peirats (2006, 81).

entire processes of extraction, cultivation, production, distribution, and administration (JH1–JH6).[26]

Throughout the conflict, anarchists in the Republican zones worked tirelessly to found schools and libraries in remote villages. In most of the villages, these educational centres were established in confiscated villas baptized with names such as Villa Kropotkin or Villa Montseny (JH1, JH3, JH4, JH6).[27] In addition, many small rural communities carried out their own experiments in libertarian communism.[28] In metropolitan areas, agrarian land was being collectivized (JH1, JH3, JH4, JH6).[29] In Barcelona, the central fruit and vegetable market in the Born neighbourhood was collectivized, and distribution from the countryside was facilitated through collectives.[30] In Montblanc, articles were purchased with a new collectivized currency (JH1, JH3). Some collectives developed central storage areas where everyone took what they needed (JH3). At other collectives, such as Llombay (Castellón), goods were distributed based on family need (JH3).

In most of the collectivized areas, when shortages existed, priority was given to children, the sick, the elderly, and women (JH3). In Peñalba, medical experts chosen by the community allocated rations (JH3). Most transactions between collectives were conducted by barter (JH3). For example, Calanda exchanged oil for textiles with Barcelona.[31] Currency in collectivized communities lost much of its value as most

---

26 In cases where an entire industry was collectivized, the population referred to this as socialized industry. Such industries included the Sindicato de Madera de Barcelona (Wood Syndicate of Barcelona), bakeries, and the train network in Cataluña and Aragón. In Asturias, the fishing industry and its offshoots were also fully socialized. A distribution cooperative (Consejo de Cooperación Provincial) was created to guarantee delivery from the coastal towns to the interior of the region; see Peirats (2006, 82, 87).

27 In Amposta, for example, the school offered public baths, classes for almost illiterate adults, a canteen for kindergarten children, and a school for arts and trades; see Peirats (2006, 103, 104).

28 On 1 May 1933, *La Revista Blanca* reported on examples of such communities in Burgos, Santander, Lleida, Soria, Asturias, Andalucía, and Extremadura. In that same article, a peasant is quoted as saying: "We have no rich and poor, no social problem, and no unemployed workers. Production is shared equally, and we all live happily and in peace" (in Peirats 2006, 97).

29 In Barcelona, for example, 1,000 acres were collectivized. In Hospitalet de Llobregat, 15 square kilometres were collectivized. In Sueca (Valencia), 3,600 acres of rice, 320 of vegetables, and 115 of orange groves were collectivized. In Belvis del Jarama (Castilla la Nueva), 2,400 acres were collectivized. In Brihuega (La Alcarria), almost the whole municipality was collectivized (Peirats 2006, 98).

30 Peirats (2006, 101).

31 Peirats (2006, 102).

people refrained from using it (JH4, JH6).[32] In Seros, unmarried people were fed in communal kitchens and given clean clothes (JH3). When they married, the community helped them set up their new homes (JH3). In Graus, the population paid for newly-weds to go on honeymoon (JH3).[33]

Relationships within collectives were deeply democratic. In Hospitalet de Llobregat, the people held general assemblies every three months; in Ademuz, every Saturday; in Alcolea de Cinca, whenever anyone in the community deemed an assembly necessary (JH3).[34] A social revolution was taking place in the broader context of a civil war, and while many collectives supported the Republican war effort, most of them focused mainly on developing constructive programs toward a new society based on non-violent, cooperative, and democratic principles (JH1, JH2, JH3).[35]

The Spanish Civil War was intensely violent. Even so, collaborative, cooperative, and democratic traditions coalesced in the trenches and in society at large. In *Homage to Catalonia*, George Orwell writes about the Spanish militias on the Aragon Front, referring to what he witnessed there as an experiment in classless society: "In theory it was perfect equality, and even in practice it was not far from it" (JH1–JH6).[36] However short-lived it turned out to be, what Orwell experienced in the trenches (and during his time in Barcelona) made him eager to see more exemplars of this kind of horizontality.

Transition to Democracy Traditions and Events

On 20 November 1975, Francisco Franco died and Spain began its transition from dictatorship to democracy. In 1977, the country held its first post-dictatorship democratic general election. In 1978, the country's

---

32 Peirats (2006, 105).

33 Peirats (2006, 106).

34 Peirats (2006, 106).

35 In addition to this exemplary developmental work, some groups in Spain were advocating publicly for a non-violent resolution to the conflict. An example was La Liga Española de Resistentes a la Guerra (Spanish War Resisters League). Affiliated with the American War Resisters League, it called for non-violent revolution and carried out relief work in war-torn areas. Founded by Professor José Brocca, the league provided humanitarian aid to refugees. It distributed food and other necessities, opened orphanages and refugee centres, and helped children escape to other countries. See S.H. Bennett, "Pacifismo socialista y revolución social no violenta: La WRL y la Guerra Civil Española," presented at the Congreso Internacional Sobre la Guerra Civil Española, Madrid, 2006.

36 Orwell (1952, 103–5).

constitution was approved. Without a doubt, this was the time most often referenced by those being 15M. It seemed quite apparent during my research travels that the people I met being 15M generally understood their struggle as not simply against austerity, political corruption, territoriality, or identity. There was within 15M a profound realization that the foundational contract that was meant to bind the society together legally and politically was illegitimate. At the very least, it was rapidly losing all legitimacy.

By late 2013, within 15M, official narratives about the transition were being strongly contested. It seemed clear that many of the struggles then being waged were rooted in, and could trace their direct lineage to, the post–civil war era. Decades later, people still viewed the transition period as a missed opportunity, as a time when the population was cheated out of a truly constituent process. From within 15M, it appeared as if *la cultura de la transición* (the Spanish identity constructed during the country's transition to democracy and reinforced until today) had been broken. With that rupture, ideas of the possible and preferable had somehow mutated, transformed, and expanded.

In Spain, a "pacted" transition acknowledged the legality of the institutional framework inherited from Franco.[37] Through an amnesty law, that pact exempted the regime from any responsibility for the atrocities carried out during the civil war and throughout the years of dictatorship. Many organizations (including the United Nations, Human Rights Watch, and Amnesty International) have made repeated requests for the derogation of this law, yet it is still in place today.[38] During the transition, while elites were deciding the institutional fate of the country, people on the streets were contributing to a creative process of direct action, a process that had been gaining momentum since the 1950s. Since then, there had been strong popular pressure

37 Transitologists like John Higley and Richard Gunther describe "pacted" transitions as "elite settlements." The Spanish transition is broadly viewed as a clear example of a pacted transition. Students of democratic transitions view this kind as exclusionary and undemocratic. Guillermo O'Donnell and Phillippe C. Schmitter describe such pacts as being negotiated by a reduced number of actors representing established institutions. According to them, such pacts "tend to reduce competitiveness as well as conflict; they seek to limit accountability to wider publics; the attempt to control the agenda of policy concerns; and they deliberately distort the principle of citizen equality." See O'Donnell and Schmitter (1986, 38); see also Higley and Gunther (1992); and Rigby (2000, 76).

38 For detail on this law, see Amnesty Law 46/1977 of 15 October, Published in BOE on 17 October 1977. The law protected political prisoners as well as numerous political crimes and acts of sedition and rebellion.

for democratization to begin. Neighbourhood groups, clubs, and associations spearheaded these mobilizations (JH4–JH6). Hiking groups, sports clubs, and blood donor associations were among those most active (JH1–JH3). Together they promoted interpersonal relationships with co-workers, family members, neighbours, and friends (JH1–JH3). A social discourse different to the one presented by the regime began to surface, and much constructive work was carried out in many different areas of social life.[39]

As part of this transformative process, dissident Catholic movements closely connected with the working class began to appear. These included Les Germandats Obreres d'Acció Catòlica (Worker Brotherhoods of Catholic Action) in the 1950s and Solidaridad in the 1960s (JH1–JH3),[40] the latter being comprised of an eclectic mix of Christian and syndicalist revolutionaries.[41] "At the time, there were many priests that used the priesthood like a political space. They were working-class first, priests second" (IA 11). Whenever people needed to hide, they hid in the churches: "without the parishes there would have been no anti-Francoism" (JH3, JH6) (IA 94).

By the 1960s, the dictatorship had been severely weakened; students had even created "free zones" in universities across the country (JH1–JH3) in which the legality of the dictatorship was systematically transgressed: "People do not talk much about the 1960s, but a lot of people were being killed by the dictatorship. They could not be a part of the staged transition that was being prepared" (IA 60). Around this time, an anti-militarist, non-violent movement surfaced. It was a "non-institutionalized, coordinated, and collective movement. It did not end until its objectives were met" (IA 8). It was a movement of conscientious objectors and draft-dodgers who rejected the country's compulsory military service (JH1, JH4). It integrated a strong Christian base with groups such as Pax Christi and Justicia y Paz. It was comprised of informal networks the encompassed self-governed social spaces, libertarian groups, radical-leftist collectives, and environmentalist groups (JH1–JH6). In 1971, the son of a Lieutenant Colonel of the Francoist army, Pepe Beúnza, became the first conscientious objector: "He was part of a non-violent civic resistance movement with strong links to the

39 For a good study of the period, A. Calle Collado and M. Jiménez (2008) "Transiciones en movimiento: La cultura de protesta en España y el ciclo de movilización global," 2008, 21. This unpublished document was prepared for the Informe Foessa.

40 Fontana, (2005, 105).

41 The roots of these Catholic currents can be traced to liberation theology and the Second Vatican Council of 1962–5, initiated by Pope John XXIII.

extra-parliamentary left in Germany and Italy" (IA 103).[42] By 1975, the country had witnessed the first collective conscientious objection in the neighbourhood of Can Serra (JH1–JH6). This happened in L'Hospitalet de Llobregat (Barcelona), a small neighbourhood in which activists practised non-violence, rejected militarism, and demanded democratic freedoms.

By the 1970s, the regime realized that its survival was being threatened by the activities of workers, working-class priests, and students. The authorities claimed that groups were "attempting to set the working-class population against the established order."[43] After years of hibernation, the public realm had been rekindled: "There were whole neighbourhoods into which the police could not enter. Autonomous spaces were proliferating" (IA 108). In addition, the housing situation had surfaced as a serious social concern. Many neighbourhoods were shantytowns, and "once big property owners were identified, whole neighbourhoods demonstrated 24/7 in front of their houses" (JH3, JH6) (IA 27).[44] Badia del Valles (province of Barcelona), a town of brand-new government-subsidized housing, was occupied largely by squatters (JH1, JH3), since "corruption had made it impossible for those in need to access a property" (IA 210).

During these last stages of the dictatorship, teachers marched across the country: "They demanded public education for everyone, creating links and showing alternatives" (JH3, JH6) (IA 203). This radical push for public education flourished in working-class neighbourhoods everywhere. In Barcelona, for example, it took place in neighbourhoods like La Sagrera, San Andrés, and Ciudad Meridiana. In response to the shortage of places for children in public schools, commissions of parents, teachers, and neighbours organized (JH1–JH3) to demand that the Ministry of Education commit itself to building schools, guaranteeing free public education, and allowing schools to be managed by communities (JH4–JH6).[45] A movement grew around the Soller, Pegaso, and Ferrer i Guardia schools, and many buildings were occupied and transformed into assembly-run, self-governed schools. The children, the parents, and the teachers organized these institutions (JH1–JH3).[46]

---

42 To learn more about conscientious objectors in the Spanish state, see: Ajangiz (2004, 2); and Soríano Díaz (2000, 530).

43 García Cotarelo (1987, 15).

44 In 2013 the PAH began to carry out these kinds of actions, which were given the name *escrache*. The term is borrowed from the social protests of 1995 in Argentina.

45 Cuevas (2010, 108).

46 Cuevas (2010, 108).

Among those being 15M, there was little doubt that the Spanish transition to democracy had been a fraud. The demonstrations of May 1968 in France took a little while to spread to Spain. Nevertheless, during Spain's transition period, the same questions were being asked: "If the revolution is not now, when? If it is not here, where?" (IA 206). The transition period clearly held an important place in the collective imaginary, and it was understood that "power lay in the ministry of protest" (IA 162). It was the time of the cooperatives boom in the Basque Country, the time of the Proceso de Burgos (Burgos Process), and the time of the Green March of 1975.[47] "Franco died in bed, but Francoism died on the streets," as one of my interview subjects so eloquently stated, and songs were key in raising the popular spirit that brought down the dictatorship (IA 31).[48]

1980s Non-violence, Associations, and Occupations

In the 1980s, working-class Christians organized and neighbourhood associations boomed (JH1–JH3). Closely tied to the neighbourhood activities surrounding housing, Spain saw the emergence of the okupa movement, which followed in the footsteps of the neighbourhood groups of the 1960s and 1970s, occupying buildings to denounce the country's housing situation (JH1, JH4). The movement grew exponentially, and a new social discourse began to evolve. Its demands for housing were mixed with calls for autonomous social spaces for political expression. The movement joined hands with the environmental and peace movements, embracing strong countercultural currents and anti-capitalist ideas stemming from autonomous movements in Italy (JH1–JH3).[49] It

---

47 The Burgos Process was a trial in which members of ETA (Euskadi Ta Askatasuna; Basque Homeland and Freedom) faced the death penalty. "This was 1970, and my generation was faced with the responsibility, of taking an anti-repression stance and standing up to defend these youths" (IA 170). In the Green March of 1975, the Moroccan government orchestrated a mass march to pressure Spain to hand over to Morocco the disputed Spanish province of Sahara: "During that Colonial dispute a lot of arrests were made in Las Palmas de Gran Canarias. It was an explosive moment for my generation" (IA 74).

48 When discussing the importance of music during the period, the interviewee had in mind Chicho Sanchez Ferlosio, a songwriter whose anonymous songs had become popular anthems during the fight against General Franco's dictatorship. One could argue that some of his songs, like *Gallo rojo, gallo negro* (Red rooster, black rooster) and *La Paloma de la Paz* (Peace Dove), were key in raising the popular spirit that brought down the dictatorship.

49 A. Calle Collado and M. Jiménez, "Transiciones en movimiento: La cultura de protesta en España y el ciclo de movilización global," 2008, prepared for the Informe Foessa (unpublished), 21.

was also greatly inspired by the activities of German social movements: "*okupas* were learning from German citizen initiatives, squatters in Germany, and the early stages of the German green party" (IA 87). Throughout the 1980s, community-run television and radio stations enjoyed a boom (JH1–JH3), mass collectivization of land was under way (the town of Marinaleda spearheaded this process) (JH1, JH4), and the popular struggle against the entry of Spain into the North Atlantic Treaty Organization (NATO) was in full swing as conscientious objectors rejected military conscription (JH4–JH6).

As Spain entered the 1980s, its admission to NATO was viewed an imminent threat. By 1981, large demonstrations were taking place across the country (JH6). These followed calls to action from pacifist organizations such as MPDL (Movimiento por la Paz; Movement for Peace), APD (Asociación por la Paz y el Desarme; Association for Peace and Disarmament); and Mujeres por la Paz (Women for Peace). Collectives from the environmental movement, Christian organizations, the Communist Party, and radical leftist organizations supported these calls (JH3, JH6).[50]

In 1982, the PSOE began to govern Spain, led by Prime Minister Felipe González. His time in power was marked by utter disinterest in revisiting the past. Those years have been referred to by Spanish scholars as "the years of great silence and of no memory."[51] Yet "the social mobilizations of that period inspired many of the practices we see in 15M today" (IA 184). By this point, it was clear to many that politics could not be conducted solely through official and institutional channels. Neighbourhoods were undergoing deep transformations, and the social upheaval that had been silenced during the transition had never really ceased.

After González was elected prime minister, Spain formally joined NATO, even though he had campaigned on an anti-NATO ticket. González ignored the clamour rising from the country's streets. The peace movement continued to gain traction as it struggled to free Spain from NATO and the citizenry from the grip of the country's military: "When we see the exemplary non-violence of those being 15M, we are seeing the influence the MOC [Movimiento de Objeción de Conciencia; Conscientious Objection Movement] has had on the country's *demos*" (IA 46).

According to opinion surveys conducted during this intensely anti-militarist period, 63 per cent of the population rejected a mandatory

50 Calle Collado and Jiménez (2008, 8).
51 Encarnación (2008, 440).

draft.[52] Opposition was so blatant that, encouraged by the Asamblea Andaluza de No Violencia (Andalucian Non-Violence Assembly), thousands of Spaniards demonstrated against military expenditures by deducting them from their taxes.[53] That same year, the CEOP (Coordinadora Estatal de Organizaciones Pacifistas; State-Wide Coordinator of Pacifist Organizations) began coordinating the activities of various peace organizations across the country. In 1985, a conference was held in Barcelona that concluded with an intensified call for a referendum on military conscription and Spain's membership in NATO (JH4–JH6).[54] In 1988, after years of being ignored by the political elite, the Spanish public responded with the largest anti-militarist protests in the country's short post-dictatorial history (JH6).[55]

Today, Spain is still a member of NATO. Nevertheless, by 1996, this non-violent anti-military movement had succeeded in forcing an end to compulsory military service.[56] Equally important, its non-violent methodologies and exemplarity have been passed down to subsequent movements: "The capacity to create local committees and to organize mass protests was exemplary, I can assure you that the climate was very similar to that of 15M" (IA 184).

1990s Societies in Movement

In the early 1990s, social mobilization in Spain began to acquire traits that would be foundational to 15M: "Understanding 15M as a shout of indignation would be ignoring the fact that it is really the result of an accumulation of struggles. At the very least, this accumulation runs from as early as the 1990s" (IA 33). A different kind of political subject was coming into being, one that "allowed every individual a voice and was based on a hyper-sensibility towards power-over politics of any kind" (IA 46). It was using technology to facilitate new forms of global mobilization while at the same time developing new ways of interaction (JH1–JH3). It began to develop multiple ways to co-think and co-create alternative economies, politics, and cultures.[57]

---

52 Calle Collado and Jiménez (2008, 20).

53 People deducted from their tax bills their share of the military budget and then filed their taxes with the deduction and an explanation.

54 Pastor (1991).

55 See Calle Collado and Jiménez (2008, 20).

56 Real Decreto 247/2001, 9 de marzo, *por el que se adelanta la suspensión de la prestación del servicio militar*, http://noticias.juridicas.com/base_datos/Admin/rd247-2001.html.

57 The imaginary of the Zapatistas influenced many being 15M who had participated in various movements of the 1990s. In 1994, when the North American Free Trade

This new political culture was visible in the campaign Desenmascaremos el 92 (Unmasking 92), which aimed to unmask global capitalism at a time when Spain was hosting a series of "world" events (JH6).[58] It could be identified in the Euromarchas (Euromarches) against unemployment and precarious labour conditions across Europe (JH6).[59] It was present in the Movimiento Anti-Maastricht (Anti-Maastricht Movement) that flowed from the protests against Spain's presidency of the EU in 1995 (JH6).[60] It was also present in the more local struggle of the workers of the Bruguera publishing house in Barcelona. To save their jobs, these workers had started a financial services cooperative called COOP57. By 2005 it had evolved into a financing web for social and cooperative organizations across the country (JH1, JH3) (IA 65).[61]

In 1993, a new movement appeared called Plataforma 0.7% (Platform 0.7%). Its main aim was to push the government to adhere to the deal reached with United Nations of committing 0.7 per cent of the country's gross domestic product to supporting development (JH6).[62] In 1994, demonstrations in support of the platform's demands spread throughout the country. From within the network of the international campaign 50 Years Is Enough, citizen-participants in Plataforma 0.7% established encampments in numerous cities across Spain (JH3, JH6). This happened just as Madrid was hosting the World Bank summit.[63] During that event, an alternative summit was organized and symbolic blockades were raised. This alternative summit received support from a broad array of collectives and small political parties. Six years later, on 12 March 2000, coinciding with the country's general election, the

---

Agreement (NAFTA) came into effect, the Zapatista rebellion began. It did not seek to take control of the state through armed struggle; rather, it worked to create autonomous, democratic, self-governing communities that would become allies through a global network of informal treaty federalism. The Zapatistas thus set out to weave together strains of counter-modernities that were by then beginning to enter into deep dialogues of reciprocal elucidation. See Graeber (2009, 11).

58 To view the manifesto and call that was made in the early days of the movement, visit http://www.revistacienciassociales.ucr.ac.cr/manifiesto-de-convocatoriadesenmascaremos-el-92.

59 For more information on the *Euromarchas*, see Navascués (2000)..

60 A. Calle, "Nuevos movimientos globales: sedimentando e impactando," 2003, http://fundacionbetiko.org/wp-content/uploads/2012/11/Nuevos-movimientos-globales1.pdf.

61 For more information, visit http://www.coop57.coop.

62 A. Calle (2003) "Nuevos movimientos globales: sedimentando e impactando," 2003, http://fundacionbetiko.org/wp-content/uploads/2012/11/Nuevos-movimientos-globales1.pdf, 11.

63 Calle Collado and Jiménez (2008), 12).

platform held a public consultation across most of the Spanish state (JH3) to address the possibility of abolishing external debt: "More than one million people across the country voted in favour of abolition, but the event ended in front of congress with police hitting and arresting people indiscriminately for organizing a referendum" (IA 103).[64]

In 1997, Rompamos el Silencio (Breaking Silence) came into being.[65] A citizen-led initiative that practised civil disobedience and non-violent direct action (JH3, JH6), Rompamos el Silencio attempted to influence political, economic, and social decisions. The following year saw the birth of ATTAC (Asociación por una Tasación sobre las Transacciones Financieras Especulativas para la Ayuda a los Ciudadanos; Association for a Tax on Speculative Financial Transactions in Order to Help the Citizenry).[66] It proposed a tax on speculative financial transactions (JH5). By the late 1990s, events and movements of this kind were expanding their efforts to cooperate with more and more Spaniards.

Stemming from initiatives within Rompamos el Silencio, MRG (Movimiento de Resistencia Global; Global Resistance Movement) began meetings in the Church of Entrevías in Vallecas (a working-class neighbourhood of Madrid). The meetings saw the coming together of collectives that included communists, members of autonomous movements, anarchists, and progressive sectors of the Catholic Church (JH3).[67] Around the same time, MJG (Movimiento de Justicia Global; Global Justice Movement) began to present alter-globalization proposals, through practices similar to those of the okupa movement (JH1), such as creating self-governed occupied social centres, engaging in horizontal decision-making, and critiquing the tenets of capitalism (JH1, JH4). Civil disobedience and the search for alternative approaches to debate and public communication characterized their actions.[68]

In Spain at this time, the alter-globalization movement was very strong. Indeed, many participants in 15M had been highly active in the alter-globalization movement. For them, 15M could not be understood without Genoa, Prague, and Seattle. The struggle was the same

64 To learn more, visit the platform's website: http://www.plataforma07.org/historiadel07.html.

65 Morán (2000).

66 To learn more about ATTAC, visit http://www.attac.es/about-2/historia.

67 Iglesias and Jerez (2005, 83).

68 Their actions and platforms included informal referendums about foreign debt in 2000, the Iraq War in 2003, and the European constitution in 2004. It also included the creation of new virtual spaces for information and debate, such as http://www.Nodo50.org and http://www.barcelona.indymedia.org.

in Puerta del Sol as in these localities. The scenarios might be different, but the same struggle was at their core (IAs 123 and 119).[69]

For many, 15M was simply one more episode in the alter-globalization struggle: "the search for a different way of being political, of being in the street, and of communicating" (IA 197). The main difference was that, while the alter-globalization movement demanded rights for those who were far away in the global South, "15M focuses on the miseries generated by the crisis in this country" (IA 108). For many being 15M, these movements that prefigured 15M were not social movements but rather "societies in movement" (IA 111).

Twenty-First-Century Horizontality and Assemblies

The year 2001 saw the emergence of a movement for greater regulation and better treatment for Spain's "illegal immigrants." This movement was characterized by demonstrations, lock-ins, occupations, hunger strikes, and blood donations (JH3, JH6). Having begun in Murcia, it expanded rapidly to other cities – Barcelona, Madrid, Valencia, Almería, Melilla, indeed, most of the country. In Murcia alone, 20,000 migrant workers succeeded in resolving their legal status.[70] Local churches played a strong supporting role in many cities and became occupied spaces with support from the clergy (JH3). In support of immigrants, Spanish citizens joined in the protests with collectives such as Desobedecer la Ley and Asociación Pro Derechos Humanos (JH3, JH6).[71] In Barcelona, African workers camped in Plaça Catalunya, remaining there for days until they were evicted (JH3, JH6).[72] In Madrid, the offices of the ombudsperson were occupied (JH3, JH6). With student support across the country, lock-ins took place at many universities (JH3, JH6).[73] The movement was characterized by horizontal decision-making through assemblies. Most occupations were open to the public in order to promote dialogue between occupiers and neighbours (JH3).[74]

69 The interviewees are referring to Seattle N30, which occurred on 30 November 1999 during the World Trade Organization (WTO) meetings in Seattle; protests in Prague during the International Monetary Fund (IMF) and World Bank summit of September 2000; and the Genoa Group of Eight Summit protests between 18 and 22 July 2001.

70 Laubenthal (2005).

71 Laubenthal (2005, 167).

72 Suárez-Navaz (2007, 191).

73 Suárez-Navaz (2007, 192).

74 Three years later, in 2004, the movement collaborated with movements present at the European Social Forum in Athens and occupied Barcelona's cathedral (Suárez-Navaz 2007, 225).

In 2002, students and professors came out to the streets against a new law regulating universities. Those in the movement claimed that the LOU (Ley Orgánica de Universidades; Organic Law for Universities) was aimed at destroying public education. Chanting slogans such as "Otra universidad es posible" (Another university is possible), they advocated for a different university model (JH3, JH6).[75] The movement was horizontal in its decision-making and focused on mass protests and non-violent civil disobedience: "In the city of Sevilla, we camped for sixty-five days in front of Town Hall" (IA 14).

Also in 2002, the oil tanker *Prestige* sank off the coast of Galicia. The subsequent oil spill became the largest environmental disaster in the history of Spain. In its aftermath, the movement Nunca Máis (Never Again) was born.[76] Thousands of people from across Spain travelled to Galicia to support the clean-up effort while denouncing the government's mishandling of the disaster (JH3, JH6). "The solidarity between people cleaning up those beaches felt the same as the solidarity in the 15M encampment. We all had differences but worked together from our similarities" (IA 200).

The year 2003 saw impassioned protests against the war in Iraq that drew millions of people. No a la Guerra (No to War) organized twenty-six demonstrations across Spain; the six largest drew 1.5 million people each (JH6).[77] During those demonstrations, people "occupied buildings that we called 'liberated spaces against war'" (JH1, JH4) (IA 205).The self-organizing later encountered with*in* 15M was already evident in No a la Guerra: "One could see it when people were printing their own posters and T-shirts from templates found on the Internet" (IA 103).

On 11 March 2004, a terrorist cell inspired by al-Qaeda carried out a set of orchestrated bomb attacks on trains in Madrid. This happened three days before Spain's general elections and was referred to as 11M. When the government tried to link the attack to ETA (Euskadi Ta Askatasuna; Basque Homeland and Freedom), people organized spontaneously to expose the government's lies. Many people were certain the attacks had been in retaliation for Spain having entered the Iraq war. On 13 March, someone sent a text message asking friends to meet at the PP headquarters to demand the truth; that text went viral.[78] Consequently, the "day

75 Iglesias and Jerez (2005, 80).

76 To learn more about Nunca Máis, visit http://plataformanuncamais.wordpress.com.

77 Calle Collado and Jiménez (2008, 3).

78 To learn more about the PP, visit http://www.pp.es.

of reflection" preceding Election Day was broken by millions of people demonstrating against the government in an act of civil disobedience (JH6). This event is referred to in Spain as 13M.[79] Although it came and went (it was really only one night), it left many people thinking: "Who were these people? How had they decided to come together on the street? Where were they coming from? This was the first appearance in the Spanish state of the 'power of collective anonymity'" (IA 194).

In 2005, the EuroMayDay network came together to unite marginalized people fighting for a free, open, and radical Europe (JH3).[80] People "were trying to use Facebook to organize a Europe-wide movement" (IA 183). By 2007, V de Vivienda had come into being.[81] At the height of the country's housing bubble, an anonymous email calling for a demonstration against the housing situation was picked up by thousands of people. Following from this, through self-organization, city squares across Spain filled with people practising a power-with kind of politics (JH3, JH6): "V de Vivienda began with sit-downs at public squares; from there large demonstrations were initiated" (IA 197).

The year 2008 was intense in terms of activities within CSOs (Centros Sociales Okupados; Occupied Social Centres): "Those practices tied to open culture, to being self-managed and to working on the margins of institutional politics, are something that I first saw in CSOs in 2008" (IA 134). That same year, the student movement was active throughout the country in response to the EU's Bologna Process (JH6).[82] Finally, this was also the year when the PAH launched its activities against evictions from mortgaged properties (JH3, JH6).[83]

By the start of 2011, social tensions in Spain were clearly mounting. On 11 February of that year, Estado del Malestar[84] gathered together

---

79 With 13M in 2004, just as with 15M in 2011, the protesters ignored the day of reflection prior to the country's elections. For a good description of 13M, see Flesher Fominaya (2011).

80 For more information on EuroMayDay visit http://www.euromayday.org/about.php.

81 To learn more about V de Vivienda, visit http://www.sindominio.net/v.

82 This constituted a set of ministerial meetings and agreements between European countries regarding the quality of higher education qualifications. For more information on the Bolonia Process, see Fernández and Serrano (2009).

83 To learn more about the PAH, visit http://afectadosporlahipoteca.com.

84 People active in Estado del Malestar described their movement in the following manner: "We are people of all ages and with numerous ideological differences, but we have a common denominator. We are pissed-off and full of indignation against the current political and financial system. We feel betrayed by this system and we believe it needs to be changed." For more information, visit *#15Mpedia at* 'http://wiki.15m.cc/wiki/Estado_del_Malestar.

people in different cities to agitate against the political and financial system (JH6). That movement had emerged out of an event created on Facebook (JH1–JH3). Although it was not a mass movement, it established links between individuals, many of whom would later converge within 15M.

On 15 February, the Sinde Law (an attempt to curb internet piracy) was approved by congress. When the law was first tabled, 200,000 people signed a public call against it in a single day (JH5) (IA 183). Before it was approved, discussion on the internet had centred on ensuring that if the government approved the law, those governing would not be re-elected (JH5). After it was approved, No Les Votes (Do Not Vote for Them) asked people not to vote for those responsible. No Les Votes was "a kind of social movement in which nobody had seen each other's face, which openly asked people not to vote for those considered to be at the heart of the country's problems" (IA 138).

On 20 February 2011, Plataforma de coordinación de grupos pro-movilización ciudadana (Pro-citizen Mobilization Coordinating Platform) was created as a Facebook page (JH1–JH3).[85] Representatives from different collectives joined the group with the objective of organizing a mass protest and developing a manifesto; by 16 March 2011, the group had transformed itself into DRY.[86] A website was activated showing a manifesto, political proposals for the future of Spain, and a call for a mass demonstration on 15 May 2011. On 23 March, a mass student protest took place throughout the country (JH5): "this demonstration was already calling for people to come out as individuals and not as members of unions or parties" (IA 213).

On 7 April of that same year, JSF (Juventud sin Futuro; Youth without a Future) was born in Madrid: "Members of IA [Izquierda Anticapitalista; Anti-Capitalist Left), together with people from autonomous movements and close to Patio Maravillas [Playground of Marvels] created JSF" (IA 169).[87] By then, the youth involved in the movement were chanting this slogan: "Sin casa, sin curro, sin pension, sin miedo [Without a house, without work, without a pension, without fear]" (IA 134). This lack of fear ignited the 15M climate that ensued and that persists to this day, albeit in subtler, less easily perceptible ways.

85 To learn more about the platform, visit http://wiki.15m.cc/wiki/Plataforma_de_coordinaci%C3%B3n_de_grupos_pro-movilizaci%C3%B3n_ciudadana.

86 To learn more about DRY, visit http://www.democraciarealya.es.

87 To learn more about JSF, visit http://juventudsinfuturo.net; to learn more about IA, visit http://www.anticapitalistas.org; to learn more about Patio Maravillas, visit http://patiomaravillas.net.

Conclusion

Diverse voices have contributed to this genealogical map of events and traditions, which helps describe what 15M is today. Through their individual histories, those being 15M have brought to the surface knowledges, ways of being, and events that today are part of a people's history of Spain. Silenced histories, once excavated, help carve new understandings of our present. In that sense, this is not a chapter *of* history, but a chapter *on* the history of the present. As such, it provides important information about the phenomenon that calls itself 15M.

By unearthing this multiplicity of traditions – of historical moments, historical characters, historical songs, historical languages, and historical struggles – we discover the multiverse that nurtures the complex and ever-shifting collective imaginary of 15M. Individuals being 15M establish symbolic connections with disparate times and places through an exercise of historical imagination that conveys an emotional empathy for them. The perspectives on Spanish history presented here cover the multiple pasts underlying individual interviewees' "15M beingness." This is a powerful resource for their political and ethical self-interpretation.

Without implying that these pages have presented a single ongoing tradition, this chapter has shown that the struggles of 2003, the events in the 1980s, the challenges of the 1960s, the victories and losses of the 1930s, and so on, are not just memories. In the narratives of those being 15M, traditions and events actually exist. In fact, in contemporary Spain, there are still active cooperatives, and there is still a cooperative spirit that has survived and has animated generations of engaged citizens.

Horizontal organizations in Spain have one-and-a-half centuries of living history. This history reveals the multiple ways in which civic and civil citizens have, over time, persisted in joining hands. Grasping this reality is important when discussing collective presences like 15M. Doing so shows the resilience of these modes of being and crystallizes the fact that, despite their spontaneity, 15M participants possess and are motivated by the historical living memory of the disparate events presented herein.[88] When we explore the deep roots and routes of 15M, we find that its multifariousness flourishes.

---

88 Speaking of 15M as spontaneous does not fully capture what happened in the squares of 15M. As Raúl Zibechi points out, this is one of the ways that critics of particular actors/actions attempt to discredit civic activity. See Zibechi (2005, 24).

Chapter Three

Constructing Alternative Futures on Shoestring Budgets

In the years since the occupations of 2011, the resilience of the 15M mode of being has been revealed through multiple instances of different *demoi* trying to be the change they seek at the civic level and linking these efforts to good relations with civil citizens (six joining-hands relationships).[1] Yet most critics have failed to grasp the Gandhian premise behind 15M beingness that true democracy and peace can only come about through truly democratic and peaceful *means*.[2] While those being 15M have continued to be the change they seek – to move their society from a stage of low-intensity democracy toward one of non-violent cooperative democracy through non-violent means – numerous voices have suggested that 15M has not been able to present and articulate solutions to multiple problems that have been pointed out.

Most critics of 15M have failed to grasp that when citizens self-organize democratically, exercise self-government together, reason with one another as equals, and commit to non-violent dispute resolution, they are in fact enacting solutions to the problems they are addressing.

1 These civic citizens are in effect attempting to auto-generate a transformative, autotelic being-with ethos. They are enacting together a kind of citizenship whose end or purpose is itself; the way in which they engage with one another and with others (mode of citizenship) is the primary transformation they are seeking.

2 This is something I have come to really appreciate through a careful reading of some of the literature in the broad field of non-violence. Tully's work offers an entry into this field in a manner that highlights the correlation between non-violence and democracy in a helpful manner. See Tully (2012, 2). For a theoretical defence of the Gandhian premise that non-violence and democracy (not violence and non-democracy) are the only means to peace and democracy, see Bondurant (1988); Christensen (2010); Ackerman and DuVall (2001); and Sharp (2005). It is important to mention that during interviewing for this study, those being 15M often referenced Gandhi when speaking about their mode of being.

Taking a non-competitive world view, people being 15M actively cooperate with one another.[3] In this way, they are regenerating a social fabric that has been destroyed by years of rampant neoliberalism. Reasoning and acting together, they generate "citizenization," a virtuous self-sustaining and self-extending process that allows the citizenry to heal their wounds.[4] Those being 15M are also able to enact "civicization," that is, governor–citizen relationships anchored in participation. By enacting civic citizenship, 15M citizens actually lead the way in expanding it, in this way creating a world in which a multitude of worlds are embraced.[5]

None of this can be understood if we view 15M through the lens of conceptual frameworks that have developed alongside the dominant institutional structures it is contesting. Only by approaching 15M as an epistemic community in its own right can we avoid discounting, obscuring, and misapprehending the alternatives 15M is showing us through its ideas and practices. So in this chapter I ask those being 15M what alternatives they are proposing. In the previous chapter, we were able to see "where we have come from"; in this one, I suggest "where things are going from here and at what pace." In this sense, I continue as a facilitator of a dialogue between different 15M voices. I do this by presenting different visions and constructing "stories" pertinent to where these voices think Spain is heading and where they think it should be going. In part as a response to those who criticize the dearth of alternatives proposed by those being 15M, this chapter crystallizes the multiple and intricate ways in which individuals being 15M are thinking through and enacting the reconstruction and reconstitution of Spain.

This chapter offers a selection from the many visions of Spain's future that were shared with me in dialogue with individuals being 15M.[6]

---

3 Mattei (2012, 121).

4 Tully (2019b, 39).

5 Tully (2008a, 281, 298).

6 Hereafter, SD signifies "Stemming from dialogue with interview with anonymous" (for example, SD 206). The word *dialogue*, Bohm reminds us in "On Dialogue," "comes from the Greek word *dialogos*. Logos means "the word," or in our case we would think of the "meaning of the word." And *dia* means 'through.'" Bohm points out that dialogue can happen between more than two people, and he presents dialogue as "stream of meaning flowing among and through us and between us." According to Bohm, this makes "possible a flow of meaning in the whole group, out of which may emerge some new understanding." This understanding of dialogue, which sees it as being "aimed at going into the whole thought process and changing the way the thought process occurs collectively," is really in alignment with the way dialogue is understood and enacted within the 15M climate that I experienced. Bohm (2004, 6–7, 10).

By approaching the country's future in this manner, I am moving from a space in which those being 15M have narrated their histories toward one in which they explain the futures they are co-constructing and the ones they are seeking to avoid. In selecting and translating seemingly shared understandings of these futures, I am acting as a storyteller.[7] That is, I am narrating my own 15M-vision of the challenges and opportunities the people of Spain may soon face and the solutions that may reveal themselves.[8] The imagined futures I present have evolved from a flow of meaning co-generated by all the co-participants in these dialogues of reciprocal elucidation.[9] They reveal that 15M voices have much to say about alternatives to the status quo.[10] But before we start imagining futures with 15M, it is useful to understand the present from which these futures were being enacted and imagined in 2013.

Contesting the Status Quo

Months before I finished my interviewing in November 2013, Joan Subirats, professor of political science at the University of Barcelona, published an article in the newspaper *El País* in which he described Spain as approaching a permanent state of emergency in which demanding a democratic political life would soon be considered an act of insurrection.[11] The accuracy of his description became clear to me as I interviewed

7 Perhaps to some readers the imagined futures presented in this chapter resonate with the call David Graeber makes for a political ontology of the imagination. See Graeber (2009, 516).

8 In this process of storytelling those being 15M are creating a different logic. Holloway's description of moving beyond the now through different ways of talking and different ways of organizing our doing resonates with what I witnessed in numerous 15M spaces. See Holloway (2019, 218).

9 Numerous participants in this dialogue are very public or/and active figures whose efforts have had a profound influence on the country's social, economic, and political climate. This has been especially true since the appearance of 15M. In this sense, some of the future visions they presented in 2013 have already taken root at the time of writing.

10 What I present in this chapter, from my dialogues with 15M individuals, is storytelling, not specific quotes from given interviews. I am presenting the essence of the dialogue. By selecting elements to bring into the discussion for this section, I am trying to capture the tone, the mood, and the essence of what was discussed.

11 J. Subirats, (28/07/2013) "La democracia como revolución," *Elpais.com*, 28 July 2013, https://elpais.com/ccaa/2013/07/27/catalunya/1374938675_852943.html.

people across Spain. While walking around Melilla, I found myself being tailed by what activists described as secret service agents; near the town of Marinaleda, the licence plate of my van was photographed by Guardia Civil officers; as I walked the streets of Barcelona, I saw activists being intimidated by Mossos d'Esquadra (the Catalan regional police). All of this helped me grasp the oppressive environment those being 15M had been enduring since the square occupations of 2011.

While I was interviewing, two major pieces of legislation were working their way through parliament: a reform of the Penal Code, and a modification of the Citizen Security Law. The Penal Code reform, first tabled in congress in September 2013, called for what Amnesty International described as serious and unjustified restrictions on freedom of speech and freedom of assembly. It also rendered migrants more invisible and pointedly ignored international recommendations in the area of terrorism.[12] Legal experts warned that the Penal Code reform was moving Spain in the direction of "Enemy Penal Law."[13]

The proposed new Citizen Security Law was quickly and variously nicknamed the "ley de patada en la boca" (kick-in-the-mouth law); the "ley antiprotesta" (anti-protest law); the "ley mordaza" (clamp law); the "ley anti-15M" (anti-15M law); and the "ley Fernández" (Fernández law, in reference to the Interior Minister, Jorge Fernández Díaz).[14] Under this new law, it would be illegal to offend or insult Spain, its autonomous communities, local entities and their institutions, symbols, and anthems. Offenders could be fined as much as 30,000 euros.[15] In

12 "El proyecto de Código Penal pone en riesgo el derecho a la libertad de expresión y reunión pacífica y se olvida de los crímenes de derecho internacional," *Amnesty.org*, 11 April 2014, https://www.es.amnesty.org/en-que-estamos/noticias/noticia/articulo/el-proyecto-de-codigo-penal-pone-en-riesgo-el-derecho-a-la-libertad-de-expresion-y-reunion-pacif.

13 A penal code that seeks to punish not what one does but on what one might do based on who the government considers they are. See E. Sanz de Bremond and N. Trillo, "Nuevas formas de represión: de la modificación del Código Penal a la modificación de la Ley de Seguridad Ciudadana," *Diagonalperiodico.net*, 25 November 2013, https://www.diagonalperiodico.net/blogs/laconquistadelderecho/nuevas-formas-represion-la-modificacion-del-codigo-penal-la-modificacion.

14 "¿Quién teme al manifestante feroz?," *Eldiario.es*, 27 November 2013, https://www.eldiario.es/piedrasdepapel/teme-manifestante-feroz_6_200939922.html.

15 This would mean, for example, that an insult to a police officer could cost citizens 30,000 euros. These fines would be administrative fines rather than fines set by the courts. Therefore, if a police officer said that a citizen had insulted her or him, the citizen would just receive a fine via mail. See "Guía práctica para manifestantes bajo la nueva Ley de Seguridad Ciudadana," *Eldiario.es*, 30 November 2013, https://www.eldiario.es/politica/respuestas-nuevas-multas_0_201930639.html.

addition, those who demonstrated in front of Parliament without permission, or who recorded a police officer doing her or his job, could be fined up to 600,000 euros.[16]

Nevertheless, despite this hardened climate of repression, contestation and constructive programs continued along multiple routes as people acting in concert insisted on bringing into being this 15M mode of citizenship. Networked forces continued to organize and make decisions collectively through popular assemblies organized in city, town, and village squares (JH3).[17] People continued to halt attempts to evict families from repossessed homes (JH3, JH6). Occupations of abandoned public or repossessed buildings persisted as a means to house homeless families (JH3). Police were continually impeded from arresting "illegal" immigrants in poor neighbourhoods (JH1, JH4). After governments implemented drastic public spending cuts, people continued trying to stop the closing of public hospitals (JH3, JH6). Neighbourhood committees continued their reorganizing with the aim of rebuilding the social fabric that had been destroyed by two decades of neoliberal economics (JH3). Entire neighbourhoods continued to organize to welcome refugees (JH3, JH6). Legal persecution of those deemed responsible for the crisis continued, financed through popular initiatives such as "crowd funding" (JH3, JH6). Boycotts mushroomed and fiscal disobedience intensified (JH1, JH4).[18]

As the government continued rapidly implementing unpopular austerity measures, and despite the fact that many people being 15M

---

16 By December 2013 the Human Rights Commissar for the Council of Europe, Nils Muiznieks, was expressing deep concern regarding the impact of such a law on the fundamental rights of Spanish citizens. Muiznieks was seeking someone to convince him that a 600,000-euro fine for demonstrating in front of a governmental institution without authorization was balanced. See E. Escribano Claramunt, "El Consejo de Europa considera que la 'Ley Fernández' es "desproporcionad,a"' *Elpais.com*, 3 December 2013, https://elpais.com/politica/2013/12/03/actualidad/1386070943_426348.html.

17 As in chapter 2, here I continue to identify in brackets different joining-hands relationships as they appear within these 15M imagined futures. These will be identified as follows: civic citizens joining hands with one another (JH1); civil citizens joining hands with one another (JH 2); civic and civil citizens joining hands (JH 3); civic citizens working with representative governments in numerous ways (JH4); civil citizens working with representative governments in numerous ways (JH5); and civic–civil citizens joining hands with one another in myriad ways in order to influence their governments (JH6).

18 Fiscal disobedience has been carried out in many different ways by those being 15M. A useful document explaining various alternatives for fiscal disobedience is the *Manual De Desobediència Econòmica* (Economic Disobedience Manual), available at https://www.autogestio.cat/tags/insubmissi%C3%B3-fiscal.

continued to face government repression, cooperative examples of non-violent mutual aid continued to be created, ranging from websites, communal libraries, radio and TV channels, and magazines and newspapers to vegetable gardens, schools, hospitals, alternative currencies, and assembly-based political parties (JH1–6). So it is not surprising, given the resilience of their mode of citizenship, that when those contesting and constructing alternatives from within 15M were asked to anticipate future scenarios in Spain, they had a clear understanding on their own intentions, the many obstacles they might encounter, and the multiple ways in which these might be overcome.

A Critique with Alternatives

At the time of my last interview in November 2013, austerity was the single greatest concern for Madrid's elites; for elites in Catalonia, it was independence. Meanwhile, for those being 15M, with*in* and between different *demoi*, debates were beginning to rage over whether it was time for an anonymous, decentralized, horizontal, and radically democratic transformation or, conversely, for the formation of a single political party to capture political institutions and radically reform them from within. All the while, 15M continued its constructive programs.

Those whom I interviewed maintained that 15M had "rescued" dialogue in Spain and thereby had also rescued politics. But they also generally understood that the struggle would have to continue if they were going to acquire the formal, legal right to be truly political (JH4–6) (SD 114). There was clear consensus that the country needed to make a transition of some sort. Most individuals felt that horizontal, consensus-based assemblies together with digital democracy were going to be the cornerstones of that transition. Most also acknowledged that despite the strong support for deeper democratization, there was also strong opposition to it (SD 42). That said, they were well aware that consensus-based assemblies had a long and strong tradition in Spain, and they were adept with modern-day communication technologies that would permit them to initiate permanent constituent processes. Many within 15M viewed the melding of civic traditions and technological advances as key to bringing about an intergenerational societal transformation (JH3, JH6).

Individuals being 15M imagined a day when permanent constituent processes would make it possible for citizens to enact change to governing structures and processes based on the real-time demands and needs of the population (JH6). They envisioned the internet as enabling open, permanent, and continuous assemblies where millions of people would be able to discuss the issues, vote their preferences, and arrive at a consensus without too high a cost. Some even suggested that this process could be implemented at a fraction of the cost of current elections (SD 37). The more technology-oriented within 15M – the "digital natives," as they referred to themselves – saw the internet as prefiguring what a Republic of the 99 per cent could look like. Inspired by squatter traditions, those within 15M understood collectives like the PAH (Plataforma de Afectados por la Hipoteca; Platform of Those Affected by Mortgages) as institutional or instituting in nature.[19] When thinking about the convergence of these two perspectives, many within 15M imagined an integral democracy in which everyone would have a permanent say in decisions that affected them.

The older generations within 15M – those who had been politically active during the dictatorship and the transition to democracy – were convinced that the force of 15M, the force of anonymity, this force without a name, would appear in another tomorrow and would be stronger when it did. Older interviewees seemed to have little doubt that a 15M-like collective presence would surprise the country again (SD 194). Many were getting ready to drive it forward just as they had done with 15M, through their ongoing dedication to love and social justice (JH1–3). Yet there was also a deep awareness that the culture of vanguards still dominated – that is, many being 15M saw their political space as one in which individuals with a political vision proposed and the majority followed (SD 206). They viewed this as an outcome of deeply embedded representative systems that needed to be rooted up. Those being 15M had already experienced how such representative systems were fostering a sense of impotence among most citizens.

Numerous voices within 15M contended that the citizenry was being disempowered by this vertical approach to urgent societal change. So in order to maintain their humanity in the face of their society's multiple crises, those being 15M called for and enacted horizontality as a virtuous response (JH3). Yet there was within 15M circles an awareness that some people were more practised than others at creating collective projects. Many being 15M understood the need for soothing, welcoming spaces where people could learn collectively to act together. From the perspective of those being 15M, as things stood, those who were already working within such experiences were articulating their

19 This interpretation is justified by numerous interviewees, given that since 2011, in Spain, people who are about to lose their home call the PAH first when seeking a solution.

frustrations and fighting their own revolutions to the extent they could, even while those waiting for political leaders to guide them felt ever more powerless (SDD 206).

Without a doubt, many within 15M understood that they were engaged in a many-sided struggle between competing truth-claims. At the same time, they realized that present-day hegemonic discourses had rather bleak prospects. Many within 15M viewed Spain's plight as getting worse every day (SD 205) and contended that it would continue to do so until majorities began to demand and enact alternatives. Indeed, some individuals thought that the country was heading toward collapse and that discussions on risks and alternatives should be broader and more serious. Could we *avoid* collapse? Some people asked themselves that question and were amazed that the word "collapse" had not seriously entered mainstream debate (SD 108). Given the planet's limited resources and ongoing geopolitical conflicts, the world seemed to be locked in a vicious cycle of perpetual war. On an equally menacing note, those being 15M could see that fascism had been emboldened and was expanding around the world. As they pointed out, when security becomes more important than freedom, fascism has taken root (SD 42).

During most of my dialoguing with 15M, people acknowledged that society had made great strides in digital communication. Others, though, cautioned that we were still in the prehistory of "real" communication (SD 162). Even so, there seemed to be a consensus that Spanish society had found itself immersed in folly because citizens were still trapped in their own memories and struggles. A number of interviewees thought that this was the main reason why citizens had been unable to organize (SD 206). Yet for those being 15M, it was clear that attempts at alternative modes of organization were here to stay and would continue to take root. They also had little doubt that nationalist, localist, and libertarian tendencies long present in Spain's political culture would continue to be reflected in the tendency of organized citizens to resolve problems from below rather than from above.[20] As those being 15M continuously emphasized, there was ample popular support for these traditions in Spain. Those within 15M saw them as part of the subconscious political imaginary of numerous *demoi* from which alternative Spains were being understood and enacted (SD 108).

---

20 When speaking of nationalism in this context, those being 15M are referring to regional nationalisms in opposition to the centralized Spanish state.

Where to Go from Here

During interviewing, it became apparent that while they made use of institutions, legal rules, and rights, *demoi* across the country refused to understand these as a prerequisite for citizen action (JH1, JH4). It was unimaginable for interviewees to understand these as constituting a limited space within which citizens could act. In the years since the square occupations, many within 15M had come to view institutions as rooted in interactions and agreements reached by communities of practice (JH1, JH3). That is why many people understood procedures as always open to negotiation – such negotiations always took place "in, with, against, and over" such procedures.

Arising from this, one of the greatest concerns expressed by those being 15M was the possibility of regression in terms of social, political, and economic rights. Long-standing rights were being reorganized without the citizenry having a say, and this was identified as an immediate problem (SD 199). Different voices now proposed urgent issues to be addressed. A majority, for example, agreed that banks must work to benefit the productive economy and that the economy must operate within the limits of the planet. This was understood as necessary for the common good; in this way, the health of the environment would determine social, political, and economic frames (SD 42). Across Spain, 15M voices emphasized how important it was for this idea to enter mainstream understandings (SD 165). In addition to this, within 15M I found a general agreement that people needed to be seen as more important than governments. Moreover, *people* had to include undocumented or excluded people, not only citizens (SD 191). Those being 15M saw an urgent need to decolonize all forms of power (SD 162).

Interviewees spoke of a climate of change that was slow to evolve partly due to fear. Many described a ruthless ideological war that had been waged for decades (centuries, when taking a long-term view) and to which it was difficult to respond. Nevertheless, within 15M there was a clear intent to invite a change of epoch by making changes in language (SD 148). People spoke of welcoming leadership and thought of it as a way out of modes of patriarchal leadership.[21] Many within 15M cautioned that even when it started out as soft or semi-soft, patriarchal leadership inevitably hardened (SD 129). Many interviewees thought that through discussion and consensus, the hegemony of organized

21 Marcela Lagarde points out that leadership is not about imposition but about convincing; such leadership is also action-based. For more on this topic, see Lagarde (2000).

groups could be avoided (JH1) (SD 130). Many also grasped that if alternatives were developed, with great synchronicity and with everyone taking their own responsibility, an engaged citizenry could work without leaders. Nevertheless, this was understood as a slow transformation; much work needed to be done at the grassroots level by learning together and overcoming individual and collective fears (JH3) (SD 125).

In many of the cities I visited and events that I attended, people being 15M attempted to think in terms of the immigrant paradigm (SD 128). This point of discussion was raised throughout Spain, from square to square. It was a position most strongly defended by individuals being 15M who described themselves as feminists. For them, it was important that citizens imagine themselves in the position of the displaced so that they could empathize with their needs. This stemmed from the caring-with ethos that characterized the 15M in which I was immersed in 2013.

Those being 15M attempted to create alternatives that did not reproduce the logic of current hierarchical structures of power. This effort did not always succeed, and many viewed it as one of the traps of our current representative democracies (SDD 102). Those being interviewed noted that they were always being told they could bring about change only by entering existing hierarchical institutions. They disagreed, though they knew perfectly well that reorganizing dominant systems of societal organization would take a long time. They also understood that though the imagined futures they were constructing were primarily horizontal, political parties would still play an important role (JH3, JH6). Within 15M, most embraced the mantra "We go ever so slowly because we are going on forever" (SD 139). Thus, alternatives were being imagined and enacted one ethical step at a time.

It was obvious from within 15M that the dominant social, political, and economic systems were immersed in processes of transition and mutation moving in a different direction. Interviewees described a shift toward totalitarianism that was manifesting itself in the concept of the War on Terror. For those being 15M, the fact that in mainstream political discourse the "other" was being portrayed as a potential terrorist typified the way in which morality had become institutional politics. Understanding this was considered key when thinking about how to reconfigure resistances (SD 169).[22] Despite the challenges posed by this new socio-political scenario, 15M voices insisted there were possibilities

22 In an attempt to overcome the us/them dichotomies so prevalent in politics, people in the squares focused not so much on demands to the "other" but primarily on joining hands with one another. This resonates with descriptions by Marina Sitrin of certain events in Occupy. See Sitrin (2018, 317).

for contesting unjust power relations while constructing alternatives (JH1–6), alternatives regarding the economic crisis, the political crisis, the crisis of democracy, the crisis of autonomous communities, and the crisis of the monarchy (SD 188).

Moving toward Constituent Assemblies

During the 2013 interviews, what was clear, as mentioned in the previous chapters, was that the social contract stemming from the transition to democracy had been broken. At the same time, within 15M there was an overarching sense that the territorial conflicts with Catalonia, the Basque Country, and Galicia were going to make it difficult for a new, elite-led transition to happen quickly. When the encampments began in 2011, it seemed that growing economic inequality would break once and for all the country's present institutions. By 2013, within 15M there was a sense that the national question raised in Catalonia was accelerating that process (JH1–6) (SD 112). In 15M circles, a constituent process was being acknowledged as a real possibility (SD 101), and people within 15M were working tirelessly to facilitate it.

From my interviews, it was clear that within 15M, such a process was understood as a space where the Spanish people would determine whether they wanted to belong to the Europe of capital or to something different (JH3) (SD 133). Through such a process, everything would be decided, and this was where the narrative of the 99 per cent converged with the narrative of independence (JH3). This reading stemmed from the fact that both processes were about seeking the right to decide (SD 121). The key, as interviewees described it, was to apply the right to decide to more than just issues of territory and nationality; such a right must be *transversal* – that is, people must be allowed to decide about *everything* that affected them (SD 120).

Across the country, whether in land occupations in Andalucía, publishing collectives in Asturias, or municipalist projects in Catalonia, people I interviewed understood the importance of recognizing transition initiatives already in motion in Spain. Generally, people being 15M were keen to share with fellow citizens the value of understanding that transition initiatives were everywhere. They described their relevance to democracy, economics, and our ways of life. The transition of 1978 had been an agreement to move from dictatorship to formal democracy. The process now in motion was understood from within 15M as deeper and far more transformative (SD 42). For many within 15M, the key was to stop elites from steering social discontent toward a process that would grant *just enough* reform without changing much at all H6) (SD 49). The

2011 square occupations had taught those being 15M that elites were eager to demonstrate that nothing could be changed by people mobilizing in city streets. Clearly, the elites were trying to bring people back into the world of institutional representation in an orderly manner (SD 162).

According to those being 15M, the sovereignty of the people had been lost, whether speaking of Spain or of the Spanish state's diverse peoples. Thus, organizing with one another and continuing to build alternatives was considered vitally important (JH1–3). Autonomous and interlinked initiatives for coexistence and sustainability needed to expand, multiply, and be protected. Interviewees were adamant that connections needed to be strengthened. Concrete struggles were viewed as the fundamental basis of organization. Nevertheless, those being 15M understood that the sum of all the struggles together gave the whole (SD 69). Not shying away from intensifying their activities, many within 15M felt that at the right junctures, boycotts should be contemplated (JH4–6) (SD 43). Most interviewees suggested that a civil war was unlikely. They emphasized instead the need ask to what degree elites were willing to hollow out democracy. Were they going to hollow it out so much that it would need to be called something else? Would they hollow it out so much that citizens would be forced to refer to it as fascism in order to be intellectually honest? (SD 47). These questions were raised when interviewees thought about future scenarios.

It was very easy to detect in 2013 how 15M had planted a seed of hope. By the time of interviewing, those within it were aware of the nurturing needed within their common spaces to help the seed grow (SD 67). There was a deep awareness that the kinds of changes envisioned would take a generation or two to be interiorized in the collective imaginary and thus become part of collective practices. Transformations in education, in culture, in the generating of new collective spaces would all take time (JH1–6). Those being interviewed could see these happening. Nevertheless, they understood the need for amplification (SD 65). To achieve this, porous common spaces would be necessary in order to generate possibilities for those who came from existing organizations to dialogically co-create new meanings and understandings with those who did not aspire to be members of organizations (SD 65). It was understood that from such spaces of confluence, new understandings of politics and of being political could emerge. New stories about what it might mean to be political could be narrated. Those being 15M sought to prefigure whether and how an institutionality of the commons could be created, and they did so through creative dialogue (JH3) (SD 82).

By 2013, those being 15M were adamant that their collective presence had moved from "agonistic-protests" to "agonistic-proposals"

(SD 125). There was a clear awareness that on the institutional front, new political parties were going to be founded. Yet these would not be like the earlier ones; they would be new projects with different conceptions of the "beingness" of political parties (JH3, JH6). At the same time, those being interviewed understood that old parties were going to reconfigure their discourses. Many interviewees expressed concern that ideas emanating from civic and civil organizations would be co-opted (SD 120). This co-opting of transformative discourses was imagined as going hand-in-hand with the destruction of those spaces within which self-organization and mutual aid were gestating (SD 110). Those being 15M saw that whatever happened, no matter how serious, little was being changed in the institutions; very few people were actually resigning from office after committing serious offences. Such responses by governing institutions were viewed as seeds of hatred being planted among those outside the institutions. There was a concern that this could lead to more violent forms of revolt. According to those interviewed, there was a concern that those who felt isolated and abandoned might one day torch a bank (SD 131). For those being 15M, Spain had become a failed state. Yet the fact that those most mobilized were predominantly children of the regime of 1978 made the search for an exit difficult (SD 13).

In Spain in 2013, there was no extreme fascist force as powerful as the Greek Golden Dawn.[23] Those being 15M felt that this was because the right-wing PP (which had fascist roots) was still governing in the country. Many interviewees felt that whenever this changed, forces already existing in Spain would be positioned to launch a Golden Dawn-like party-movement of the extreme right (SD 120).[24] The interviewees did not downplay this threat, which they understood as extreme, and many pointed to the benefit of rethinking some of the narratives that had placed Spain at the centre and not the periphery of geopolitics. For those being 15M, the country was part of the global South, not the global North. Following from this, many being 15M contended that by acknowledging this reality, the country could learn from those spaces that had been actively organizing as the global South (SD 137). From within 15M, there was clarity on the need for more unity and coordination among those contesting and

23 For more information on Golden Dawn, see Ellinas (2013).

24 Some extreme right-wing parties in Spain include the following: DN (Democracia Nacional, National Democracy), Plataforma per Catalunya (Platform for Catalonia), España 2000 (Spain 2000), and VOX. In April 2019, VOX won twenty-four seats in the Spanish parliament. After the elections were repeated in November 2019, due to a failure in government formation negotiations, VOX won fifty-two seats and became the third-largest party in parliament, overtaking Podemos.

building alternatives in southern European states. 15M responses along these lines envisioned joint strikes, coordinated occupations, and more extended joint repertoires across the south of Europe (JH1–6) (SD 28).

Regarding how to continue contesting within Spain, there was broad consensus on the need to keep mobilizing. Concerns were apparent during the interviews about the possibility that people's disillusionment would drive them back into the resigned silence of their homes (SD 133). Interviewees understood that the more isolated people were, the more frightened they would become (SD 161). Stemming from this, the underlying idea behind all the proposals that those being 15M presented rested on everyone continuing to work on their own political projects while remaining committed to the collective imaginary of 15M. This diversity-binding unity was a virtuous 15M approach to oppressive systems (JH1–3). Those being 15M grasped that established formulas were unable to offer solutions to the multiple crises Spanish citizens were facing. Given this, constituent assemblies seemed a more humane way out of this paradox (SF 108).[25] Interviewees acknowledged that anticipation, together with a deep and honest recovery of memory, would be necessary if this process was going to avoid the fate of the country's 1978 transition from dictatorship to democracy (SD 155).

Non-violence and Violence

In 2013, the global media reported that Spain's poorest had been the most affected among OECD nations by the global financial downturn. While the country's wealthiest 10 per cent saw their incomes fall only by 1 per cent, the income of the poorest 10 per cent had fallen by 14 per cent.[26] According to a report from Spain's National Statistics Institute, more than 1 million people in the country had not had a job since 2010. The report stated that the country's "very long-term unemployment" (more than three years without work) had risen by more than 500 per cent since 2007.[27]

---

25 The term paradox is used here in the sense that David Bohm suggests in "On Dialogue." Our multiple crises are not problems that can be systematically solved, but paradoxes in that they are to be approached through relationality. Paradoxes have no discernible solutions, and new approaches are required. Sustained attention to the paradox is vital. See Bohm (2004, xxiii).

26 S. Burgen, "Spain's poor affected the most among OECD nations in financial downturn," *theguardian.com*, 18 March 2014, https://www.theguardian.com/world/2014/mar/18/spain-poor-affected-most-among-oecd-nations-financial-downturn.

27 "'National disaster': Spain sees 500% rise in 'very long-term unemployment,'" *Rt.com*, 30 May 2014, https://www.rt.com/news/162640-spain-unemployment-rate-increase-report/

Also in 2013, UNICEF reported that 27.2 per cent of infants in Spain were living in poverty. This was attributed to a 65 per cent reduction in public expenditures for basic social services.[28] According to Intermón Oxfam, if austerity measures continued down the same path, by the year 2025, 20 million people (42% of the population) would be poor. The Oxfam report, with an introduction by Nobel Prize–winning economist Joseph Stiglitz, highlighted that by the end of 2012, more than 12 million people (27 per cent of the population) were living in poverty. The report described how every year more than half a million people in Spain crossed the poverty line.[29] The situation of most Spanish citizens was rapidly becoming unsustainable. Yet as those being 15M tried to confront this reality, government institutions were applying their full force to stop them as it pressed on with its austerity program.

As the situation in the country continued to deteriorate, some considered leaving the country altogether (SD 45). There was a deep awareness about where things stood politically, economically, and socially. People understood that repression could be overcome only if there was a large amount of support and if individuals were willing to assume shared responsibilities (SD 189). After a civil war, forty years of dictatorship, and thirty years of a "silent majority," many people had stopped attending demonstrations out of fear of being attacked by police. No longer – 15M had opened up new possibilities. This was something that most interviewees were very proud of – 15M had taught people that they should stand up to this violence, albeit in a non-violent manner (JH4–6) (SD 162).

In the 15M I encountered, there was a clear preference for a new societal pact that embraced from non-violent agonisms rather than violent antagonisms. Nevertheless, many believed that it would be difficult to achieve a non-violent pact if things continued along the current path (SD 13). The spirit inspiring 15M protests and constructive programs was a non-violent one. However, some interviewees pointed out that a lot of what looked like non-violence was actually absolute fear of the state and the force it could wield (SD 184). As a consequence, even while fear was being lost, in many spaces non-violence as a moral position useful for revealing the wrongs of state institutions had slowly given way to an array of possible legitimate actions (SD 134).

---

28 "Malnutrición infantil en España: 'Jamás había visto casos tan desgarradores como este año,'" *Huffingtonpost.es*, 21 September 2013, https://www.huffingtonpost.es/2013/09/21/malnutricion-infantil_n_3959806.html?ncid=edlinkusaolp00000003.

29 M.J. Esteso Pove, "La austeridad ha puesto a España en el mismo camino que Grecia," *Diagonalperiodico.net*, 2 October 2013, https://www.diagonalperiodico.net/global/19997-la-austeridad-ha-puesto-espana-mismo-camino-grecia.html.

In 2011, energy, anger, frustration, and discontent had converged around and with*in* 15M encampments, where they materialized in the form of open, consensus-based popular assemblies. Yet many were aware that such collective energies could turn out to be far less constructive (SD 131). As those being interviewed pointed out, not everyone could put up their hands and shout '¡Estas son nuestras armas!' (These are our weapons!) (SD 139).[30] Those being 15M understood that the struggle waged by those working within networks of mutual aid would need to focus on creating constructive alternatives in order to avoid everything descending into absolute nihilism (JH1–3) (SD 130).[31]

During interviewing, many people expressed concern that 15M had closed the violence–non-violence debate too soon (SD 155). There had been such a broad adoption of non-violence as the only way forward that participants from different traditions felt that their modes of struggle were not being adequately acknowledged, engaged, or explored. Albeit without advocating for violence as the correct approach, different *demoi* within the 15M I engaged with expressed interest in keeping the debate open to ensure that the adoption of non-violence would be adequately critiqued and not blindly adopted. Their main point was that 15M could not be monolithically inclined toward non-violence (SD 60). Some individuals within certain spaces within 15M felt that some traditional forms of struggle, such as barricades, had lost legitimacy with the closing of the violence–non-violence debate, and advocated for their reappearance in a recomposed and rearticulated manner (JH4–6). To help empower the citizenry, violence and non-violence needed to be broadly discussed. Many hoped that through such a dialogue, principled non-violence would be ever more broadly embraced through acts of conviction (SD 162).

Work outside of Official Institutions

At the time of interviewing, collective work toward a paradigm shift was being done within official institutions as well as outside of them. The efforts of those working *within* institutions will be discussed in the following chapter. In this section, I explore the imagined futures of those

30 "Estas son nuestras armas" is a popular slogan shouted during the moments when police are attacking non-violent protesters. It was popularized during the 15M encampments.

31 In this part of the dialogue this discussant used the concept of absolute nihilism. Prior to his passing away I had the pleasure of meeting Jonathan Schell at an informal workshop held at the London School of Economics. In the workshop, he used the same term in a similar sense.

working outside of official institutions. In 2013, their imaginary revealed that there was little interest in creating strong organizational structures. There seemed to be more interest in creating consensus-based structures suitable for collective strategic planning (SD 69).[32] 15M had shown that it was possible to popularize assembly-based organizing. Following from this, at the time of interviewing there was a drive toward extending and generalizing these practices as a way of life (SD 8. Some groups organized citizen-led assemblies that would be held at polling stations during regional and national elections (JH1, JH3) (SD 62). Others worked on extending their assemblies by planning to occupy institutional buildings and bank branches (JH1). This was being done with the idea of being able to hold people's assemblies on a permanent basis, in key areas in different cities across Spain (JH1, JH3) (SD 89).

While I was interviewing, I found ample support for occupying abandoned properties, land, offices, factories, and schools (JH1). There was a push to build parallel networks of alternative economies and self-run, self-managed spaces (JH1) (SD 8). There was a growing network of individuals looking to collectivize factories (JH1, JH3) (SD 36). There were initiatives working toward municipal strikes, figuring out ways to paralyse cities by working from within neighbourhoods (JH1, JH3) (SD 25). Interviewees described networked initiatives that gave legal and emotional support to people who refused to pay protest-related administrative fines. These initiatives were becoming highly efficient (JH1, JH3) (SD 46). Interviewees in the south of Spain spoke of campaigns being planned during which thousands of people would demand food at the doors of chain supermarket (JH1, JH3) (SD 26).

Through interviewing, it became clear that many being 15M understood the dangers for Spain of a run on the bank. Seeking creative ways to pressure banks into changing their practices, some interviewees were working to create citizen-led platforms of savers, who would threaten to withdraw their savings from banks on specific dates unless particular demands were met (JH1–6). Many being 15M believed that if these platforms attracted millions of people, a new form of pressure would be exerted on banks (JH3, JH6) (SD 2). Similarly, different groups were collectively exploring the legal and financial consequences of mortgage holders joining hands and collectively withholding mortgage payments on given months. The idea, as with coordinated bank withdrawals, was that

32 Within 15M squares, consensus is understood as a process whereby citizens can avoid impositions from group members, and which facilitates relating with one another through mutual respect and creativity. For a good discussion on consensus-based politics, see Graeber (2009, 312).

millions of people not paying their mortgages at the same time could force changes in banking practices (JH1–6). (SD 38). Finally, also related to the relationship between citizens and banks, different collectives were exploring ways of building citizen-led civic-shareholder platforms that might creatively pressure banks to "communize" (JH1, JH3–4, JH6) (SD 66).

In the meantime, political, financial, and corporate figures identified by different groups as responsible for the political, economic, and social crisis would continue to be ridiculed in public, including outside their homes (JH6). At the same time, constructive programs were ongoing in the form of self-organized, self-financed pedagogic missions by activists travelling around the country, to cities, towns, and small villages; exchanging practices; co-learning; and co-creating in networks of co-responsibility (JH1–3) (SD 67). Those being 15M intended to continue expanding these kinds of practices without forgetting preparations for worst-case scenarios. Along these lines, certain groups within the 15M that I engaged in 2013 were working on thinking through what citizen-organized strategic plans could look like for self-organizing crisis refugees (JH1–3). As the number of victims of this economic, political, and social crisis continued to grow, mutual aid consolidated as the preferred approach moving forward among those more focused on transforming Spain through working outside of official institutionality (SD 15).

Conclusion

This chapter has been anticipatory. The broad and forward-looking questions interviewees were asked presented a tremendous opportunity to treat the "intersubjective space of dialogue … as a space of storytelling or the exchange of narratives" in its truest sense.[33] This approach constituted a valuable tool that facilitated the anticipation of future events.

A lot of what was said during interviewing was drawn out by me as a dialogue partner asking individuals to dream. I asked them to expunge from their minds conditioned fears about what could and could not be said. I hoped that in this way, they would be able to share with me the "deepest" and "truest" essence of their vigorous contestation and construction of alternatives. During interviewing, the dialogical space quickly became a place from which individuals being 15M shared in detail ideals related to the future, frustrations, fears, expectations, and limits. I wanted to know what they really thought was possible as well as what they anticipated. My aim was to facilitate a view of the dreams that comprise the imaginary of the possible that make 15M what it is.

33 Tully (2016).

I wanted to get from those being 15M a sense of the kinds of thoughts they entertained in their contemplative solitude. In terms of collectives, I wanted to know what was being planned and strategized in the subtlest spaces of 15M knowledges and practices.

By engaging in story-sharing and story-building with individuals deeply engaged in the transformation of Spain, I hoped to narrate a story of where we might be going as understood through dialogue with them. This chapter has captured the tenacity of those being 15M and shown their ability to construct imaginatively and under the guidance of their own temporality. The future-oriented judgments made by those being 15M have revealed how they are able to think through and construct alternative worlds on shoestring budgets even while the full force of the state clamps down on them.[34]

As this chapter has shown, individuals being 15M dream about possible futures, but they do so without dreaming like hopeless optimists. Instead, their optimism is saturated with the hopes of those who are already seeing other Spains taking form. They are already co-constructing and co-creating the futures they project and that they hope will inspire others. Those being 15M are not predicting the future for all of us. They are telling us future stories about the Spains in which they inhabit. These Spains feel different from the Spain of official narratives. In this sense, these alternative visions and futures offer necessary insight if we are to understand the phenomenon that calls itself 15M.

Following from this, the chapter has contributed valuable insights about 15M's long-term thinking and constructing, as well as its deep grasp of the challenges and opportunities faced by Spanish citizens today. Hearing what futures 15M envisions is important because such collective presences are often dismissed for not providing an alternative to the capitalist state and representative democracy. Often, they are portrayed in the media as a critiques without alternatives. Here, individuals being 15M are presenting what they see as the future (or the alternative) they are trying to construct by being the future they want to see. A future in which all current social, political, and economic structures and norms become more inclusive, more horizontal, more non-violent, and, ultimately, more democratic.

34 This clampdown was tied to a clear commitment from the elite-owned media establishment to rapidly silence 15M efforts and achievements.

Chapter Four

Engaging State-Based Representative Government

During the first weeks of the 15M encampments, millions of people across Spain defied electoral laws by congregating in public squares on the day of reflection prior to the municipal elections. Yet they were unable to reach consensus on whether to recommend voting for alternative parties or abstaining from voting all together. From day one of 15M, the unresolved question of how to deal with institutions has been at the centre of the dialogue in public squares, virtual meeting spaces, and assemblies of various collectives, parties, and movements. Since 2011, 15M individuals have been opening up debates and prying into spaces that were traditionally closed to public discussion. This has generated a whole new ecosystem of thought centred around reimagining traditional spaces of political contestation.[1]

15M has behaved as an open-source community one can enter and exit at will, giving one's soul and body to multiple activities (IA 44). 15M has transformed knowledges and recombined politics (IAs 134 and 37). Within 15M, practices have merged, spread, and multiplied, thus giving form to a plethora of alternatives. Some participants think of 15M as a question more than an answer – as a great conversation arising from a collective fear (IA 93). Others have suggested that 15M has diagnosed the problems our societies face (IA 57). Personally, I read 15M as a prefiguring of alternatives to the power-over model of order proposed by nation-states, modern representative governments, populist political

1 I am thinking here of spaces in which the never-ending and necessary contestation found when the carving out or challenging of citizen–governor relations finds expression. As mentioned in the introduction, Antje Wiener defines contestation as "a norm-generative social practice, which – depending on the environment – entails four different modes (arbitration, deliberation, contention and justification)." See Wiener (2014, 1).

parties on the left and the right, and the so-called international community with its multiple formal and informal organizations.[2]

15M invites us to construct modes of governance for our societies that draw inspiration from the horizontality enacted in the Spanish public squares of 2011. Those being 15M have empowered themselves to govern together with their fellow human beings, and in their exemplarity they have revealed that in our present societal transformation there may be no need for a *condottiere* (Gramsci).[3] Instead, 15M citizens enact the fact that with trust, with dialogue, with kindness, and with understanding, we can envision other ways of co-inhabiting this earth and governing ourselves in a more peaceful, loving, compassionate, empathetic, and power-with manner.

Prior to the square occupations of 2011, social movements, trade unions, and small political parties had been saying, "Our lives do not fit into your ballot box." It turned out that the lives of those who congregated in urban 15M encampments did not fit into the old institutionalized contestatory structures (IA 163). Yet by the end of the encampments, those old structures and their ways had begun to enter the squares. People in 15M assemblies watched their discussions being "absorbed, manipulated, and monopolized by elite structures of power" (IA 133). Some participants felt that established organizations were compelling them to dissolve the squares; there seemed to be no space for the kind of horizontal politics they were enacting (IA 105). Also, 15M individuals who had amassed sociopolitical capital through influential Twitter and Facebook accounts began to drift away from the idea of horizontal participation. Distancing themselves from their civic colleagues in the squares, they began to promote a reformed representative politics (IA 113).

During the last days of the encampments, 15M came under constant pressure. Some pushed it to radicalize, others to define itself, many wanted 15M to propose a state-based representative alternative, and most wanted it to do things faster. At the time, numerous commentators suggested that 15M had failed to adopt a clear position regarding

2 The distinction I have been making throughout this text between "power-over" and "power-with" differs from the one proposed by John Holloway between "power-over" and "power-to." Holloway is pointing to the difference between power *from* authority (power over someone else) and the power *to do* something (the capacity for action). Here I am contrasting power-over relations with power-with ones (working together as equals in a horizontal manner). For a better understanding of Holloway's point, Holloway (2019).

3 Drawing from Niccolò Machiavelli, Gramsci describes the *condottiere* as the person "who represents plastically and 'anthropomorphically' the symbol of the 'collective will.'" See Gramsci (2005, 125).

the regional elections. This, they argued, had led to 15M broadening its transformative social imaginary while the institutional arena remained unchanged (IA 168). Nevertheless, for those being 15M, this inability to reach consensus on how to approach elections amounted to a healthy disagreement that fitted perfectly within the agonistic civicness they were practising. For 15M, steps toward representation needed to be made in such a way as to ensure that the power-over politics of state-based representative government did not threaten the power-with spaces that had been created collectively (IA 12).

Civic–Civil Agonisms

Many within 15M understand representation as a modality of government whereby citizens govern over their governors through dialogical and horizontal accountability mechanisms and practices.[4] This interpretation of representation reveals how the practices of 15M citizens are different in kind from those we conventionally associate with political participation in a system of representative governance. As I have suggested throughout the previous chapters, 15M is a dialogical space in which, and through which, civic and civil citizens are (among many other things) communally constructing new understandings of how to engage with official institutions. How should these institutions be treated if the aim is to have "real democracy now"? How important should their role be? When should they be engaged, and why? Individuals being 15M ask these the kinds of questions as they explore and construct institutional alternatives.

Such questions have certainly brought to the surface complex agonisms that have crystallized the fissures between civic and civil approaches to representation. Yet within 15M, members of these overlapping traditions are working through these fissures in a dialogical manner. Notwithstanding, two important agonisms are worth highlighting. The first arises in regard to how the two traditions understand the way in which representation should be generated and should

4 When thinking of accountability, I am thinking of a kind of dialogical and horizontal accountability that is beyond legal or social accountability. Following my dialogues of reciprocal elucidation *within* 15M, it became clear to me that individuals being 15M when thinking of accountability are thinking of an ability to revoke collectively granted powers at any time; and to be able to discuss issues deemed important at any given moment with those having been granted temporary representative powers. This kind of accountability gets lost when a power-with relationship becomes a power-over arrangement.

operate. The second relates to how each tradition understands the role of official representative institutions.

Civic citizens within 15M feel that representation should always be generated and should always operate in a horizontal manner. In this sense, in its most radical articulation, civic approaches within 15M cannot envision any power structure that is not horizontal in nature (power-with). In other words, 15M civic approaches construct power structures in which decisions are always made via assemblies, and these assemblies always try to advance through consensus. Even if someone is chosen to be a representative for a particular issue, that role can always be revoked through horizontal decision-making mechanisms. This is 15M's civic understanding of accountability. Thus, within 15M one can readily observe civic citizens encouraging the constant rotation of visible figures. One also notices how, although seeking to engage with the representative question, civic citizens within 15M seek to change the way in which representation is approached. They do this through exemplary engagement with existing representative institutions: they seek to enact the changes they want to see with*in* the institutions with which they are engaging.

Civil citizens within 15M have a different understanding of representation. They are keen to incorporate themselves into representation mechanisms that offer spaces for collective discussion and decision-making. Nevertheless, they seem to take for granted that representation is central to the attainment and exercise of political power. So it is often the case that within 15M, civil citizens demand visible leaders and promote them into positions of power. Civil citizens being 15M hope that in this way, their leaders will steer a successful course through traditional institutions of representation. They feel that they will then be able to institute the transformations they deem necessary for the majority of Spain's population.

Following from this, for *civil* citizens the institutional form of modern representative citizenship reveals the central means by which citizens and governors relate. If power relations are to be altered, citizens' attempts to transform society must be channelled through official institutions of representation. In contrast to this view, *civic* citizens are aware of the central role these institutions are currently playing, but they also suggest that this centrality should end. For them, institutions are part of a multitude of interlinked and/or parallel governor/citizen relationships with different histories and meanings.[5] Civic transformation,

5 Tully (2014b, 223–4).

therefore, often implies going beyond the limits established by state-based representative government.

These civil/civic tensions surfaced early on in the squares as citizens attempted to join hands and address the question of institutional engagement. Working together has never been a simple task. Yet their relations have always been agonistic, not antagonistic; instead of confronting one another, they engage in a continuous game of mutual provocation. Civic and civil citizens within 15M see each other not as enemies who must be destroyed but rather as potential partners with whom they must coexist and cooperate to collectively improve their situation. This is revealed by the six joining-hands relationships presented in the previous chapters. Because of these and other agonisms, they strive to build relationships of trust. On the one hand, civil citizens with leadership aspirations within 15M have "mistrusted" the capacity or/and good judgment of those they are seeking to represent. Conversely, civic citizens have tended to "mistrust" the goodwill and/or vertical strategy of those seeking to be representatives.[6] This agonistic mistrust between civic and civil citizens has been visible in Spanish politics since the beginning of the 15M encampments. It has shaped post-encampment social movements and new municipal governments across the country, and it is reflected in the 2014 rise of the party-movement Podemos and its relationship to 15M.

"Commoning" Representation

From January 2012 to August 2014, 9,629 demonstrations took place in Madrid alone.[7] The situation in Spain resembled an endless march. Mutual aid outside of official institutions kept society in movement and millions of people afloat as the country's elites continued to implement austerity measures. Yet those within 15M were still faced with the challenge of figuring out how to approach institutions of representation through the practice of mutual aid. That is, given that mutual aid

6 According to Tully, whereas "distrust" implies lack of trust, "mistrust" stems from misjudging, misunderstanding, misinterpreting, or misrepresenting. We may question the trustworthiness of our partner even while acknowledging that it may be the case that we misunderstand them. In fact, we may even hope this is so. Furthermore, even if we haven't misunderstood, with mistrust there is always an open invitation and an encouragement for the partner to change his or her attitude and behaviour. See Tully (2019a, 43).

7 "Descienden un 38 por ciento las manifestaciones en Madrid," *Abc.es*, 11 August 2014, http://www.abc.es/madrid/20140810/abci-descenso-manifestaciones-madrid-201408091647.html.

is implicitly "power-with," how could mutual aid organizations "engage-with" an electoral system that explicitly presented "power-over" institutions? How could mutual aid be genuinely represented in official institutions? And ultimately, how could mutual aid flourish in its engagement with*in* state-based representative government? In the initial occupations of 2011, 15M was unable to recommend whether to vote for alternative parties or abstain from voting altogether. By 2012, a decision had been reached to recommend voting, and 15M worked collectively to develop its program.

In the 2012 regional elections, Galician social movements began their "communing" of state-based representative governments.[8] Only one year after the 15M occupations began, civil and civic citizens in this autonomous region joined hands and obtained an unexpectedly positive electoral result in the elections to the Galician parliament. They did this through AGE (Alternativa Galega de Esquerda; Galician Leftist Alternative).[9] Three months after that party was founded, aided by its 15M discourse, it garnered 200,000 votes (IA 129). In Galicia, those advocating for a representative option had learned that in post-encampment Spain, to engage representative government effectively one needed to understand the phenomenon of 15M.

This experience served as an example to many of how to utilize the space opened up by 15M to reclaim governmental institutions from elites. After this, in 2012 and 2013, through a broad-based multilogue among *demoi* across Spain, those being 15M engaged in discussions of how groups could join hands.[10] There was broad agreement that the identities of pre-15M parties, trade unions, and collectives need to horizontalize. There was also a sense that joining hands needed to happen around a set of issues that could be assembled into a platform (IA 166).

---

8 I am using the idea of "communing" in alignment with David Bollier to describe the way in which social movements in Galicia joined hands to generate a web of mutual support for negotiating, communicating, and experimenting with institutional engagement. Working toward an integrated system to manage shared resources, these citizens did not shy away from state-based institutions. Instead, they understood them as one of the sites of struggle that needed to be engaged in the management of the commons. D. Bollier, "Commoning as a Transformative Social Paradigm," *Next System Project*, 2016, https://thenextsystem.org/commoning-as-a-transromative-social-paradigm.

9 AGE is an anti-capitalist and Galician sovereigntist coalition created for the Galician parliamentary elections of 2012. In the elections, it became the third political force in Galicia, with nine representatives and 14 per cent of the votes.

10 The CUP (Candidatura d'Unitat Popular, Popular Unity Candidature) obtained a very positive result in the Catalan elections one month later. It was viewed as an experiment from which to learn and with which to dialogue.

While the space generated by those being 15M remained open, the collective imaginary of what was possible now began to transmute. The common processes and other '"common senses" of 15M began to lose popularity while somewhat older discourses and "common senses" began to reclaim the ground they had lost since the public square occupations (IA 131).[11]

By December 2013, a debate had developed within Spain's diverse leftist community about the model of state to be defended. Three main themes marked the conversation: first, how to fight for a republic; second, how to approach territorial organization; and third, how to think about the right to self-determination.[12] In support of this discussion, Espai en blanc (Blank Space), a Catalan critical theory collective, offered the text *Un esfuerzo más* (One More Effort). In it, the group sketched the way toward preserving "the opening of a new world that is already in this world." Taking this path would require ensuring that the processes begun by 15M were not locked into the "one-dimensional political code of the electoral system and its electoral processes."[13] Their message was clear: enter representative institutions to address all these issues, but do not make these institutions central to political practice.

As the year came to a close, there were clear indications that new political options were emerging, many of which had arisen within 15M collective spaces. Ahora tu decides (Now You Decide) polled people asking whether a candidate from the social movements should run in the European elections of May 2014. On the basis of this poll, a decision was made to present a "citizen-candidate."[14] Confluencia (Confluence) was formed with the objective of bringing together collectives opting to engage the institutional question. Alternativas desde abajo (Alternatives from Below), launched by IA (Izquierda Anti-capitalista; Anti-Capitalist Left), suggested that social movements work with*in* official institutions. It

---

11 Discourse as a common process is one of the elements inspiring this book's approach. This common process of 15M is part of the common sense I am trying to learn with.

12 D. Rey, "Proceso constituyente, República y Estado Federal," 4 December 2013, *Luchadeclases.org*, http://www.luchadeclases.org/inicio/118-izquierda-unida/1671-proceso-constituyente-republica-y-estado-federal.html.

13 "Un esfuerzo más," *Espaienblanc.net*, 3 September 2013, http://www.espaienblanc.net/UN-ESFUERZO-MAS-UN-ESFORC-MES.html.

14 "La plataforma 'Ahora tu decides', ligada al 15M, avanza en la creación de una 'candidatura ciudadana' para las europeas," *Lainformacion.com*, 3 October 2013, http://noticias.lainformacion.com/politica/elecciones-europeas/la-plataforma-ahora-tu-decides-ligada-al-15m-avanza-en-la-creacion-de-una-candidatura-ciudadana-para-las-europeas_h6jBOUL7Ff41YvMVa7cbA3.

called for open electoral initiatives that would be transparent and confluent in nature.[15] Parallel to this, the Consejo de la Juventud (Youth Council) had put out a call for "steps towards a *frente amplio* [broad front]."[16] And the Partido X (X Party) presented itself as a group of "normal and anonymous citizens" with a program based on four pillars: transparency; binding referendums; executive and legislative citizen power; and a permanent right to a real vote.[17] All this criss-crossing and overlapping activity made 2013 an exemplary year of multiple *demoi* experimenting with "communing" approaches to representative government.

The Rise of Party-Movement Podemos

January 2014 began on a different note with the appearance of a new political formation called Podemos (We Can). In one day – aided by his popularity as a talk show guest on mainstream television and as the host of his own political show – political scientist Pablo Iglesias collected 50,000 signatures to lead a "popular and open candidacy" that would run in the European elections. Podemos presented a manifesto titled "Making a Move: Transforming Indignation into Political Change."[18] The party went on to win five seats in the European parliament in the elections of May 2014. Then, in the October 2014 municipal elections, although it did not stand directly, it supported local grassroots political formations that won numerous town halls as well as seats in regional governments.[19]

Following the launch of Podemos, Madrilonia, the critical reflection collective, reminded its readers that political structuring and sedimentation are slow processes. The collective was aware of the strong bonds such processes are able to consolidate; it also acknowledged that those processes often generated high doses of impatience. It was in terms of

15 "Los indignados del 15-M se preparan para dar el paso a la política," *Nuevatribuna.es*, 8 September 2013, http://www.nuevatribuna.es/articulo/espana/indignados-15-m-preparan-dar-paso-politica/20130908130404096210.html.

16 A. Barba, "Convocatoria: Nuevos pasos hacia el Frente Amplio," *Cronicapopular.es*, 9 September 2013, http://www.cronicapopular.es/2013/09/convocatoria-nuevos-pasos-hacia-el-frente-amplio.

17 J. Vargas, "Partido X: 'Empecemos por lo más fácil: echémosles de ahí,'" *Publico.es*, 8 October 2013, http://www.publico.es/actualidad/partido-x-empecemos-mas-facil.html.

18 J. Vargas, "Pablo Iglesias consigue en un día los 50.000 apoyos que pedía para seguir adelante con Podemos," *Publico.es*. 18 January 2014, https://www.publico.es/politica/pablo-iglesias-dia-50-000.html.

19 The most notable of these being Guanyem Barcelona, the citizen platform led by anti-evictions activist Ada Colau in Barcelona, and Ahora Madrid, led by ex-judge Manuela Carmela, which won town halls in Barcelona and Madrid respectively.

this impatience that the collective understood the launch of Podemos: "In some sense, the game we were all thinking together has begun with a knight jumping the line of pawns."[20]

Many members of the political party IA were rattled by the appearance of Podemos. Some of IA's executive committee met with Iglesias, along with members of the Fundación CEPS (CEPS Foundation) and Juventud sin Futuro (Youth without Future). Soon after, the IA attendees decided to launch a new party without discussing it with the other members of IA. In fact, the name Podemos came from the title of an internal IA document. That document had presented points to be worked on before the European elections, and though it belonged to another party whose membership had not agreed to share it, Podemos decided to use it as their initial manifesto.[21] An article in the political magazine *Rebelion.org* described how for months everyone had been tirelessly working on a Trojan horse to enter institutions. Yet one morning everyone had woken up to an unexpected reality: those they had been working with shoulder-to-shoulder had announced on television a different political project with the same aim. The article, by Miguel Álvarez, finished on a cautionary note: "With mistrust we board this train, but we remain close to the emergency exit because change is so urgent that wasted time generates incalculable damage."[22]

By the end of January 2014, Madrilonia had asked the following question: Is a political party or organization possible that is born out of a process from below, is grown by those below, and that once on top remains true to being from below?[23] Podemos responded to that question by creating its own party circles. In these political spaces, citizens who enjoyed absolute autonomy and who did not need to renounce membership in other political parties could gather together to carve the way forward for this new political project.[24] The announcement

---

20 "Algunas preguntas sobre Podemos e Izquierda Anticapitalista," *Madrilonia.org*, 21 January 2013, http://www.madrilonia.org/2014/01/algunas-preguntas-sobre-podemos-e-izquierda-anticapitalista.

21 "Un boletín interno de Izquierda Anticapitalista preparó el terreno a Podemos," *Eldiario.es*, 21 January 2014, http://www.eldiario.es/politica/nacimiento-Podemos-candidatura-Pablo-Iglesias_0_220478302.html.

22 M. Álvarez, "Mover ficha desde abajo. Apoyos críticos al Podemos de Pablo Iglesias," *Rebelion.org*, 25 January 2014, http://www.rebelion.org/noticia.php?id=179934. In this quote, we already see people involved talking about mistrust.

23 F. Guerrero, "¿Sois los nuestros? ¿Estáis seguros?," *Madrilonia.org*, 29 January 2014, http://www.madrilonia.org/2014/01/sois-los-nuestros-estais-seguros.

24 "Círculos Podemos," *Publico.es*, 24 January 2014, http://blogs.publico.es/pablo-iglesias/760/circulos-podemos.

was followed by a statement from Iglesias in which he emphasized that 15M could not be represented and that Podemos was represented by 15M.[25] Nevertheless, by this time, many who cautiously embraced the new party were beginning to worry about its rapid "verticalization." Commentators suggested deflating the media attention received by its leaders while calling for a broadening of the search for alternatives.[26]

As the months passed, Madrilonia reflected again on the project. This time, the collective asked itself: "Podemos, ¿pero que exactamente?" (We can, but what exactly?). While confirming their support for the initiative, the collective suggested that Podemos was not ready to take advantage of the opportunities opened up by 15M in this terminal crisis of the regime of 1978.[27] At the same time, Movimiento por la Democracia (Movement for Democracy) published an open letter about Spain's general elections of 2015. The letter stated that MS's objective was to transform the elections into "a great citizens constituent assembly that could lead to a new democratic pact."[28] This letter was followed by a second one in which the movement defined the only legitimate form of democracy as "that which grows out of citizens deliberating; organization between equals; and the direct control of institutions."[29]

In April 2014, public philosopher Amador Fernández-Savater offered his thoughts on the political move toward institutional representation. He emphasized that a new type of political party could be only one more point in the sociopolitical constellation crystallized through 15M.[30] This reflection was followed by the suggestion from Arturo Puente in his blog *Síntesis ni Análisis* (Neither Thesis nor Analysis) that we remove our 15M lenses. Doing so, he continued, would help us

---

25 P. Machuca "Entrevista a Pablo Iglesias: 'No es izquierda o derecha, es dictadura o democracia,'" *Huffingtonpost.es*, 16 February 2014, http://www.huffingtonpost.es/2014/02/16/pablo-iglesias-entrevista-podemos_n_4787408.html.

26 J. Vargas, "'En Europa no hay democracia, hay fascismo electoral' Entrevista a Antoni Aguiló," *Publico.es*, 15 March 2014, http://www.publico.es/politica/europa-no-hay-democracia-hay.html.

27 M. Rodriguez et al., "Podemos, pero qué exactamente," *Madrilonia.org*, 12 March 2014, http://www.madrilonia.org/2014/03/podemos-pero-que-exactamente.

28 "El Movimiento por la Democracia presenta su hoja de ruta para un proceso constituyente," *Eldiario.es*, 12 March 2014, http://www.eldiario.es/politica/Movimiento-Democracia-presenta-proceso-constituyente_0_237977208.html.

29 "La Carta por Madrid: A por las municipals," *Movimientodemocracia.net*, 31 March 2014, http://movimientodemocracia.net/2014/03/31/la-carta-por-madrid-a-por-las-municipales.

30 A. Fernández-Savater "Notas para una política no estadocéntrica," *Eldiario.es*, 11 April 2014, http://www.eldiario.es/interferencias/Notas-politica-estadocentrica_6_248535164.html.

better understand how the inauguration of this electoral phase opened up by Podemos adhered to a different set of rules. We would now seek results, not ways of doing, and meeting objectives would become far more important than constructing alternatives.[31]

While this debate continued, the European elections of May 2014 underscored the decay of Spain's political regime in Spain. On the one hand, there was almost 55 per cent abstention and Spain's "bipartisan democracy," in which two parties (PP and PSOE) had long alternated governance, had lost three of every five voters. On the other, the newly formed parties Partido X and Podemos had garnered 100,000 and 1.25 million votes respectively as well as five parliamentary seats.[32] After the elections, Madrilonia published an article addressing those who were critical of Podemos. It invited them to exert pressure from the outside so that social movement elements could enter the organization; alternatively, it could participate directly in this newly created institutional tool: "The point is to 'movementalize' Podemos. We need to push against the unavoidable consolidation of the party structure."[33] By this time, Podemos had become a national phenomenon. Yet the party's founders were facing strong internal criticism for their non-democratic practices.[34] Podemos co-founder Juan Carlos Monedero responded to this criticism by suggesting that such discourse would lead the party down the road of 15M: "radically democratic, but radically inoperative."[35]

Monedero's language and tone were indicative of what Podemos was rapidly becoming. After visiting the square in front of the Reina Sofia (Queen Sofia) Museum in Madrid – where Podemos was celebrating its victory – José Miguel Fernández-Layos described the transmutation. For him, the space shared family resemblances with 15M. It felt like being in a 15M-type space, but some things were very different: "15M had not only had unexpected mutations, but seemed to have also mated with creatures of a different kind."[36] For Fernández-Layos, some of the

---

31 "Podemos y el repliegue del 15M," *Sintesisnianalisis.com*, 27 May 2014, http://sintesisnianalisis.com/2014/05/27/podemos-y-el-repliegue-del-15m.

32 "Lo que las Europeas abren," *Madrilonia.org*, 28 May 2014, http://www.madrilonia.org/2014/05/lo-que-las-europeas-abren.

33 "Lo que las Europeas abren."

34 J. José Precedo, "Las bases de Podemos se enfrentan a sus fundadores para exigir democracia interna," *Elpais.com*, 9 June 2014, http://politica.elpais.com/politica/2014/06/09/actualidad/1402295920_514605.html.

35 J. José Precedo, "Las bases de Podemos."

36 J.M. Fernández-Layos, "Todos los 15M que sus ojos no ven," *Diagonalperiodico.net*, 3 June 2014, https://www.diagonalperiodico.net/global/23113-15m-sus-ojos-no-ven.html.

ways of Podemos seemed very new and others a little older. John Holloway added that while the party might meet some of the aspirations of social movements, it was destined to participate in the aggressive practices of capital once it governed.[37]

A few months after this sombre analysis, according to CIS (Centro de Investigaciones Sociológicas; Centre for Sociological Research), Podemos had become the third political party in Spain and might win 15.3 per cent of the vote in the next general election).[38] The newspaper *Público.es* suggested that at this juncture, Spanish and European oligarchies could either denaturalize and domesticate Podemos or impede its rise through coalition governments.[39] The online newspaper *ElDiario.es* joined the conversation with an article by Javier Gallego, who acknowledged that the new party was generating the same excitement as the PSOE (Partido Socialista Obrero Español; Socialist Workers Party of Spain) had generated in 1982. Yet, as had happened with the PSOE, he thought that Podemos was being forgiven for its numerous mistakes: "its lack of definition; its contradictions; its slips and silences." Remembering the deep frustration generated by 1982, he hoped that Podemos would navigate the process without arrogance so as to avoid a collapse from which mobilized citizens might take thirty years to recover.[40]

While warnings against arrogant practices by Podemos executives continued, and demands for more internal democracy within the party continued to mount, Iglesias offered the way forward for Podemos. Its aim, he said, was to end the political system of the regime of 1978 and to open the way for a constituent process. In his statement, he sent a message to those within 15M who were critical of the new party: "We have not created Podemos so that some people can feel good engaged in discussion, we have created Podemos to change the country and we will have to adapt the organization to that goal."[41] University of

---

37 A. Fernández-Savater, "John Holloway: 'Podemos o Syriza pueden mejorar las cosas, pero el desafío es salir del capitalism,'" *Eldiario.es*, 30 July 2014, http://www.eldiario.es/interferencias/John_Holloway_Podemos_Syriza_capitalismo_6_287031315.html.

38 "Podemos es ya la tercera fuerza y el PP aumenta suventaja con el PSOE, según el CIS," *Publico.es*, 4 August 2014, http://www.publico.es/politica/ya-tercera-fuerza-y-pp.html.

39 "Podemos es ya la tercera fuerza."

40 J. Gallego, "Todos los caminos llevan a Podemos," *Eldiario.es*, 7 September 2014, http://www.eldiario.es/zonacritica/caminos-llevan-Podemos_6_299980007.html.

41 O. Osuna, "El cambio político es posible en España y Podemos será determinante," *Nuevatribuna.es*, 14 September 2014, http://www.nuevatribuna.es/articulo/espana/cambio-politico-espana-posible-y-podemos-sera-determinante/20140914120019107102.html.

Córdoba professor Ángel Calle Collado responded to Iglesias, suggesting that "citizenry-parties" like Podemos needed to be marketplaces for both debate and sociopolitical action if they were going to be relevant: "Without these traits it is difficult to think of Podemos as being an emerging and interdependent part of the cycle of protest anchored in the radicalization of democracy."[42]

By November 2014, Víctor Alonso Rocafort, professor of political theory at the University of Alicante, was describing Podemos as a vertical political party that was concentrating power in the figure of the General Secretary. The party seemed to have drifted away from its declared intentions. According to Rocafort, Iglesias would become General Secretary, determine the list of sixty-two people for the citizen council, and select the people tasked with running the party's "Guarantees Committee." Rocafort's article signed off with the following message: "To any person choosing to be an adviser to princes – currently the only *parrhesia* possible in Podemos – I would ask that they do not ask for a just monarch, and [e]specially not for a *politólogo rey* [political scientist king]."[43] Writing for the politics blog *Politikon.es*, Pablo Simón followed up these comments, noting that it was clear that political scientists with a deep experience in assemblies and political parties were directing Podemos. This, he claimed, was allowing them to configure the rules of the party so as to control it from the top down.[44]

Nevertheless, despite Podemos's growing pains, 2014 ended with the party rapidly positioning itself as Spain's left, social-democratic option poised to combat neoliberal austerity. Considering its short history, its success was impressive. The polls showed that Podemos might actually attract the most votes in the general election of 2015. The CIS predicted that Podemos might obtain 27.7 per cent of the vote.[45] Metroscopia enthroned Iglesias as the most respected politician in the country.[46] Furthermore, while

---

42 A. Calle Collado, "De los Partidos-Ciudadanía a los Círculos Sociales: Podemos en la encrucijada," *Tercerainformacion.es*, 15 September 2014, http://www.tercerainformacion.es/spip.php?article73971.

43 V. Alonso Rocafort, "La Carta VII y la fundación de Podemos," *Eldiario.es*, 8 November 2014, http://www.eldiario.es/zonacritica/Carta-VII-fundacion-Podemos_6_322377765.html.

44 P. Simón, "La vieja elección de Podemos," *Politikon.es*, 24 November 2014, http://politikon.es/2014/11/24/la-vieja-eleccion-de-podemos.

45 T. Bolaño and F. Moreno, "El CIS anuncia un terremoto: Podemos, primera fuerza en intención directa de voto," *Cronicaglobal.com*, 29 October 2014, http://www.cronicaglobal.com/es/notices/2014/10/el-cis-anuncia-un-terremoto-podemos-primera-fuerza-en-intencion-directa-de-voto-12559.php.

46 "La 'semana negra' de la corrupción tiene un ganador: Podemos," *Elconfidencial.com*, 2 November 2014, http://www.elconfidencial.com/espana/2014-11-02/la-semana-negra-de-la-corrupcion-tiene-un-ganador-podemos_433856.

in Spain the party continued to attract criticism, on the international front it continued to gain support for its project. By the end of 2014, intellectuals like Wendy Brown, Judith Butler, Noam Chomsky, Costas Douzinas, Eduardo Galeano, Michael Hardt, Naomi Klein, David McNally, Chantal Mouffe, Antonio Negri, Slavoj Žižek, and Jacques Rancière had signed a document in support of the initiative.[47] For Monedero, it was clear that Podemos would sooner or later govern the country. Regarding how the party would be organized to achieve this, he presented a clear position: "You have two, or three solutions: trusting always and fully in assemblies; trusting in a vanguard; or searching for mechanisms that work between both spaces. The latter is what we are trying to do."[48] This outline of Podemos's intentions was received cautiously by many within 15M as a set of promising messages, though the party executive's execution was open to question.

Gramscian Imaginary[49]

With the rise of Podemos in 2014, various currents within the European intellectual left suggested that the creative project necessary for confronting the question of representation had arrived. For example, Boaventura de Sousa Santos described Podemos as "the biggest political innovation in Europe since the end of the Cold War."[50] For him, the new party was the culmination of a creative process initiated in the global South, which had arrived to Spain and was now channelling the outrage that 15M had generated in public squares. According to de Sousa Santos, in the internal life of Podemos, one could find the genetic code of the "complementarity between participatory and representative democracy that ought to guide the workings of the political system."[51]

---

47 See online the list of international supporters at http://apoyointernacionalapodemos.wordpress.com.

48 P. Batalla Cueto, "Es evidente que vamos a gobernar este país," *Asturias24.es*, 7 July 2014, http://www.asturias24.es/secciones/politica/noticias/es-evidente-que-vamos-a-gobernar-este-pais/1404666352.

49 When speaking of a Gramscian imaginary, I am thinking about what Mustapha Kamal Pasha describes as neo-Gramscians holding on to an implicit notion of an imaginary outside of capitalism from which they formulate their strategies of counter-hegemony. See Pasha (2013).

50 B. de Sousa Santos, "The Podemos Wave," *Telesurtv.net*, 6 December 2014, http://www.telesurtv.net/english/opinion/The-Podemos-Wave-20141206-0025.html.

51 de Sousa Santos, "The Podemos Wave." It is important to mention that in the *Eucanet.org* webinar, "The Crises of Democracy: Boaventura de Sousa Santos and James Tully," 15 March 2019, de Sousa Santos had radically changed his position and was very sceptical regarding Podemos. https://www.youtube.com/watch?v=-i9aFUsTipk.

Without a doubt, by 2014 Podemos had become the most successful alternative in Spain regarding the question of how to enter state-based institutions of representation. Nevertheless, its operations generated unexpected disillusionment in terms of how party-movement executives were executing their plans. Podemos was also disappointing people in the way it related with existing networks of mutual aid. For these reasons, criticisms of what Podemos was and what it could achieve remained active. Yet the perceived need for a left populist party to "become a state" meant that many public intellectuals of the European left supported Podemos without much public critique. Instead of joining hands with those from 15M who sought to encourage an open societal dialogue about how best to enter institutions, many chose to close ranks around the party executive.

To understand where this sense of urgency and the ensuing strategy came from, Chantal Mouffe's recent work is useful. According to Mouffe, since the economic crisis of 2008, the neoliberal hegemonic formation has been challenged from both the right and left. She argues that this is a new conjuncture, one she calls the "populist moment," in which the type of politics required to recover, deepen, and extend democracy is left populism.[52] Only such an option, she suggests, can stop the expansion of right-wing parties. She anticipates that left populism will be able to do this by developing a "properly political answer" that federates "all the democratic struggles against post-democracy."[53] The objective of such a project is "the creation of a new hegemony that will permit the radicalization of democracy."[54]

Mouffe emphasizes that to radicalize democracy, we first need to recover it. We can learn from Margaret Thatcher's populist tactics and apply progressive values to them. In this manner, Mouffe writes, we can "bring about a transformation of the existing hegemonic order without destroying liberal-democratic institutions."[55] In Spain, for Mouffe (as for de Sousa Santos), the answer to this challenge has materialized with the birth of Podemos. Attributing the party's meteoric rise to the young academics and intellectuals who took advantage of the space opened

52 Mouffe (2018, 16).

53 For Mouffe, post-democracy refers to a moment in which due to neoliberal hegemony, liberal democracy has lost its constitutive agonistic tension (between liberal and democratic principles). Mouffe differentiates her use of the concept from that of Colin Crouch and Jacques Rancière. She believes that in order to challenge post-democracy, democratic demands can come together into a collective will that allows for the construction of a "we," a "people" that confronts oligarchy as its common adversary. Mouffe (2018, 24, 36, 39).

54 Mouffe (2018, 40).

55 Mouffe (2018, 55).

up by 15M, she suggests that the creation of a new hegemony requires intervening on multiple fronts. Nevertheless, she quickly verticalizes these fronts by subsuming 15M under Podemos as an instrument of mobilization for the party to win electoral power. This she does by suggesting that movements that are not articulated through institutional channels are only the beginning of the process required to transform relations of power.[56] For Mouffe, movements like 15M are an expression not of the crisis of representative democracy but rather of its current, post-democratic incarnation.[57] She understands that movements like 15M have raised important issues and have helped transform political consciousness. But for her, the important political work begins when the representative option is addressed.[58] Thus, for her, we must understand the paramount importance of political parties in this process.

What is important is that Podemos developed within the 15M climate and has branded itself as a possible option for bringing a 15M spirit to Spain's representative government. The attempts at confluence arising within 15M are what made it possible for Podemos to force its way into the institutional arena. Nevertheless, the state-centric research framework used by Mouffe (and others defending the rise of Podemos) has a tendency to reconstruct movements like 15M in ways that conceal the lived experience of 15M.[59] From within its Gramscian imaginary, 15M's infrastructure of power-with organizations appears to drop out of the picture. When viewed in these terms, 15M resembles a "discussion

---

56 This is how Mouffe frames it: "Movements have helped to raise important issues and this can hopefully motivate people to call for an alternative, but this is only the beginning, to effectively transform power relations the new consciousness that arises out of those protests requires institutional channels." See Mouffe, "How to Interpret the Recent Protest Movements?: An Agonistic Approach, at the 6th Subversive Festival," *The Utopia of Democracy*, 6 May 2013, https://www.youtube.com/watch?v=4sWK2KRhBjo

57 See Mouffe (2005).

58 Mouffe thinks that significant results have only been achieved when these movements "have been followed by structured political movements, ready to engage with political institutions" Mouffe (2018, 33).

59 When speaking of state-centric research frameworks I see two types of state-centrism: The *first*, like the one that frames this book, takes state borders as spatial borders worth taking into consideration because of the reality of an existing politics of the nation-state. The *second* gives central importance in politics to state institutions. In the first reading, the state is considered when thinking about politics because of the abuse of power by people holding on to the power of the state. In the second reading, politics is defended as a way of fighting for state power. Through this second reading collective presences such as 15M are seen as proto-political. It is in this second sense that state-centrism is critiqued throughout this book.

group" – a sort of proto–civil citizenry. Interpreting 15M's horizontal political practices as being all talk and no action, state-centric analysts misunderstand how those being 15M are actually practising politics.

According to Mouffe, 15M's refusal to engage political institutions has limited its impact and sapped its energy.[60] Mouffe sees horizontalist currents within 15M as "withdrawing from" institutions instead of "engaging with" them. Viewing 15M through her theoretical lens, she fails to see how it *is* in fact "engaging with" in the way that she describes this type of politics – but is doing so in a much broader sense.[61] 15M "engages with" institutions by addressing the question of how best to enter state-based representative government. Yet those being 15M also engage with one another and with all other living beings in a multiplicity of equally important political spaces. Institutional representation is only one more plane for those being 15M. As Fernández-Savater suggests: "There is no privileged space setting rhythms, positions, or the meaning of the action to the rest … What exists is a plurality of tempos, spaces and subjects, all precious and necessary."[62] In this regard, I find it helpful to think of their mode of citizenship as one that aspires to a civic integral engagement. Within 15M, the question is not *whether* to engage or withdraw, but about *why* to engage, *how* to engage, *whom* to engage, and *when* to engage.[63]

---

60 See Mouffe (2018, 33). It is important to emphasize that according to Mouffe, in 15M there are people expressing total rejection to representation who yearn for a direct democracy (withdrawal from). Yet, she points out, this position is by no means the typical one held by those being 15M. See Mouffe, "How to Interpret the Recent Protest Movements."

61 In her defence of agonistic confrontation as a necessary condition of vibrant democracies, Mouffe counterpoises two different ways of envisioning radical politics. On the one hand, she speaks of a strategy of "withdrawal from" and on the other she speaks of "engagement with." She describes "withdrawal from" as a position that understands being political as not engaging with official institutions. Existing institutions cannot be changed; therefore, assemblies of peoples must organize and "try democracy in presence, in act." See "'A vibrant democracy needs agonistic confrontation' – An interview with Chantal Mouffe," CITSEE Research Project, 22 June 2013, http://www.citsee.eu/interview/vibrant-democracy-needs-agonistic-confrontation-interview-chantal-mouffe.

62 A. Fernández-Savater, "Notas para una política no estadocéntrica," *Eldiario.es*, 11 April 2014, http://www.eldiario.es/interferencias/Notas-politica-estadocentrica_6_248535164.html

63 It is important to point out that the majority of "withdrawal from" networks of autonomous people, which are widespread throughout Spain, and which are coming from long traditions within these territories, *did* not and *do* not identify as being 15M. Instead, they sympathize and collaborate with (engage with) civic and civil citizens working from within the 15M climate. It must be noted that these autonomous networks do not feel as if they are "withdrawing from"; instead they see themselves as "engaging with" different spaces of the political.

Mouffe's concepts of "withdrawal from" and "engagement with" presuppose a state-centric framework/orientation. These are what limit understandings of what 15M is and how it relates to Podemos. Such descriptions presuppose that representative politics is primary and thus to not engage in such politics is to "withdraw from" this primary site. Conversely, "engaging with" implies that we are addressing the primary site of politics. Yet this interpretation generates a blind spot when we think about possible alternative strategies. It channels all energies toward entering the power-over infrastructure of the state, but only because it fails to see or hear 15M's infrastructural alternatives. So removing the centrality of representative institutions is key if we are to recover the infrastructure of 15M's power-with organizations.

Through 15M's civic world of power-with and mutual aid, we can see how, when they engage-with the government, the police and courts, or Podemos, they are engaging-from or from-within a whole infrastructure of mutual aid organizations. This infrastructure is broad, connected, historical and intergenerational. It presents opposition to the power-over infrastructure of the Spanish state, and it is different in kind from the organization presented by the state. Thus, disclosing the field of 15M through reciprocal elucidation crystallizes 15M as a political phenomenon in its own right that is overlooked by state-centric framings. 15M is neither a discussion group nor an instrument in the service of Podemos. By orienting oneself to the practices of 15M, one can see another world of political engagement that in Spain goes back at least one-and-a-half centuries. As the first three chapters have shown, this mode of being political is experiencing a renaissance in Spain.

Once we are able to orient ourselves to the practices of 15M in this manner, we are also able to see beyond 15M and examine Podemos. This allows for a different interpretation of the party as potentially giving rise to a relationship of subordination (power-over) rather than a democratic relationship of equality (power-with). This is because theoretical frames that present 15M as instrumental to Podemos foster an unequal and authoritarian Podemos–15M relationship (*condottiere*). Most pro-Podemos voices have tended to make this move, and in most cases their analyses have been grounded, one way or another, in the work of Gramsci. Since 2014, their imaginary has gained a foothold in broad segments of the Spanish and European left. Within Podemos, this imaginary was already hegemonic by the end of 2014.

The problem I see is that, as Podemos continues in its struggle toward "becoming state," agonistic mistrust between civil and civic citizens in Spain has amplified since the party's launch. This is cause for concern, for the mistrust risks becoming antagonistic distrust and such a turn of events could have negative consequences for civic and civil citizens in Spain. It could jeopardize ongoing attempts to join hands around institutional engagement. We already know that, in regard to state-based representative government, civil and civic relationality has historically – and from the inception of this particular spiral of mutual aid that Podemos executives are aiming to steer – started from a position of agonistic mistrust. So it is in the interest of Spanish citizens that this mistrust becomes trust, instead of distrust.[64]

Following from this, it is likely a healthy option to only cautiously accept Podemos's empty signifiers.[65] Perhaps we can entertain the idea that Ernesto Laclau is correct when he suggests that "once we have a series of unsatisfied demands, these must crystallize symbolically around a leader."[66] Yet it is important to acknowledge that civic citizens tend to think in terms of "exemplars" that lead by example rather than Machiavellian "leaders." This 15M view of leadership can be contrasted to Mouffe's Machiavelli–Gramsci–Prince–hegemony model. For Mouffe, the leader articulates a program that unites all the diverse movements under a big tent program in which every group finds some of its concerns addressed. This is hegemony in her technical sense: everyone finds something worth supporting in the program the leader develops, so they support her/him for these different reasons, and thus "coercion" or "domination" is not needed. Mouffe sees this in both Gramsci and Thatcher. In the Anglo-World it is referred to as a *modus vivendi* coalition or model.

A 15M program is different.[67] The program of those being 15M is one that they themselves articulate together, and when they reach the point that they can all endorse it sufficiently for it to be a platform, they then

---

64 As Tully suggests, "trust is the aspect of these social relationships that renders them 'sociable' (*socialitas*) rather than unsociable or anti-social" (2019a, 6).

65 Learning with Ernesto Laclau, I see empty signifiers in the ambiguity of the positions expressed by party executives as part of their left-populist option. Laclau (1996, 36).

66 E. Laclau, "El populismo en América Latina está creando nuevas formas de legitimidad política." Conference in Quito, Ecuador, 2012. Notes by Fernando Arrellano Ortiz, http://www.cronicon.net/paginas/edicanter/Ediciones72/NOTA01.htm.

67 The way in which leadership is understood is an important means to distinguish civic and civil modes of citizenship.

select a leader to fight for it in elections for representative institutions. Of course, the potential leader can play a role in these discussions, but merely as one member among others. The leader is understood as bound to the platform as it has been collectively articulated and as it continues to be rearticulated *en passant*. If the leader breaks the trust they have put in her/him in working within the platform, then 15M citizens can withdraw their support. At that point, they can turn away from institutional politics or find a new leader to start again. Clearly, then, a platform is actually a binding agreement between the two parties – 15M and the representative party.[68] And, of course, the creation of the platform by 15M is itself direct democracy prior to and underpinning and legitimating representative democracy.[69]

War of Position

Mouffe finds the equivalent to what she is referring to when speaking of "engagement with" in Gramsci's concept of a "war of position."[70] When there cannot be a total revolution, energies are channelled toward transforming existing institutions.[71] For Gramsci, this is the pinnacle of the struggle, for the war of position "once won, is decisive definitively."[72] The unprecedented need to generate hegemony among disparate subjects forces the defenders of that hegemony to practise a more interventionist form of government; and the state and financial elites need to focus on avoiding internal disintegration. To exploit the

68 Rodrigo Nunes emphasizes that the party-form, in order to be, useful must emerge from existing networks. See Nunes (2014, 12).

69 Mouffe's Machiavelli–Gramsci–Prince–hegemony model sees the program drafted from above, whereas for 15M the path is not set – it is neither permanent nor continuous. Instead, as with the Zapatistas, there is a flow that adapts and grows through the path of dialogue. For useful insights on Zapatista practices see Zibechi (2005, 25).

70 Gramsci, in his prison notebooks, when speaking of a war of position, first refers to it in terms of military warfare and then moves the concept into the realm of politics. According to Gramsci, in military warfare a war of position takes place in the following manner: "[It] is not, constituted simply by the actual trenches, but by the whole organizational and industrial system of the territory which lies to the rear of the army in the field. It is imposed notably by the … armed strength which can be concentrated at a particular spot, as well as by the abundance of supplies which make possible the swift replacement of material lost after an enemy breakthrough or a retreat." Gramsci (2005, 234).

71 "A vibrant democracy needs agonistic confrontation," http://www.citsee.eu/interview/vibrant-democracy-needs-agonistic-confrontation-interview-chantal-mouffe.

72 Gramsci (2005, 239).

situation and fight effectively, those seeking to challenge the state need to act strategically and with "lightning speed."[73]

In 2014 the Podemos civil citizens who proposed themselves as representatives in the state-based institutional arena presented their analysis of the situation at hand: post-15M Spain was facing an unavoidable war of position. Many 15M civic and civil citizens opted cautiously to join hands with them. Nevertheless, they engaged with Podemos as a confluence of power-with organizations that embodied a completely different view of relations between means and ends. That is, means and ends from within 15M were understood as requiring a constitutive or prefigurative relationship of "being the change." In this sense, insofar as for 15M citizens it was a war of position of some kind with the state, the two parties organized differently and engaged differently (non-violently rather than repressively). This was the field of struggle as understood by those being 15M. It was from within this space that they joined hands with the civil citizens who were spearheading Podemos. In walking this path, 15M citizens aligned themselves with theorists of non-violence, who had long presented contestation in this manner.[74]

Conclusion

In 2014, Spain seemed to be at a critical historical juncture. State-centric public intellectuals and engaged civil citizens were arguing that the path out of the status quo was through a confluence of forces channelled, under leadership, toward attaining institutional control. They seemed to assume that actors needed to seize "power-over" and exercise it within a kind of "crisis time" framework. 15M spoke of a different temporality, one of "amassing in slow tempos."[75] By this means, 15M had already amassed knowledges, practices, bonds, and victories, and many felt that all of these together would lead toward tipping points.

In *Cesar Chavez and the Common Sense of Nonviolence*, Antonio Orosco criticizes the idea of "crisis time."[76] Seeing it even in the work of Martin Luther King Jr, he argues that it blocks the "long time" that is necessary

73 Gramsci (2005, 129–30).

74 For examples on this non-violent tradition, see Gregg (2018); Huxley (1941); Gandhi (2008); and Merton (2003). The ideas of these thinkers will be introduced in the following chapter.

75 "Algunas preguntas sobre Podemos e Izquierda Anticapitalista," *Madrilonia.org*, 21 January 2013, http://www.madrilonia.org/2014/01/algunas-preguntas-sobre-podemos-e-izquierdaanticapitalista.

76 Orosco (2008).

for real transformation. That theme has run through this chapter, and in this sense, it has helped vindicate the power of the "ever so slowly" time of 15M: "'We go ever so slowly because we are going on forever' means that we refuse to close the openings that people are presenting with their struggles."[77]

Slow steps allow for healthy multilogues among citizens whose practices and ideas share family resemblances. Virtuous joining-hands relationships are facilitated when people understand their similarities and dissimilarities. These relationships are greatly needed in Spain as its citizenry addresses multiple crises. The situation seems to be calling for a space of/for transformative political action imbued with an "ethics or ethos of trust."[78]

As things stand, there is a genuine risk that Podemos will hijack the processes that have been picking up pace with 15M. It is also possible that Iglesias is hoping to become Spain's charismatic *condottiere*. Taking note of this, it is important to acknowledge that a careful reading of Gramsci warns against precisely this kind of unequal and authoritarian relationship that state-centric theories uncritically enable. In fact, Gramsci suggests that even if a project like Podemos comes out victorious, it will not create another world but simply duplicate the present.[79] It is true that the concept of a "war of position" fails to grasp the magnitude of civic alternatives presented by those being 15M. Yet despite being a state-centric theorist, Gramsci is clearly aware of the limits of this power-over approach to politics.

In agonistic tension with this approach, the dialogical power-with public philosophy I practise has helped capture how 15M shifts the state from the centre of politics. Broadening the space of the political, 15M dissolves assumptions regarding the primacy of representative institutions and leaders on the one hand and the powerlessness of power-with direct democrats on the other. State-centric theories are blind to the myriad ways in which citizens are being political in

---

77 "Un esfuerzo más," *Espaienblanc.net*, 3 September 2013, http://www.espaienblanc.net/UNESFUERZO-MAS-UN-ESFORC-MES.html.

78 According to Tully this ethics or ethos of trust guides the ways in which members of a relationship exercise judgments of trust and mistrust. See Tully (2019a, 1).

79 This is how Gramsci describes what the figure of the *condottiere* is capable of achieving: "[A]n improvised action of such a kind, by its very nature, cannot have a long-term and organic character. It will in almost all cases be appropriate to restoration and reorganization, but not to the founding of new States or new national and social structures ... It will be defensive rather than capable of original creation." Gramsci (2005, 129–30).

Spain. Nevertheless, once dialogue opens up to include the practices and knowledges of engaged civic citizens, representation crystallizes as simply one space among a multiplicity of political spaces. By eliminating this theoretical blind spot, reciprocal elucidation contributes to enriching understandings of both 15M and Podemos.

Throughout this chapter, I have engaged the literature about the rise of Podemos that has been developed by party members, by individuals being 15M, and by academic commentators. I have also addressed various bodies of literature on horizontality, populism, the rise of verticality, and the co-optation of power relations into relationships of subordination (power-over) rather than democratic relationships of equality (power-with). Through this engagement, the mistrustful confluences that have been developing between civil and civic citizens around the issue of official institutional representation have been presented. In addition, numerous ways in which 15M "engages with" instead of "withdrawing from" institutions have been sketched.

As a final note, and following from this, I want to think along with *For a Left Populism* and Mouffe's conception of "withdrawal from." Mouffe writes that she developed this concept as a means to describe the kind of politics defended by Michael Hardt and Antonio Negri – basically, a strategy of exodus with an end goal of a "non-representative democracy."[80] She acknowledges that in *Assembly* these two authors have significantly changed their position in that they have accepted the need to take power – albeit in a different manner. Yet for Mouffe, what this means remains unclear.

Inserting myself into this discussion, I suggest that 15M's six joining-hands relationships, with their criss-crossing and overlapping nature, point to the fact that the struggle today is not about taking power one way or another. From within 15M, the struggle appears to revolve around how to transform power-over structures of domination into power-with communities of practice. In this great transformation, 15M understands state-based representative government as a more engaged, symbiotic, and interdependent partner. 15M is attempting to break the vicious cycle in which Spanish society is immersed and turn it into a virtuous one.

Those who orient themselves from within 15M come to reject Mouffe's understanding of the political as antagonism. 15M's agonistic

80 The politics of refusal has a long history in Western political thought. One can see it, for example, in the works of Étienne de La Boétie, Henry David Thoreau, Herman Melville, and contemporary anarchists like David Graeber.

understanding of democracy resonates more with Bonnie Honig's and James Tully's understandings of agonistic politics – a politics that for Honig is always potentially "a politics among would-be friends" and that for Tully involves "always listening to the other side."[81] From within this mode of politics, 15M rejects the binary "engaging with" / "withdrawing from." Instead, it embraces a politics of the middle ground, of joining hands, as an attempt to overcome us/them conceptions of community.[82]

Along these lines, those being 15M are not presenting themselves as a perfect "we" over and against the corrupt "them."[83] Those being 15M understand their own dependence on many of the violent institutions of the modern Spanish state and the capitalist market in which they participate. Joining hands is their way of "being the change" within a complex situation they are trying to change. As they act non-violently in a power-with manner and invite comrades, bystanders, and opponents to transform their reality together, they experiment with this "joining hands" ethos. This is not to say that 15M cannot withdraw from joining-hands relationships whenever the parties involved attempt to gain hegemony over the relationship. Whenever this happens, 15M refuses consent, withdraws its hand, and continues its work with those who reciprocate.

Ultimately, those being 15M seem to concur with Kropotkin-inspired anarchists on demo-kratos mutual aid and an-arche-ism (no *arche*) and joining hands, but not on Kropotkin's violent revolution. When one spends time with*in* 15M, what surfaces is a mode of being that bears a family resemblance to Gandhi's idea of combining *swaraj* (self-government of communities) and *satyagraha* (joining hands).[84]

81 For a great analysis of the distinction between Chantal Mouffe's understanding of agonistic politics and that of Bonnie Honig and James Tully, see Michelsen (2019, 1–21).

82 This feature of 15M's mode of being resonates with what Barbara Deming argues for in Deming (1971).

83 This way of understanding joining hands and the us/them binary has crystallized in ongoing conversation with James Tully.

84 Gandhi (2008).

Conclusion

Democracy Here and Now

As the economic crisis began in Spain, representatives of the state did not hesitate to sideline democratic and legal institutions in order to exercise authoritarian power.[1] This power-over state repression was aimed at protecting the status quo and the austerity programs being imposed on the population. This behaviour is in alignment with the general thesis that European and Western representative governments tied to unregulated capitalist development – and the war machine necessary to protect them – will "hollow out" democratic institutions whenever they feel the need to do so.

There is nothing exceptional about the Spanish case in this regard. Yet the country does present a uniquely challenging scenario given its Civil War (1936–9), its forty years of dictatorship, and its relatively short span of democracy. The separation between dictatorship and democracy in this southern European state has never been fully attained; the line has always been blurred. Following from this, the ghost of dictatorship has been ever-present in my dialogues with*in* 15M. During our discussions, there has always been a prevalent understanding that what is being hollowed out is an already extremely hollow democracy.

Across Europe, and across Western states more broadly, representative democracy is being degraded. Yet in each country this hollowing

1 Individuals being 15M understand that the state has many aspects and facets (it is a complex structure and set of processes). They highlight that financial power and police power are able to control some aspects or facets of the state and repress 15M (and dissent in general) and impose austerity programs in many repressive ways. Yet they presuppose that the state is complex, multi-aspectival, and changeable. Within 15M it is clearly understood that states are multifaceted and can be many different things at the same time. It is also understood that the state is not simply the government; it is also a much more complex and contradictory bundle of public law, institutions, and social functions.

out, along with any contestation to it, is following particular local processes that have adapted to local conditions. Following from this, although activities in different countries share family resemblances, ultimately citizens around the globe are grappling with unique local realities. This is generating multiple modalities of contestation, which, although criss-crossing and overlapping, carry with them local customs and traditions.

In Spain, 15M came together in opposition to this hollowing out through the occupation of public squares in a clearly articulated and exemplary non-violent and horizontal manner.[2] As citizens organized and acted together, democratic challenges arose for elites attempting to maintain the status quo. They implemented social control strategies and tactics and shifted the boundaries of what constitutes legitimate freedom of speech. Notwithstanding, citizens continued to contest in multiple ways and the constitutional order revealed the strain it was under. Spain's institutional shift toward "illiberal democracy" exposed the country's path "out of and into authoritarian law."[3] Counterpoising non-violence to state violence, 15M showcased the country's regression toward authoritarian rule.[4]

In such circumstances, it seems that all that citizens can do is make noise and observe what the elites are saying and doing. This is a clear indication of the country's democratic deficit.[5] Yet as this book has documented, amid such a profound hollowing out, an event took place across Spain starting on 15 May 2011 that interrupted routine processes

2 Around the globe, horizontality has been historically important for a multitude of movements. For valuable examples, See Sitrin (2006); Nunes (2005a); and Juris (2008).

3 Juska and Woolfson (2012, 405). The authors are speaking of Lithuania; however, I think the concept applies also to Spain. Many studies today are critically examining the enduring nature of a form of democracy that various people are attempting to label. Examples of current labels include delegative democracy, incomplete democracy, guarded democracy, low-intensity democracy, violent pluralism, disjunctive democracy, and competitive authoritarianism.

4 For those interested in useful commentary from academics and activists regarding 15M's square occupations, as well as its responses to neoliberalism, austerity, and the far-right, see works by the following: José Luis Sampedro, Manuel Castells, Eduardo Galeano, Rubén Martínez, Jean Plantureux, Eduard Punset, Mohsen Makhmalbaf, Joaquín Valdivielso, Daniel Innerarity, Jacques Rancière, Yayo Herrero, Ernesto Laclau, Carlos Fernández Liria, Lucía Lois, Félix Rodrigo Mora, Prado Esteban, Frank G. Rubio, José Luis Martí, Félix Ovejero, Eva Botella, Eduardo Romanos, Luis Alegre, Santiago Alba Rico, Germán Cano, José Luis Villacañas, Rita Maestre, Pablo Soto, Belén Gopegui, Sandra Ezquerra, Stéphane Grueso and Jon Aguirre.

5 For a good description of what is broadly referred to as democratic deficit, see J. Tully, "Global Disorder and Two Responses," Global Order and Disorder in the History of Political Thought, Senate House, University of London, 3–4 June 2013.

and routine procedures.[6] All of a sudden, inspired by participatory practices in public squares, citizens across the country realized that they could do more than simply complain. Since then, the social world as it was thought of in the collective imaginary of Spanish citizens has transmuted and new worlds are being imagined and constructed.[7]

Since 15M appeared in the public squares, collective presences of numerous kinds have stepped forward from anonymity in collective cries of indignation, silent communion, and power-with collective co-creation. Throughout this book I have attempted to describe and understand this reality, which continues to manifest itself in Spain's current affairs.

Deep Hanging Out

The participatory spirit of this research trip began with the preparation of the 1980s VW Westfalia van with which I travelled throughout Spain. Turquoise blue with white roofing and known in 15M spaces as La Pasionaria, the van was collaboratively prepared for the road by a group of Spanish activists.[8] When I took to the road in 2013, this collaborative spirit travelled with me. I was inspired by the clear failure of institutional reform in Spain but also by the joy of seeing fellow citizens in the square occupations of 2011, coming together in a manner that appeared to break through the institutional framework of representative democracy. At the time, the democratic spaces they co-generated seemed different from and more egalitarian that the democracy I was used to. Nevertheless, I began my trip with only a vague sense of what I thought individuals being 15M were doing. I understood that to better grasp what 15M was, I needed to broaden my understanding of their field of practice. I was captivated by their exemplary commitment to dialogue, their horizontal practices, and their non-violent modes

6 As Hannah Arendt reminds us, by definition events "interrupt routine processes and routine procedures." See Arendt (1972, 117).

7 For John Holloway, the "knowing" of the revolutionaries of the last century has been replaced with the "not-knowing" of those who understand not-knowing as part of the transformation. See Holloway (2019, 215).

8 The name La Pasionaria pays tribute to Dolores Ibárruri, Basque revolutionary and Spanish Republican leader during the Spanish Civil War. After my research trip, I donated the van to a collective known as Barraca 2.0. This was a pedagogical project of reciprocal elucidation in which city activists travelled to small villages around the country, conducting workshops on urban activism and interviewing local activists on their specific struggles. Eventually, La Pasionaria was sold to a VW enthusiast, who fully restored it.

of conflict resolution and conciliation. To this outside observer, their lifeway seemed to be one of "deep democracy": prefigurative, direct, and radical. I found it deeply inviting, and it drew me in: I wanted to hear its own vernacular meanings and map out its paths toward the construction and transformation of community. As I drove and walked across Spain, my core motivation was to learn from and with 15M as crises of democracy intensified around the globe.

In 1972, Foucault reminded us that people know what they want and why they want it and are perfectly capable of speaking with their own voice. During my research, 15M's practice-based citizen enactment of governance, democracy, and citizenship confirmed for me the validity of Foucault's words. Yet the more I read about 15M in popular media, the more it became clear that cartographers were mapping 15M's field of activity in a deliberately misleading manner. 15M was being presented as an example of civil citizenship interspersed with acts of civil disobedience, yet it was enacting something different. Puzzled by this, I began my trip around Spain seeking to engage 15M in a different way, by practising the kind of public philosophy that studies practices of civic engagement through "dialogues of reciprocal elucidation." I was attempting to study the phenomenon of 15M as an empirical social scientist without disqualifying it in the process. This seemed the most appropriate path toward understanding 15M's habitus and ethos.

I discovered through this participatory process that 15M crystallizes a multiplicity of examples of civic activities and exemplars of civic citizenship. Ongoing dialogues of reciprocal elucidation serve to reveal civil and civic modes of citizenship in 15M and their complementarity. In this way, 15M appears as a living exemplar, not a living memory, of citizens enacting civic freedom. 15M citizens are immersed in constructive programs of various kinds in the course of which they develop the being-with ethos of thinking and acting with and for one another no matter how diverse the others happen to be. Those citizens wanting to reform institutions from within, work with those organizing beyond these institutions. Together, with differently situated others, they practise six different yet related ways of joining hands, cooperating, and contesting non-violently.[9]

---

9 As mentioned in the Introduction, and revealed through chapters 1, 2, and 3, the following are the six joining-hands relationships this study has identified: civic citizens joining hands with one another (JH1); civil citizens joining hands with one another (JH 2); civic and civil citizens joining hands (JH 3); civic citizens working with representative governments (JH4); civil citizens working with representative governments (JH5); and civic-civil citizens joining hands with one another in order to influence governments (JH6).

Through these criss-crossing and overlapping examples and their exemplary execution, 15M demonstrates how civic and civil modes of citizenship are not opposed to each other but are co-dependent. 15M is not struggling against representative democracy per se; rather, it is deuniversalizing representative democracy through its tightly interwoven activities. 15M citizens clearly understand democracy as a space within which their multiple heterodoxies can enter into dialogue and negotiate ways to coexist peacefully and constructively without being subsumed. Although governed subjects within the dominant governance system, 15M citizens are primarily engaged agents in the field of governance. This book has shown that.

Looking Back, Looking Forward

Chapter 1's thick description by means of reciprocal elucidation showed how 15M practices come into being and what motivates people to engage in them or even initiate them. The chapter also presented examples of the six joining-hands relationships in which 15M is immersed. Through the individual self-descriptions by participants we identified themes that are of upmost importance to those being 15M. 15M language games and the activities into which they are woven revealed how 15M is not a fad, but a way of being in the world together.

In chapter 2, we were able to appreciate the truly multifarious nature of 15M. By excavating ways of being and events that inspire and/or mark individuals being 15M, we arrived at the origins and antecedents of 15M. It became apparent that 15M did not appear out of thin air or with the advent of social media. 15M's counter-modernity grew out of knowledge of previous developments and the six types of roots and routes of Spain's counter-modernity.

Chapter 3 contributed to our phenomenology of 15M valuable insights about 15M's long-term thinking and constructing. It presented an accurate portrait of different future-visions of Spain as they were presented in dialogues with individuals being 15M. In this manner, the chapter revealed the multiple and intricate ways in which individuals being 15M are thinking through the reconstruction or reconstitution of the country. 15M is often portrayed in the media as a critique without an alternative, but in fact it is an epistemic community in its own right, and in this chapter we explored the future or alternative 15M envisions and is relationally co-creating.

In the first three chapters, we recovered the infrastructure of power-with organizations found within 15M. State-centric analysis erases this infrastructure. Once recovered, it becomes clear that 15M's infrastructure is broad, connected, historical, and inter-generational. With this established, chapter 4 showed how 15M's transformative social imaginary presents opposition to the power-over infrastructure of the Spanish state and is different in kind from the organization presented by the state. The same chapter captured well 15M's program as one that those being 15M articulate together. That program having been sufficiently endorsed, a leader is selected to fight for it in elections for representative institutions. The task at hand is to transform power-over structures of domination into power-with communities of practice.

The first four chapters greatly expanded our phenomenology of 15M. Following from this, and in order to complement the previous chapters and bring the book to a close, this chapter presents, first, a critique of 15M *by* 15M that can help 15M learn from itself, and second, a critique of Podemos *by* Podemos so that the party can listen to its own self-critiques. Third, it presents two hypotheses that crystallize 15M's mode of being and *raison d'être* and help overcome the paradox of a democracy-to-come: (1) the "virtuous versus vicious democracies hypothesis," which offers a cautionary note pointing out that when elites attempt to steer "societies in movement" toward institutional politics of the kind practised by those defending the status quo, power-over methods leave leaders who employ them without reliable bases of accountability; and (2) the "ever-so-slowly hypothesis," which suggests that individuals being 15M remind us through their actions that for their mode of democracy to be enacted, they have to take into account both their way of being (power-with) and their temporality (one step at a time).

The transformative mode of being outlined in this second hypothesis presents a way to transmute the predator–prey relationship – which power-over means attempt to create in the first hypothesis – into a civic/civil democratic relationship. The chapter concludes with some remarks on democratization here and now and the power of joining hands.

A 15M Critique of 15M

The exemplarity of 15M has been highlighted throughout this book. It is important now to explore some of the areas in which 15M could do better. As I mingled with*in* 15M, I had many opportunities to ask about the things that had gone wrong, the things that did not work, and where things could have been done better. Certain themes resonated across locales. Presenting those that were most often discussed will provide a sense of the kind of ongoing self-critique in which 15M engages and which is integral to its mode of being.

Power within 15M is meant to be distributed in a networked manner, but toward the end of the encampments mistrust grew within 15M as conflicts mounted over leadership, organization, and trappings (IA 33). Although many contend that centralization is not in 15M's DNA, the fact is that many within 15M felt that the movement had started collectively in all cities but eventually centralized in Madrid (IAs 5 and 195). As a result, tensions mounted between the various encampments across Spain and the one in Madrid's Puerta del Sol (IA 26).[10] Organizing in a distributed manner had the drawback of allowing certain nodes to amass a lot of power. With the "first attempt at a minimum consensus it became apparent that the power resided in the Twitter account of Puerta del Sol (IA 39).

This triggered conflicts in various regions. In Galicia, for example, 15M was accused of being a copy of Madrid. Many Galicians saw it as a branch of a centralized Spanish movement and rejected it for not being Galician (IA 132). Many participants "found problematic that the main language being used in 15M assemblies was Spanish" (IA 130). This led to a declaration emanating from the square "emphasizing Galician as the language of the general assembly" (IA 123). On a similar note, in Valencia, because of the "Spanish symbolism associated to 15M, numerous independence inclined neighbourhoods rejected 15M assemblies" (IA 86). In Catalonia, there were many attempts to "appropriate 15M in a Catalan Independence key. When these failed, 15M was attacked for being too Spanish" (IA 200). Across Spain, 15M struggled to articulate a united Spanish resistance. This was a response to the different regional conflicts brewing in the country and the agonisms that existed between different understandings of what it meant to be 15M.

Equally challenging, a different set of conflicts arose within 15M revolving around anarchism. In most of the cities I visited, there was a clear acknowledgment and deep appreciation of Spain's anarchist traditions. Yet many in the squares felt that the anarchist and libertarian spirit of Spain in the late nineteenth and early twentieth centuries was better represented by 15M's collective presence than by those claiming to be anarchism's inheritors. According to many in the squares, those claiming to be anarchists were behaving more like counter-revolutionaries

---

10 At the start of the square occupations, a document was circulated around the encampments across Spain suggesting a set of points all assemblies should agree upon. The idea behind the document was to converge 15M's strange multiplicity into a single set of 15M political demands. This was understood by many people in different squares across Spain as an imposition from Madrid; it generated much division.

attempting to take control of the spirit of rebellion sweeping the country. For most in the squares, there were no predefined paths toward revolution, and this meant that everything had to be decided together in a democratic power-with manner. Contrary to this, long-term anarchists (individuals who, prior to 15M, had participated in anarchist collectives or groups) often felt and acted as if they were the ones with the correct strategy for moving things forward; this, quite obviously, generated unproductive tensions.

Long-term anarchists participated in 15M and brought much-needed skills to the encampments: facilitation of assemblies, direct action tactics, and expertise in horizontality, to name a few. Nevertheless, they often accused 15M of not being radical enough, and in many squares they were resented for their patronizing attitude toward non-anarchists: "Certain people did not have any patience with those that were learning about politics through 15M" (IA 149). Although many people coming from traditions of autonomous anarchism attended 15M assemblies, they often behaved in the exact same manner as those in the institutionalized political system they had always criticized. They went to the squares to tell people what to do, not to listen and dialogue (IA 134).

The path toward bureaucratization also raised challenges for 15M. As encampments progressed, dynamics and structures that had at first been criticized began to be reproduced: "Commissions and sub-commissions sprung up. You wanted to work in a commission and you were told that it was already full. This was contrary to the idea that 15M belonged to everybody. I was very disappointed" (IA 155). 15M was faced with the challenge of maintaining its momentum. Having to think about new forms of organization and lacking a new language, 15M began to specialize: "When the chant became an expert discourse, people began to leave the square" (IA 205).

Regarding the idea of transformation, many within 15M thought that this was the revolution of the healthy and pure and that their purity would spread to the rest of society. But "it turned out that the social crisis, the ecological crisis, frustrations, rage, and violence were present in all of us" (IA 162). There was a lot of internal conflict within 15M, and sometimes agonism became antagonism and mistrust turned into distrust. For example, in many squares people complained that different collectives were boycotting the encampment with the intention of dissolving it (IA 78). Similarly, 15M efforts were often destabilized owing to a lack of loving dialogue (IA 67). At the same time, within 15M there was always "a worrisome absence of immigrant participants in a political and economic juncture marked by immigration" (IA 102). In some encampments, people were rejected or marginalized and divisions began to grow: "Women, immigrants, and whole neighbourhoods were excluded but always within a dialogue of inclusion" (IA 65).

This exclusion was visible in some of the language used in the squares. The sexist language, for example, shocked many feminists: "We were so used to our spaces in which care of the other is such an important element that being in the square one felt unnecessary hostility" (IA 161). Although individuals being 15M often addressed one another as sisters in an attempt to challenge patriarchal language, many women felt excluded and/or ignored. Many women felt alienated from the power-with horizontality that 15M was claiming to uphold. Many female interviewees recounted that it was impossible for them to be empowered through a collective presence that was essentially sexist and anti-feminist.[11] These voices suggested that adequate channels for dealing with feminist issues had been rejected. They also claimed that feminist commissions were ignored when they tried to raise concerns in general assemblies (IAs 114, 97, and 104). In many cities, women abandoned the encampments in order to continue their struggles within feminist collectives and groups.

Communication was yet another area in which conflict arose within 15M. Communication efforts were not always exemplary, and transparency and/or horizontality did not always prevail. Without a doubt, conversations were going on between and within squares. Yet individuals in the encampments were aware that this multi-square multilogue was not always fully transparent. "Like in any dialogue, there were lapses and misunderstandings. Sometimes one square would speak and another one would not listen; or did not hear; or simply would not respond" (IA 111). The same prevailed as individuals communicated with one another within squares.

Finally, there were always tensions within 15M between those who argued that violence was justified and those who adhered strictly to non-violence. As a result, the legal commission in Barcelona's Plaça Catalunya ended up having to dissolve. It became "two separate commissions. One commission that defended those with a history of violence, and a second, that only defended people without criminal records" (IA 209). Similar divisions arose in encampments across Spain. Once the encampments were dismantled, these tensions continued and mistrust took root.

11 David Graeber points out that although consensus processes tend to generate spaces in which honesty, generosity, and good intentions thrive, unfortunately, deeply internalized forms of oppression can also thrive in consensus-based spaces. This certainly resonates with what was repeated to me across Spain during the interviews. See Graeber (2009, 296).

These kinds of critiques of 15M, by 15M, were often raised within the different locales I visited across Spain. Across cities, these themes bore a family resemblance. In this sense, presenting some of the concerns being raised within 15Ms across the country helps us understand how 15M and other communities of practice can learn from 15M's weaknesses, limitations, and mistakes. This is a useful area of analysis in which much work remains to be done. That work is important as representative and participatory democrats in Spain continue to contest and construct alternatives by joining hands.

A Podemos Critique of Podemos

It has been five years since the founding of party-movement Podemos. In the country's general election of 2015, Podemos received 21 per cent of the vote and became the third largest party in parliament, with 69 out of 350 seats. In the general election of 2016 it won 71 seats. Since 2016, however, the party has lost votes in every one of the elections in Spain. Podemos is going through a profound crisis. In the autonomous communities of La Rioja and Cantabria, court orders have suspended the party's primaries due to irregularities.[12] In addition, in Cantabria, the national executive has imposed a management committee following serious accusations of sexual assault against a member of Podemos in the regional parliament.[13]

In Galicia, there is a risk of rupture in the coalition EnMarea, within which Podemos participates. In the midst of this potential rupture, the party's Galician primaries in December of 2018 ended up in the courts after accusations that party membership lists had been manipulated. An external audit concluded that the integrity of the results could not be guaranteed.[14]

---

12 For a detailed description of the reasons for this suspension in La Rioja, see "Un juez paraliza de forma cautelar las primarias de Podemos en La Rioja," *LaRioja.com*, 7 November 2018, https://www.larioja.com/la-rioja/juez-paraliza-forma-20181107192535-nt.html. For a detailed description of the reasons for the suspension in Cantabria, see "Un juzgado suspende cautelarmente las primarias de Podemos en Cantabria," *LaVanguardia.com*, 12 November 2018, https://www.lavanguardia.com/politica/20181112/452882270262/un-juzgado-suspende-cautelarmente-las-primarias-de-podemos-en-cantabria.html.

13 R. Piña, "Madrid, la punta del iceberg de los conflictos de Podemos," *ElMundo.es*, 19 January 2019, https://www.elmundo.es/espana/2019/01/19/5c4238fcfdddff439e8b46d6.html.

14 Piña, "Madrid, la punta del iceberg."

In Catalonia, the party has had four general secretaries in only four years.[15] In Navarra in May 2018, Podemos broke in two and the General Secretary left to found a new party called Orain Bai (Now We Can).[16] In Andalucía, the coalition between Podemos and Izquierda Unida (United Left) known as Adelante Andalucía (Forward Andalusia) won only 17 seats in the regional parliamentary elections of 2018. That was only five more seats than the new far-right political party VOX, which won seats in a regional parliament for the first time in these Andalusian elections. On 28 April 2019, Podemos lost 29 seats out of the 71 it held in the Spanish parliament.[17] After that election was repeated the following November, Podemos lost another 7 seats. Podemos now holds 35 seats in the Spanish parliament.

Podemos has always been an audacious political party that tries to surprise its opponents. But in the process, its leaders have been surprising one another. Out of all the founders of Podemos, only Pablo Iglesias, the General Secretary, remains in the executive. Out of the twelve people Iglesias originally picked to join him, only four remain. It has been obvious to observers over the past few years that something has not been working properly in Podemos. And it has been through the departures of party executives over time that we have been able to glean what Podemos actually looks like from within. When co-founder Juan Carlos Monedero left the executive, he said that Podemos sometimes resembled the parties it was trying to replace.[18] When co-founder Luis Alegre left, he described the executive as a group of conspirators seeking to exclude anyone who was not part of their clan.[19] In 2018, co-founder Carolina Bescansa used her Telegram account to publish a plan to oust Iglesias from the post of General Secretary. When that plan failed, she tried to win the General Secretary position in the autonomous community of Galicia. After losing, she announced in 2019 that she would be abandoning the parliamentary seat she holds with Podemos.

In January 2019, Podemos co-founder and candidate for the Madrid regional government Iñigo Errejón, and retired judge Manuela Carmena (the mayor of the city of Madrid), announced that they were

15 Piña, "Madrid, la punta del iceberg."

16 "La grave crisis de Podemos en Navarra obliga a la presidenta del Parlamento foral a dejar su cargo," *ElMundo.es*, 20 December 2018, https://www.elmundo.es/espana/2018/12/20/5c1bc8acfdddff4b9b8b4700.html.

17 For the 2019 general election, Podemos ran in a coalition known as Unidas Podemos, which included Podemos, Izquierda Unida (United Left), and Equo.

18 B. Asuar Gallego, "Los caídos de Podemos: ninguno de los fundadores continúa en el equipo de Iglesias," *Publico.es*, 17 January 2019, https://www.publico.es/politica/aniversario-caidos-ninguno-fundadores-continua-equipo-iglesias.html.

19 Asuar Gallego, "Los caídos de Podemos."

joining forces to launch a new political project called Más Madrid (More Madrid). They would be putting together a new platform and running for election to the regional government of the autonomous community. Their open letter stated that their program would be participatory and would encourage political parties to open up and reach beyond their brands.[20] Interestingly, Errejón and Carmena made the announcement through the media only minutes after sharing the news with the General Secretary of Podemos. Equally important, the announcement coincided with the fifth anniversary of the founding of Podemos.

Immediately following the announcement, Iglesias responded with his own open letter. In it, he banished Errejón from Podemos and announced that the party would be presenting its own candidate. Iglesias described the shame he felt that the party was once again in the news for political manoeuvres of this kind. He also expressed how offended he felt by the way in which Errejón had disrespected the collective space of Podemos: "Doing things in secret, by surprise and without taking into account collective spaces is incompatible with being a part of Podemos."[21] He ended his letter by describing the party's birthday as an unhappy one.[22]

An ex-member of the executive, Monedero, followed Iglesias, expressing indignation at Errejón's decision and accusing him of breaking the basic rules of political courtesy.[23] According to Monedero, Errejón was putting at risk the confluence of forces needed to reclaim the country from its corrupt elites. Judging Errejón's move as a miscalculation, he warned him about the risk of having a strictly populist program as an alternative to the status quo. Monedero ended his intervention with a critique of a politics based on friendships: "When electoral candidates are selected amongst friends, those with an aura of charismatic legitimacy end up placing their own family members in positions of trust."[24]

After a few days of uncertainty and recriminations from both sides, Errejón made a second move and abandoned his parliamentary seat. He was

---

20 "Carta de Manuela Carmena e Íñigo Errejón," *MásMadrid*, 13 January 2019, https://www.masmadrid.org/carta_de_manuela_carmena_e_igo_errej_n.

21 A. Romero, "Iglesias considera a Errejón un 'aliado', pero advierte de que los adversarios de Podemos quieren una 'izquierda amable,'" *Publico.es*, 30 January 2019, https://www.publico.es/politica/iglesias-considera-errejon-aliado-advierte-adversarios-quieren-izquierda-amable.html.

22 C.E. Cué, "Podemos: el partido en el que no caben dos amigos," *ElPais.com*, 21 January 2019, https://elpais.com/politica/2019/01/19/actualidad/1547925666_294597.html.

23 A. Riveiro, "Errejón ha estado acumulando fuerzas desde Vistalegre 2 para asestar este golpe," *Eldiario.es*, 22 January 2019, https://www.eldiario.es/politica/Errejon-acumulando-fuerzas-Vistalegre-asestar_0_859865128.html.

24 Riveiro, "Errejón ha estado acumulando fuerzas."

leaving to connect again with those who had not joined Podemos, with those who had lost their trust in political parties, and with those whom Podemos had been unable to convince.[25] In a wink to both 15M and the mayor of Madrid, he closed his speech with these words: "This path finished where everything always starts, in Puerta del Sol."[26] In subsequent media appearances, Errejón attributed this move to the lessons he had learned while co-founding Podemos: "When things are not working out, people are more important than parties and we need to open up."[27] According to Errejón, nobody could argue that things in Podemos were going well. Things needed to change, and for him the comfort of being in the party was working against his ability to bring a lot of people together.[28]

Carmena, the mayor of Madrid, was not left out of the controversy. She had been mayor since 2015, when she headed Ahora Madrid (Now Madrid).[29] Ahora Madrid is comprised of various citizens' platforms and political parties, including Podemos. Iglesias had proposed Carmena as candidate for mayor in 2015. Nevertheless, early on, Carmena had her doubts about the party. According to Alegre, a co-founder of Podemos, "attempts by Podemos to impose and blackmail Carmena generated absolute distrust."[30] Since that time, Carmena had described her links with Podemos as almost non-existent. Later, when asked about her new project with Errejón, she responded that she had always been grateful to Podemos

25 "Íñigo Errejón deja su escaño en el Congreso: 'Yo no vine a estar en política, vine a hacer política,'" *Antena3noticias.com*, 21 January 2019, https://www.antena3.com/noticias/espana/inigo-errejon-deja-escano-congreso-video_201901215c45c6470cf290657b0091f6.html.

26 "Íñigo Errejón deja su escaño en el Congreso." Puerta del Sol is both where the first 15M occupation happened and where the Madrid Town Hall is situated. By December 2018, there were clear signs that Errejón was making important political moves. In early December, he appeared in Puerta del Sol in support of the mayor of the city as she was putting up a plaque in the square commemorating the 15M encampments of 2011. Soon after, he recorded his first video as candidate for the presidency of the autonomous community of Madrid without mentioning Podemos or showing the party's logo. See J. José Mateo, "Errejón lo apuesta todo a Carmena," *ElPais.com*, 16 January 2019, https://elpais.com/ccaa/2019/01/15/madrid/1547573264_159640.html.

27 "Errejón dice que actuó como Podemos le enseñó: 'Si la cosa no va bien, hay que abrirse,'" *Publico.es*, 27 January 2019, https://www.publico.es/politica/errejon-dice-actuo-le-enseno-cosa-no-hay-abrirse.html.

28 "Errejón dice que actuó como Podemos le enseñó."

29 Ahora Madrid is a citizen platform of popular unity that was constituted as an instrumental party without organic internal life.

30 A. Riveiro, "El intento de Podemos de imponer y chantajear a Manuela Carmena rompió una confianza decisiva," *Eldiario.es*, 23 January 2019, https://www.eldiario.es/politica/Podemos-chantajear-Manuela-Carmena-confianza_0_860215012.html.

for its support but had always emphasized her independence. As she put it, she did not take orders or advice from anyone.[31] For her, the launch of Más Madrid amounted to an acknowledgment that the ways citizens were thinking about political parties were evolving in important ways. Finding concepts like "militant" too strident, she suggested that "trying to find representative structures that work for the citizenry requires parties behaving like intermediaries rather than as elements of direct intervention."[32]

In the days following the announcement by Errejón and Carmena, more Podemos executives and past executives commented on the move by Errejón and Carmena. Bescansa simply stated that she saw it as more evidence that Podemos had gone adrift.[33] Alegre took this thought one step further, suggesting that once a common understanding has been established, politicians should strive to generate power and momentum, not within a central party or authority, but in the power-with locales on which representative power depends.[34] With no end in sight to the controversy, Ramón Espinar, the General Secretary of Podemos in Madrid, announced that he was abandoning institutional politics. He made clear his reason for abandoning Podemos and electoral politics more broadly: "When you have no room to manage and you do not share the direction of the party, you have to leave."[35]

The departure of Errejón from Podemos and his partnering with Carmena to run for the presidency of the community of Madrid undoubtedly damaged the party, setting off a string of resignations across the country. But this does not signify the end of Podemos.[36] The party is learning how to remain connected to its base, and its executive is

---

31 B. Asuar Gallego, "Matar al padre: 'Carmena ya no cuenta con Podemos,'" *Publico.es*, 23 January 2019, https://www.publico.es/politica/matar-al-padre-carmena-ya.html.

32 Asuar Gallego, "Matar al padre."

33 M. Vilas López, "¿Puede nacer un 'Más Galicia' del conflicto en Podemos Galicia?," *GaliciaPress.es*, 24 January 2019, https://www.galiciapress.es/texto-diario/mostrar/1307540/anova-ofrece-bildu-erc-bng-concurrir-candidatura-elecciones-europeas.

34 A. Riveiro, "El intento de Podemos de imponer y chantajear a Manuela Carmena rompió una confianza decisiva," *Eldiario.es*, 23 January 2019, https://www.eldiario.es/politica/Podemos-chantajear-Manuela-Carmena-confianza_0_860215012.html.

35 "La política es comer 'tazas de mierda': la escena de The Wire con la que Espinar se ha despedido de la política," *Eldiario.es*, 25 January 2019, https://www.eldiario.es/rastreador/politica-The-Wire-Espinar-despedido_6_860973928.html.

36 Amidst the chaos lived within Podemos, a person close to the executive remembered the day they were told by a friendly government in Latin America that this would happen. What surprised him, however, was how quickly it had happened in Podemos: "It is shameful, this was a great opportunity for our generation and we are throwing it away." See C.E. Cué, "Podemos: el partido en el que no caben dos amigos," *ElPais.com*, 21 January 2019, https://elpais.com/politica/2019/01/19/actualidad/1547925666_294597.html.

learning to work in a more congenial and collaborative manner. Overall, this crisis serves as yet another example of civic and civil citizens joining hands. In this particular case, municipalist currents that were strong in the city of Madrid (Ahora Madrid) joined hands with dissenters from Podemos's party structure. Inventing new "public spheres," they are experimenting with yet another political alternative (Más Madrid).

I see this as part of a continuum that can be traced back to the discussions that took place during 15M's square occupations. It reflects a process of transmutation in which 15M's lifeways are emerging from within party structures. This hints at the possibility that, at least in the community of Madrid, civic and civil citizens have entered a moment of reconciliation. They came together initially through 15M in 2011 but grew distant from one another after Podemos was launched in 2014. In this sense, it is possible that the present-day moment signals the beginning of a new virtuous cycle in Spanish civil/civic relations.[37]

Virtuous versus Vicious Democracies

Throughout this book, I have tried to show that the huge civic cooperative base of 15M made possible the new "party-movement" Podemos. But 15M had not come into being with Podemos as its purpose. When individuals being 15M were asked what 15M meant to them, many expressed sentiments such as "15M is a mode of being in the world with others and exercising power together." Podemos is a different form of organization, a power-over entity that plays power politics and that has attempted to swallow 15M. Yet as this research has shown, after numerous attempts Podemos has failed to take over 15M. Instead, while Podemos has misunderstood and tried to misuse, abuse, manage, and subordinate 15M, the movement has survived and is uniquely resilient.[38]

As I hope is clear by this point, Podemos came to power (power-over) with considerable support and assistance from 15M. Yet Podemos failed to enter into a gift/reciprocity relationship with 15M that would have allowed the two groups to grow together. Instead, Podemos took advantage of

37 On a separate yet important note, these back-and-forth critiques among Podemos co-founders share a family resemblance with critiques Podemos received from 15M communities when it launched in 2014 (see chapter 4).

38 John Holloway points out that conceiving revolution instrumentally as a means to an end subordinates the multiplicity of rich traditions involved in the process of transformation. This, he says, "inevitably reproduces power-over (the subordination of the struggles to the Struggle) and ensures continuity rather than the rupture that is sought." See Holloway (2019, 214).

15M's support, did not reciprocate, and entered into a conventional struggle for electoral power-over. It did this by building on the foundations that 15M had done so much to help build. Orienting itself to gaining power-over through campaigning for office, Podemos neglected its base and tried to attract more or less *all* actors, including 15M, in a power-over manner.

Through Podemos's critique of itself, we can see that power-over struggles eventually erupted within the party. The resulting schisms were partly the cause of its electoral decline. As happens with many political parties, even while Podemos strove to attain state power, vicious internal divisions undermined that possibility. This seems to be the history of power-over movements – war by other means, as Carl von Clausewitz described it.[39] The party's martial attitude eventually shaped internal relationships within the party, and by the end, Podemos had become yet another power-over political party of the left.[40] In contrast, 15M exercised gift/reciprocity relationships within itself among its individual and collective members (power-with) and offered this kind of power relationship to Podemos (mutual aid – power-with – joining hands). However, Podemos declined and only offered 15M a position of power-under. From the perspective of Podemos, the role it could offer 15M was that of subaltern. Of course, 15M responded by declining and walking away.

Having learned from this experience, 15M has turned its attention back to citizens working within 15M. It has gone back to developing relationships with partners who understand gift/reciprocity relationships and their responsibilities. Through its experience with Podemos, 15M has grasped a crucial lesson: one can offer to join hands, but if the recipient tries to transform the relationship into that of hegemon/subaltern, it is best to step back and sustain 15M until another opportunity arises.[41]

Unfortunately, 15M has lacked the capacity to persuade Podemos to co-generate an intersubjective interaction that is "with and for each other."[42] 15M doesn't yet have the tools to sustain a long campaign and persuade through exemplarity. Fortunately, power-with democracies are resilient, and though 15M tried and failed to join hands with Podemos, those being 15M have survived and carried on their constructive programs

39 Clausewitz (1918, 1: ch. 1).

40 A second factor leading to the party's decline is that the Spanish right is so well-entrenched that it has been able to divide and defeat Podemos.

41 As Cornel West and Harry Belafonte pointed out at the time, African American 15M-like communities that supported Barack Obama to become US president then walked away when he failed to reciprocate.

42 15M did not have the training to sustain what Gandhi would describe as a *satyagraha* campaign. See Tully's introduction in Gregg (2018, xxii).

among themselves and with other responsive communities of practice. It is precisely 15M's resiliency (auto-generated sustainability) that has become apparent throughout this research. What used to be referred to as "spontaneous cooperation" has been recast by 15M as symbiotic cooperation and resiliency leading to growth and sustainability. As chapter 2 showed, this mode of being can be traced back to the 1800s in Spain.

Following from the above, the virtuous-versus-vicious democracies hypothesis should encourage members of Podemos to work out a more respectful relationship of mutual accountability with 15M (and other networks of non-violent and horizontal mutual aid). In this sense, the party-movement should radically rethink its relationship with its base. After all, as Hannah Arendt points out, power grows out of the human ability to act in concert.[43] If a group that has made power actual fractures, then the power vanishes, since it is not the property of a sole individual.

As Podemos continues to creep into state institutions, the party should work toward making its relationships of representation with 15M communities (and others) more representative of, and accountable to, an engaged citizenry (and electorate). At the same time, civic and civil citizens can benefit from remembering Mahatma Gandhi's views about representative politics. For Gandhi, "consent through elections" is never enough to govern the conduct of elected representatives: people have to be ready to exercise mass non-violent civil disobedience in order to "govern their governors" whenever those governors abuse the power conditionally delegated to them.[44] Perhaps, if Podemos ever governs Spain, the base will need to play such a role. However, this is a huge responsibility, which it might or might not take on. Clearly, to live in virtuous versus vicious democracies, engaged citizens practising power-with ways and Podemos participants enacting power-over methods will need to join hands and act in concert.[45]

---

43 Arendt (1972, 143).

44 This theme runs through Gandhi's writings. In *Hind Swaraj*, it is ever-present. For a good overview of Gandhi's thought see, Gandhi (2008).

45 When Obama became president, community-based organizations that had tirelessly worked for him to become president soon realized that he had been taken over by professional lobbyists of the banking industry and by the Pentagon's military-industrial complex. These community-based organizations at this point wished that they had a strategy of non-cooperation that would hold him to his promises. They failed to produce one. Similarly, in Egypt we witnessed how after the removal of Hosni Mubarak the power-with base that had made his fall possible had no control over the situation. Finally, in Greece, power-with channels within SYRIZA closed rapidly once it was governing the country. Considering that at the time, these three examples were understood by many as progressive exemplars, it is important to think about avoiding a similar fate if Spain is ever governed by Podemos or a party-movement of a similar kind.

Ever so Slowly, Every Step Must Embody the Ends

In this section I reflect on what has been 15M's mantra all along and what surely is this study's main hypothesis: ever so slowly, every step must embody the ends. In the previous section, we discussed the virtuous versus vicious democracies hypothesis as a reminder to political parties, including Podemos, that they must join hands with their base. This section warns of the risks of overlooking the means/ends logic of acting "ever so slowly" when considering the events going on in Spain. The point of this section is to remind Podemos executives, as well as political theorists who support such projects, not to ignore the valuable lessons offered by 15M. Through their actions, individuals being 15M remind us that ways of being (power-with) and temporality (one step at a time) both have to be taken into account if we are to enact democracy as 15M understands it – that is, democracy is in the here and now, and we must be democratic in every little step we take.[46]

Throughout this book, the ever-so-slowly, every-step-must-embody-the-ends way of being of 15M has been at work. In addition, through the multilogue presented throughout, we have been able to observe 15M's ability to adapt to and evolve in an ever changing and ever more repressive environment. In light of this, 15M's effectiveness and continuity suggest that the often-repeated objection that the ever-so-slowly approach is "ineffective" is based on a false assumption, namely that social change can be brought about by cause/effect means unrelated to their ends. Countering this assumption, through 15M's way of being and the numerous outcomes of its efforts, we are able to see two very important features of this ever-so-slow, means-in-alignment-with-ends way of being. First, it brings about real effects at each step.[47] Second, it has immediate effects in another sense: the small, non-violent, democratic, horizontal, power-with

46 In his final novel, *Island* (1961), Aldous Huxley writes about an Englishman who finds himself shipwrecked on the imaginary island of Pala. There he finds a society that enjoys universal economic and social well-being. On the island, mynah birds are specially trained to carry out the sole function of loudly repeating the phrase "Here and now! Here and now!" whenever anyone gets sucked into focusing on the progress "to come" in some imaginary future.

47 If we listen to 15M, we can see how its slow-time has had immediate effects in the present. These immediate effects lie in the fact that the day-to-day life of 15M is democratic. Foucault discovered this in his late lectures. As an example, indicative of Foucault's grasp of the idea that the way we walk is the basis of all further transformation, in *Hermeneutics of the Subject* he writes that "there is no first or final point of resistance to political power other than in the relationship one has to oneself." See Foucault (2005, 252).

steps that individuals being 15M take have kaleidoscopic, transformative, cumulative effects that can lead to unpredictable tipping points.

By aligning means and ends and acting ever-so-slowly, 15M is creating its own complex system (in the form of a set of counter-conducts), one that interacts with and alters the complex system that is society. Society, being a multiplicity of complex forces in mobile equilibrium, often finds it hard to balance itself.[48] This means that minute forces can alter the societal system. In this sense, 15M is affecting society through accumulation.[49] That is, through the repetition of stimuli far below "the threshold of response," 15M is generating a "staircase effect."[50] Since actions have no end, we cannot predict the outcome of the actions of those being 15M. As Arendt suggests, through this no-end to action, a single deed can endure through time.[51]

For those not engaged with*in* 15M, its deeds may be incomprehensible. Yet if one pays attention, the cumulative effects of 15M are visible in Spanish politics. Podemos is a clear example of this: the party would not exist were it not for the climate generated by 15M, and Podemos leaders are the first to admit it. And despite the cautionary reminder presented by the virtuous versus vicious democracies hypothesis, the arrival of Podemos in the electoral arena suggests a possible tipping point. The institutions founded during the country's transition to democracy are being seriously challenged for the first time, and that challenge is arising from within. 15M has played a vital role in this. If civic and civil citizens in Spain are able to add to this success by dedicating time to the ever-so-slowly hypothesis, there is a chance they will change the status quo in meaningful and long-lasting ways.

Those being 15M do not see humans as independent, insecure, and unable to organize without violence and domination; rather, they see the need for means and ends to align and for acting in an ever-so-slow manner. This is why they enact and defend cooperative and interdependent relationships of contestation and integration.[52] Through these kinds of relationships, systems of violent conflict can be transformed and replaced. This is the kind of non-violent agonistics that Richard Gregg and Gandhi advocated.[53] Nevertheless, this mode of being of collective presences like 15M has often been misunderstood. The problems

48 Gregg (2018, 140).
49 Gregg (2018, 140).
50 Gregg (2018, 140).
51 Arendt (1958, 233).
52 Gregg (2018, xxiii).
53 Gregg (2018, xxiv).

that arise when grassroots organizations are treated as instrumental means to gain political power rather than as ongoing and intergenerational cooperative organizations in their own right (and as the basis of representative institutions in practice) have been central throughout the twentieth century. A whole body of critical literature has developed around them.

In 1902, Peter Kropotkin spoke of mutual aid to describe the kind of power relations we see 15M enacting today. He pointed out that despite the systematic destruction of mutual aid institutions over the centuries, such institutionality survived, along with its habits and customs.[54] According to him, millions of individuals have continued to enact mutual aid institutions, reconstituting them when they perished.[55] Arguing along similar lines, Paul Hawken has suggested that these mutual aid networks constitute the world's largest informal, symbiotic fellowship of engaged citizens.[56] As Hawken put it, they make up a network of human beings "willing to confront despair, power, and incalculable odds in an attempt to restore some semblance of grace, justice, and beauty to this world."[57]

In multilogue with Kropotkin, Hawken, and millions of other participant-thinkers, 15M reveals the robust health of mutual aid institutionality in Spain. As a reminder, the popular 15M slogan "Vamos lentos porque vamos lejos" (We go ever so slowly because we are going on forever) plays tribute to the autotelic relations between means and ends found in 15M's six joining-hands relationships. I think of these joining-hands relationships as exemplary responses and antidotes to neoliberalism and right-wing populism. Through them, citizens are challenging modernity's foundational and violent forms of subjectivity and building a counter-modernity "within, around, and against" their society's dominant institutions.[58]

Through this process of "integrated small steps and tipping points," 15M and Podemos can work together to ameliorate the vicious relationship described in the previous section. That relationship can be turned into a co-generated, democratic, and mutually sustaining one capable of regenerating the system they are both contesting.[59] Through reciprocal elucidation, and by grasping how civic and civil citizens can

54 Kropotkin (2006, 215).
55 Kropotkin (2006, 189).
56 Hawken (2007).
57 Hawken (2007, 4).
58 Gregg (2018, xxiv).
59 Gregg (2018, xxv).

join hands, 15M and Podemos can transform their mutually destructive predator/prey relationship into a joining-hands democratic relationship of mutual empowerment that can serve as an exemplar for the world. An important contribution of this book is that it shows how civil and civic participants in 15M and Podemos may find a way forward and how this may serve as a model for other contexts.[60]

Conclusion

Some of Europe's leading liberal public intellectuals suggest that the idea of Europe is falling apart before our eyes. According to Bernard-Henri Lévy and other signatories of a recent manifesto, the challenges the continent faces are as severe as they were in the 1930s.[61] According to investor and philanthropist George Soros, "the dream of a united Europe could become a 21st-century nightmare."[62] Asking citizens to wake up to the reality of a period of "radical disequilibrium," Soros warns that Europe could be on the verge of collapse like the Soviet Union in 1991.[63]

As far-right parties continue to win elections across Europe, many are beginning to fear what Chantal Mouffe describes as the populist moment (see chapter 4). In Spain, the far-right party VOX is growing rapidly. It already holds 52 seats in the Spanish parliament, 13 seats in the Madrid regional parliament, 12 seats in the Andalusian regional parliament, 11 seats in the Catalonia regional parliament, and 10 seats in the Valencia regional parliament. In its program, titled 100 *Medidas para la España Viva* (100 Measures for the Spain That Is Alive), the party highlights some of the measures it wants to implement. These include suspending the autonomy of Catalonia until the coup instigators are

---

60 In his chapter on persuasion, Gregg provides powerful insight into the temporality of social change, the importance of mutual trust and respect, and the way to offer our energies for a curative societal process. Gregg (2018, 139–65).

61 I am referring here to a manifesto published in several newspapers, including *The Guardian*, in which thirty writers, historians, and Nobel laureates declare that Europe is coming apart. The signatories include Bernard-Henri Lévy, Ian McEwan, Salman Rushdie, Simon Schama, Svetlana Alexievitch, Herta Müller, Orhan Pamuk, and Elfriede Jelinek. See J. Henley and M. Rice-Oxley, "Europe 'coming apart before our eyes', say 30 top intellectuals," *Theguardian.com*, 25 January 2019, https://www.theguardian.com/world/2019/jan/25/europe-coming-apart-before-our-eyes-say-30-top-intellectuals.

62 G. Soros, "The EU looks like the Soviet Union in 1991 – on the verge of collapse," *TheGuardian.com*, 12 February 2019, https://www.theguardian.com/commentisfree/2019/feb/12/eu-soviet-union-european-elections-george-soros.

63 Soros, "The EU looks like the Soviet Union in 1991."

defeated, repealing historical memory laws, repealing gender violence laws, building walls in the Spanish enclaves of Ceuta and Melilla, deporting illegal immigrants, creating an agency to help threatened Christian minorities, and eliminating subsidized radical feminist organizations.[64]

While VOX's popularity is rising, Podemos's is declining. In 2019 the PSOE (Partido Socialista Obrero Español; Socialist Workers Party of Spain) won the country's general election with 123 seats but was unable to form a government. This led to a repeat election in which, although the PSOE lost three seats and Podemos lost seven, they were able to form a coalition government, with Pedro Sanchez as Spain's Prime Minister.

Unfortunately, in Spain, the representative space continues to be unstable. Perhaps this is best exemplified by the Supreme Court trial of Catalan politicians and civil society leaders that ended with nine of the twelve accused being sent to prison for crimes of sedition; four of them were also found guilty of misuse of public funds. The sentences range from nine to thirteen years. The remaining three accused were found guilty of disobedience and sentenced to pay fines, though not to prison terms.[65] Quim Torra, President of Catalonia at the time, described the trial as an attack on democracy and human rights and suggested that it was unworthy of the twentieth century.[66]

On the surface, the Catalonia/Spain conflict seems to have faded. There have been no large mobilizations recently, and the new pro-independence politicians coming into power in Catalonia seem to be treading carefully to avoid ending up in prison. Nevertheless, I think it is fair to say that much of the decrease in pro-independence mobilizations in Catalonia can be attributed to the COVID-19 pandemic and the restrictions that citizens have endured during the country's "state of alarm."

Political tensions in Spain keep mounting, and it is likely that as pandemic restrictions continue to ease, contestation will become more visible. Whether this happens or not, it is clear that the authoritarian hand of the state is continuing to respond to protest in Spain by clamping

---

64 A. Iríbar, "Vox, una enmienda a la totalidad de la Constitución," *ElPais.com*, 30 December 2018, https://elpais.com/politica/2018/12/29/actualidad/1546113394_554430.html.

65 R. Rincón, "Sentencia del 'procés': penas de 9 a 13 años para Junqueras y los otros líderes por sedición y malversación," *ElPais.com*, 15 October 2019, https://elpais.com/politica/2019/10/14/actualidad/1571033446_440448.html.

66 "Torra condena el juicio al 'procés y lo tilda como un 'ataque a la democracia,'" *RTVE.es*, 12 February 2019, http://www.rtve.es/alacarta/videos/telediario/torra-condena-juicio-proces-tilda-como-ataque-democracia/4983358.

down on dissent. In these challenging circumstances, Laclau's suggestion that a left-populist option can help makes a lot of sense. A new institutionalism propelled by a populist party would not break with the old institutionalism, but it might compensate for it by practising popular power.[67] This could help reduce the social misery generated by neoliberal austerity policies and in that sense could be valuable. However, such an approach would not provide the antidote that 15M presents. In marked distinction from Podemos, 15M addresses the paradox of a democracy-to-come by being democratic in the here and now.[68]

In the language and cultural imagination of 15M, the self exists in relation to the rest of the community. That summarizes 15M's silent power. Even though most citizens do not adequately appreciate it, 15M is enacting powerful changes in our practices and understandings of democracy. Its highly diverse community is negotiating complex norms of recognition and interaction relevant to its daily activities. It is enacting a powerful kind of "conviviality" that in Spain has deep roots and routes, as chapter 2 revealed.[69]

With*in* 15M, we can observe the everyday kind of agreement that is necessary to create and sustain society and sociability and that is at the core of all types of power relationships. Through reciprocal elucidation, we capture 15M's non-violence, its horizontality, its solidarity in resistance, and its construction of alternatives. Through such a dialogue, in which we make something in common, we are able to experience the confluence of disparate views that collectively embrace multiplicity with*in* 15M.[70] In this manner, the field of activity emerges "in its objectivity and visibility from all sides."[71]

At a critical juncture for Spanish citizens, 15M has crystallized alternative forms of knowledge.[72] It has also made visible an alternative mode of being political that has different rules of social time and a different temporal code (slow-time versus crisis-time).[73] 15M citizens are co-evolving, diversifying, and growing together through joining-hands

67 Laclau, "El populismo en América Latina."

68 Monological Western political theory would have it that the West exemplifies the democracy that others should follow. Yet a great deal of political thought presents democracy in a very different manner. Specifically, I am thinking of those traditions that imagine democracy as "being democracy-here-and-now." In this sense, I am writing this chapter against the conventions of Western political theory.

69 Tully (2008a, 313).

70 Bohm (2004, 3).

71 Arendt (2005, 165).

72 Sousa Santos (2006, 34).

73 Sousa Santos (2006, 34).

relationships. Through this process, they remind fellow citizens that they must be peaceful, democratic, and negotiating-with if they are to get to where they want to go in Spain. Along these lines, since 2011, 15M's lifeway has stimulated reciprocity among various *demoi*, with the result that a transformation is happening in ever-widening circles.[74] In this manner, 15M is contributing to a glocal cycle of struggles for "real democracy" that is spreading around the globe and in which modalities of contestation share a family resemblance.

Whether speaking of oligarchy, plutocracy, democratic elitism, or centralized, procedural, capitalist or bourgeois democracy, it is clear that citizens everywhere are contesting fixed systems of entrenched inequality.[75] In the multitude of sites of democratic struggle around the planet, practices of democracy are varied. It follows that we have the freedom and responsibility to listen outside of Eurocentric knowledges (global South), as Boaventura de Sousa Santos recommends. We are also free to act, like 15M or any other alternative modernity that is resurging in the global North.

As Joe Parker points out, there are many democracies and in many of them citizens are thinking of "democracy beyond the state."[76] At different registers, scales, and sites, the boundaries between democracies are being renegotiated; conflict and reconciliation between and within them is apparent.[77] If as researchers we want to study the broad field of democratization and democracies, we need to listen to individual self-descriptions in their own vernacular languages. This is a healthy approach to understanding particular lifeways and an important lesson I have learned through my dialogues of reciprocal elucidation with*in* 15M.[78]

Carole Pateman asks herself whether in the wealthy countries there is still a political will and a political culture ready to pursue deeper democratization.[79] This is an important question because in the institutional political arena, the will and political culture for this are both lacking. Nevertheless, it is clear that a critical dialogue about democracies

74 Tully (2018, 83–129).

75 Parker (2017, 114–31).

76 Parker, (2017, 5).

77 Parker, 42, 452, 462.

78 Raúl Zibechi, in 2005, invited scholars to trust that the oppressed were gaining experience and "learning to communicate without speaking, to walk without moving, to fight without fighting." See Zibechi (2005, 25). By 2013, two years after 15M's square occupations, what was clear was that while 15M citizens and others joined hands, many were left struggling to understand all that 15M was exemplifying.

79 Pateman (2012, 9).

is very much alive in the networks of those being 15M. Perhaps their position is less state-centric and more focused on joining hands. Yet these engaged citizens clearly have the necessary will as well as a multiplicity of political cultures to experiment with as they carry out their joining-hands activities.

At a time when liberal dominance is declining and a cacophony of populisms of both the right and the left are struggling to take its place, expanding our democratic imaginary strengthens our resilience and expands our possibilities. If modes of democracy enter into critical dialogues in which there is no appropriation or subordination, they will contribute to a great transformation. 15M's contribution to this intersocietal and intergenerational multilogue serves as a reminder of the meaning of "democracy here and now." That is the thread running through this book. It is what the ever-so-slowly, every-step-must-embody-the-ends hypothesis implies, and even entails, and it is what my method of reciprocal elucidation shows to be happening. Participatory democracy is the order of 15M, so to speak, and representative democracy only works well if it is based on this participatory democracy in a civic/civil gift/reciprocity relationship. That is why I view 15M in Spain as an exemplary case of twenty-first-century "democracy here and now."[80]

---

80 I would like to thank one of the readers who evaluated the original manuscript for the University of Toronto Press for highlighting the value of comparing and contrasting my work with that of two American theory schools: the new communists and the Wolinites (fugitive democracy). Although entering into an in-depth dialogue with these two schools of political theory goes beyond the scope of this book, I want to acknowledge their importance. I do see a certain family resemblance with the traditions I have been in conversation with in this text, and I do intend to communicate with these other schools in the future. Nevertheless, in the "political ethnography" character of this text, my distinctive contribution differs from the project they are carrying out. They tend to be more theory-driven, using concrete examples to illustrate a particular theory, whereas I am trying to tell the academic community what the people in the squares are *doing*, as opposed to telling fellow academics what I think the people in the squares *should be doing*. In this sense, my engagement with theorists like Chantal Mouffe, Ernesto Laclau, Antonio Gramsci, Mahatma Gandhi, and Joe Parker is of value because they help bring out important salient features of both being 15M and joining hands.

Bibliography

Ackerman, P., and J. DuVall. 2001. *A Force More Powerful: A Century of Non-Violent Conflict*. New York: St Martin's.

Agamben, G. 2014. "What Is a Destituent Power?" In *Environment and Planning D: Society and Space* 32: 65–74. https://doi.org/10.1068/d3201tra

Ajangiz, R. 2004. "Objeción de conciencia, insumisión, movimiento antimilitarista." *Mientras Tanto* 91–2 (Summer–Fall): 139–54.

Allen, J.S. 2008. "Ethnography of the Treacherous Interstices" [Review of *Battered Black Women and Welfare Reform: Between a Rock and a Hard Place*, by D.-A. Davis]. *American Anthropologist* 110(3): 373–5. https://doi.org/10.1111/j.1548-1433.2008.00046_1.x

Ancelovici, M., et al. 2016. *Street Politics in the Age of Austerity: From the Indignados to Occupy*. Amsterdam: Amsterdam University Press.

Arendt, H. 1958. *The Human Condition*. Chicago: University of Chicago Press.

– 1971. "The Abyss of Freedom and the Novus Ordo Seclorum.' In *The Life of the Mind*, 195–377. New York: Harcourt.

– 1972. "On Violence." In *Crises of the Republic*, 103–84. San Diego: Harcourt Brace.

– 2005. *The Promise of Politics*. Edited and with an introduction by Jerome Kohn. New York: Schocken Books.

Aslam, A. 2017. *Ordinary Democracy: Sovereignty and Citizenship beyond the Neoliberal Impasse*. Oxford: Oxford University Press.

Aslam, A., D. McIvor, and J.A. Schlosser. 2019. "Democratic Theory: When Democracy Is Fugitive." *Democratic Theory* 6(2): 27–40. https://doi.org/10.3167/dt.2019.060204

Avilés, J., and Á. Herrerín. 2010. "Propaganda por el hecho y propaganda por la represión: Anarquismo y violencia en España a fines del siglo XIX." *Ayer* 80: 165–92.

Bakhtin, M. 1981. *The Dialogic Imagination*. Austin: University of Texas Press.

– 2008. *The Dialogical Imagination: Four Essays by M.M. Bakhtin*. Edited by Michael Holquist. Austin: University of Texas Press.

Bohm, D. 2004. *On Dialogue*. New York: Routledge.

Bollier, D., and S. Helfrich. 2012. "Introduction." *The Wealth of the Commons: A World beyond Market and State*. Edited by D. Bollier and S. Helfrich. Amherst: Levellers Press.

Bondurant, J. 1988. *Conquest of Violence: The Gandhian Philosophy of Conflict*. Princeton: Princeton University Press.

Bookchin, M. 1978. *The Spanish Anarchists: The Heroic Years, 1868–1936*. New York: Harper Colophon Books.

– 1998. *The Spanish Anarchists: The Heroic Years, 1868–1936*. Oakland and Edinburgh: AK Press.

Byrne, J. 2012. *The Occupy Handbook*. New York: Little, Brown.

Cahm, C. 1989. *Kropotkin and the Rise of Revolutionary Anarchism*. Cambridge: Cambridge University Press.

Capra, F. 1986. "The Santiago Theory of Life and Cognition." *la revista Be-Vision* 9(1): 59–60.

Casas-Cortés M., M. Osterweil, and D. Powell. 2008. "Blurring Boundaries: Recognizing Knowledge-Practices in the Study of Social Movements." *Anthropological Quarterly* 81(1): 17–58. https://doi.org/10.1353/anq.2008.0006

Castells, J. 2015. *Networks of Outrage and Hope: Social Movements in the Internet Age*. New York: John Wiley and Sons.

Celikates, R. 2015. "Learning from the Streets: Civil Disobedience in Theory and Practice." In *global aCtIVISm: Art and Conflict in the 21st Century*. Edited by P. Weibelm, 65–72. Cambridge, MA: MIT Press. https://www.ias.edu/sites/default/files/sss/pdfs/Crisis-and-Critique-2018-19/celikates_learning.pdf.

Chin, C. 2018. *The Practice of Political Theory: Rorty and Continental Thought*. New York: Columbia University Press.

Chomsky, N. 2012. *Occupy*. New York: Zuccotti Park Press.

Christensen, K. 2010. *Nonviolence, Peace, and Justice*. Peterborough: Broadview Press.

Clausewitz, C. 1918. *On War* [1832]. Translated by J.J. Graham. Rev. ed. 3 vols. London: Kegan Paul, Trench, Trubner & Co.

Cuadras-Morató, X. 2015. *Catalonia: A New Independent State in Europe? A Debate on Secession within the European Union*. Abingdon: Routledge.

Cuevas, F.J. 2010. "La Línea Rojinegra Educativa del Anarquismo Español." *HAOL* 21: 101–9.

Dardot, P., and C. Laval. 2013. *The New Way of the World: On Neoliberal Society*. London: Verso.

Davidson, D. 1986. "A Nice Derangement of Epitaphs." In *Philosophical Grounds of Rationality*. Edited by R. Grandy and R. Warner, 157–74. Oxford: Oxford University Press.

Davis, D.A. 2006. *Battered Black Women and Welfare Reform: Between a Rock and a Hard Place*. Albany: SUNY Press.

della Porta, D., and A. Mattoni. 2014. *Spreading Protest: Social Movements in Times of Crisis*. Colchester: ECPR Press.

della Porta, D., and D. Rucht. 2013. "Power and Democracy in Social Movements: An Introduction." In *Meeting Democracy: Power and Deliberation in Global Justice Movements*. Edited by D. della Porta and D. Rucht, 1–22. Cambridge: Cambridge University Press.

Deming, B. 1971. *Revolution and Equilibrium*, New York: Grossman.

Devesa Pájaro, D. 2008. "El discurs pacifista dins de l'anarcosindicalisme: el cas de Badalona i Mataró durant la Primera Guerra Mundial." *Cercles. Revista d'història cultural* 11 (January): 154–67.

Dugatkin, L.A. 2011. *The Prince of Evolution: Peter Kropotkin's Adventures in Science and Politics*. Createspace.

Dupuis-Déri, F. 2013. *Démocratie: Histoire politique d'un mot aux Etat-Unis et en France*. Montréal: Lux Editeur.

Ellinas, A. 2013. "The Rise of Golden Dawn: The New Face of the Far Right in Greece." *Southern European Society and Politics* 18(4): 543–65. https://doi.org/10.1080/13608746.2013.782838

Encarnación, O.G. 2008. "Reconciliation after Democratization: Coping with the Past in Spain." *Political Science Quarterly* 123(2): 435–59. https://doi.org/10.1002/j.1538-165X.2008.tb00630.x

Engler, M., and P. Engler. 2016. *This Is an Uprising: How Nonviolent Revolt Is Shaping the Twenty-First Century*. New York: Nation Books.

Epstein, B. 1993. *Political Protest and Cultural Revolution Nonviolent Direct Action in the 1970s and 1980s*. Berkeley: University of California Press.

– 2017a. "The Left We Have and the Left We Need." *Jewish Social Studies* 22(3): 174–81. https://doi.org/10.2979/jewisocistud.22.3.09

– 2017b. "The Rise, Decline, and Possible Revival of Socialist Humanism." In *For Humanism: Explorations in Theory and Politics*. Edited by D. Alderson and R. Spencer, 17–67. London: Pluto Press.

Errejón Galván, I. 2011. "El 15-M como discurso contrahegemónico." *Encrucijadas: Revista Crítica de Ciencias Sociales* 2: 120–45.

Evans, R. 2016. "Achieving and Evidencing Research 'Impact'? Tensions and Dilemmas from an Ethic of Care Perspective." *Area* 48(2): 213–21. https://doi.org/10.1111/area.12256

Farnsworth, K., and Z. Irving. 2018. "Austerity: Neoliberal Dreams Come True?' In *Critical Social Policy*, 461–81. https://doi.org/10.1177/0261018318762451

Fernández, C., and C. Serrano. 2009. *El Plan Bolonia*. Madrid: Los libros de la Catarata.

Flesher Fominaya, C. 2011. "The Madrid Bombings and Popular Protest: Misinformation, Counter-Information, Mobilisation, and Elections after '11-M.'" *Contemporary Social Science: Journal of the Academy of Social Sciences* 6(3): 289–307. https://doi.org/10.1080/21582041.2011.603910

– 2020. *Democracy Reloaded: Inside Spain's Political Laboratory from 15-M to Podemos*. Oxford: Oxford University Press.

Fontana, J. 2005. "Bases per a una nova transició." *HMiC: història moderna i contemporània*. https://www.raco.cat/index.php/HMiC/article/view/22060

Foucault, M. 1977a. "What Is an Author?" In *Language, Counter-Memory, Practice: Selected Essays and Interviews by Michel Foucault*. Edited by D.F. Bouchard. Ithaca: Cornell University Press.

– 1977b. *Language, Counter-Memory, Practice: Selected Essays and Interviews*. Ithaca: Cornell University Press.

– 1982a. "The Subject and Power." *Critical Inquiry* 8(4): 777–95. https://doi.org/10.1086/448181

– 1982b. "Is It Really Important to Think?" Translated and with afterword by T. Keenan. *Philosophy and Social Criticism* 9(1): 29–40. https://doi.org/10.1177/019145378200900102

– 1991. "Govermentality." In *The Foucault Effect: Studies in Governmentality*. Edited by G. Burchell, C. Gordon. and P. Miller. Chicago: University of Chicago Press.

– 2005. *The Hermeneutics of the Subject: Lectures at the College de France, 1981–1982*. New York: Palgrave Macmillan.

– 2007. "What Is Critique?" In *M. Foucault, The Politics of Truth*. Edited by S. Lontringer. Los Angeles: Semiotext(e).

Gandhi, M. 1942. *Democracy: Real and Deceptive*. Compiled by R.K. Prabhu. Ahmedabad: Navajivan.

– 1957. *An Autobiography: The Story of My Experiments with Truth*. Boston: Beacon Press.

– 2008. *The Essential Writings*. Edited by J.M. Brown. Oxford: Oxford University Press.

Garcés, M. 2019. "From the Politicization of Life to the New Politics." In *Spain after the Indignados/15M Movement*. Edited by Ó Pereira-Zazo and S. Torres. New York: Palgrave Macmillan.

García Cotarelo, R. 1987. *Resistencia y desobediencia civil*. Madrid: Eudema Universidad.

García Márquez, G. 2014. *One Hundred Years of Solitude* [1967]. London: Penguin.

Geertz, C. 1983. *Local Knowledge: Further Essays in Interpretative Anthropology*. New York: Basic Books.

– 1998. "Deep Hanging Out." *The New York Review of Books* 45(16): 69–72.

Gibson-Graham, J.K. 2006. *A Postcapitalist Politics*. Minneapolis: University of Minnesota Press.

Graeber, D. 2009. *Direct Action: An Ethnography*. Oakland: AK Press.

Gramsci, A. 2005. *Selections from the Prison Notebooks of Antonio Gramsci*. Edited by Q. Hoare and G. Nowell Smith. New York: International.

Gregg, R. 2018. *The Power of Nonviolence*. Edited by James Tully. Cambridge: Cambridge University Press.

Gros, F. 2014. *A Philosophy of Walking*. New York: Verso.

Guareña, J.L., et al. 1999. *Sociabilidad fin de siglo: espacios asociativos en torno a 1898*. Cuenca: Ediciones de la Universidad de Castilla-La Mancha.

Haraway, D. 1988. "Situated Knowledges: The Science Question in Feminism and the Privilege of Partial Perspective." *Feminist Studies* 14(3): 575–99. https://doi.org/10.2307/3178066

Hardt, M., and A. Negri. 2017. *Assembly*. Oxford: Oxford University Press.

Hawken, P. 2007. *Blessed Unrest: How the Largest Movement in the World Came into Being and Why No One Saw It Coming*. New York: Viking Press.

Higley, J., and R. Gunther. 1992. *Elites and Democratic Consolidation in Latin America and Southern Europe*. Cambridge: Cambridge University Press.

Holloway, J. 2018a. "Think Hope, Think Crisis." In *Against Capital in the Twenty-First Century: A Reader of Radical Undercurrents*. Edited by J. Asimakopoulos and R. Gilman-Opalsky. Philadelphia: Temple University Press.

– 2018b. "The Asymmetry of Revolution." In *The Movements of Movements*, pt 2: *Rethinking Our Dance*. Edited by J. Sen. Vol. 5 in OpenWord's Challenging Empires series. Oakland and New Delhi: OpenWord and PM Press.

– 2019. *Change the World without Taking Power: The Meaning of Revolution Today*. London: Pluto Press.

Holquist, M. 2002. *Dialogism: Bakhtin and His World*. New York: Routledge.

Huxley, A. 1941. *Ends and Means: An Enquiry into the Nature of Ideals and into the Methods Employed for Their Realization*. London: Chatto and Windus.

– 1961. *Island*. New York: Harper and Brothers.

Iglesias, P., and A. Jerez. 2005. "El movimiento global y las contracumbres. Una reflexión sobre la visibilidad del conflicto social desde España." *Documentación Social* 152: 77–92.

Iglesias, P., and J.C. Monedero. 2011. *Que no nos representan. El debate sobre el sistema electoral español*. Madrid: Editorial Popular.

Iñiguez, M. 2001. *Esbozo de una enciclopedia histórica del anarquismo español*. Madrid: Fundación de Estudios Libertarios Anselmo Lorenzo.

Isin, E.F. 2002. *Being Political: Genealogies of Citizenship*. Minneapolis: University of Minnesota Press.

Ivison, D. 2019. "Liberty as a Political Value." In *Civic Freedom in an Age of Diversity: The Public Philosophy of James Tully*. Edited by D. Karmis and J. Maclure. Montreal and Kingston: McGill-Queen's University Press,

Jackson, G. 2005. *La República española y la guerra civil*. Barcelona: RBA Coleccionables S.A.

Juris, J. 2005. "Social Forums and their Margins: Networking Logics and the Cultural Politics of Autonomous Space." *ephemera* 5(2): 253–72.

– 2008. “Spaces of Intentionality: Race, Class, and Horizontality at the United States Social Forum.” *Mobilization: An International Journal* 13(4): 353–71. https://doi.org/10.17813/maiq.13.4.232j1557h7658813

Juska, A., and Woolfson, C. 2012. “Policing political protest in Lithuania.” *Crime Law and Social Change* 57: 403–24. https://doi.org/10.1007/s10611-012-9363-4

Karmis, D., and J. Maclure, eds. Forthcoming. *Civic Freedom in an Age of Diversity: The Public Philosophy of James Tully*. Montreal and Kingston: McGill-Queen’s University Press.

Klein, N. 2017. *No Is Not Enough: Resisting Trump’s Shock Politics and Winning the World We Need*. Chicago: Haymarket Books.

Kraus, P., and J. Vergés Gifra, eds. 2017. *The Catalan Process: Sovereignty, Self-Determination and Democracy in the 21st Century*. Barcelona: Institut d’Estudis de l’Autogovern.

Kropotkin, P. 1913. *Anarchist Communism: Its Basis and Principles*. London: Freedom Press.

– 2002. *The Conquest of Bread and Other Writings*. Edited by Marshall Shatz. Cambridge: Cambridge University Press.

– 2006. *Mutual Aid: A Factor of Evolution*. New York: Dover.

Laclau, E. 1996. *Emancipation(s)*. London: Verso.

Laden, A. 2020. “How Democracy Doesn’t End.” In *Cedar Trees Institute Responses to Covid-19*. https://www.cedartreesinstitute.org/how-democracy-doesnt-end.

Lagarde, M. 2000. *Claves feministas para liderazgos entrañables*. Managua: Puntos de Encuentro.

Laubenthal, B. 2005. “La Emergencia de las Protestas de Inmigrantes sin Papeles en España: El caso de la región de Murcia.” In *La Condición Inmigrante: Exploraciones e investigaciones desde la Región de Murcia*. Edited by Andrés Pedreño Cánovas and Manuel Hernández, 159–74. Universidad de Murcia: Aula de Debate.

Leydet, D. (Forthcoming). “Representative Democracy and Democratic Struggles from Below.” In *Civic Freedom in an Age of Diversity: The Public Philosophy of James Tully*. Edited by D. Karmis and J. Maclure. Montreal and Kingston: McGill-Queen’s University Press.

Liarte, R. 1977. *La C.N.T y el federalismo de los pueblos de España*. Barcelona: Producciones Editoriales.

López Petit, S., et al. 2012. *Indignados, la fuerza del anonimato.* Paris: L’Harmattan..

Maguirre, P. 2001. “Uneven Ground: Feminisms and Action Research.” In *Handbook of Action Research: Participative Inquiry and Practice*. Edited by P. Reason and H. Bradbury, 59–69. London: Sage.

Malleson, T. 2014. *After Occupy: Economic Democracy for the 21st Century*. Oxford: Oxford University Press.
Manin, B. 1997. *The Principles of Representative Government*. Cambridge: Cambridge University Press.
Mason, P. 2013. *Why It's Still Kicking Off Everywhere: The New Global Revolutions*. London: Verso.
Mattei, U. 2012. "First Thoughts for a Phenomenology of the Commons." In *The Wealth of the Commons*. Edited by D. Bollier and S. Helfrich. Amherst: Levellers Press.
Meek, D., and L. Simonian. 2017. "Transforming Space and Society? The Political Ecology of Education in the Brazilian Landless Workers' Movement's *Jornada De Agroecologia*." In *Environment and Planning D: Society and Space* 35(3). https://doi.org/10.1177/0263775816667073
Merton, T. 2003. *The New Man*. New York: Bloomsbury.
Michelsen, D. 2019. "Agonistic Democracy and Constitutionalism in the Age of Populism." *European Journal of Political Theory* 21(1): 68–88. https://doi.org/10.1177/1474885119871648
Michonneau, S. 2004. "La política del olvido de la dictadura de Primo de Rivera." *Historia y política. Ideas, procesos y movimientos sociales* 12: 105–32.
Mintz, J.R. 1982. *The Anarchists of Casas Viejas*. Bloomington: Indiana University Press.
Morán, A. 2000. "'Rompamos el silencio': siete días de lucha social." *Éxodo* 52 (January–February): 42–55.
Motta, S. 2011. "Notes towards Prefigurative Epistemologies." In *Social Movements in the Global South: Dispossession, Development, and Resistance*. Edited by S. Motta and A. Nilsen, 178–99. Hampshire: Palgrave Macmillan.
Mouffe, C. 2005. *On the Political*. Abingdon: Routledge.
– 2018. *For a Left Populism*. London: Verso.
Navascués, J. 2000. "Euromarchas 2000. De Colonia a Lisboa y Niza, pasando por Seattle." *Viento sur: Por una izquierda alternativa* 49: 43–6.
Nunes, R. 2005a. "Networks, Open Spaces, Horizontality: Instantiations." *ephemera* 5(2): 297–318.
– 2005b. "Pack of Leaders: Thinking Organization and Spontaneity with Deleuze and Guattari." In *Occupy: A People Yet to Come*. Edited by A. Conio, 98, 105. London: Open Humanities Press.
– 2014. *Organisation of the Organisationless: Collective Action after Networks*. Berlin: Mute Books.
– 2018. "Nothing Is What Democracy Looks Like: Openness, Horizontality, and the Movement of Movements." In *The Movements of Movements*, pt 2: *Rethinking Our Dance*. Edited by Jai Sen, 38–9. Vol. 5 in OpenWord's Challenging Empires series. Oakland and NewDelhi: OpenWord and PM Press.

Ober, J. 2008. "The Original Meaning of 'Democracy' – Capacity to Do Things, Not Majority Rule." *Constellations* 15(1): 3–9. https://doi.org/10.1111/j.1467-8675.2008.00471.x

O'Donnell, G., and P. Schmitter. 1986. *Transition from Authoritarian Rule: Tentative Conclusions about Uncertain Democracies*. Baltimore: Johns Hopkins University Press.

Oikonomakis, L., and J. Roos. 2014. "They Don't Represent Us! The Global Resonance of the Real Democracy Movement from the Indignados to Occupy." In *Spreading Protest: Social Movements in Times of Crisis*. Edited by D. della Porta and A. Mattoni, 117–36. Colchester: ECPR Press.

Orosco, J. 2008. *Cesar Chavez and the Common Sense of Nonviolence.* Albuquerque: University of New Mexico Press.

Orwell, G. 1952. *Homage to Catalonia*. London: Harcourt.

Owen, D. (Forthcoming). "On Exemplarity and Public Philosophy." In *Civic Freedom in an Age of Diversity: The Public Philosophy of James Tully*. Edited by D. Karmis and J. Maclure. Montreal and Kingston: McGill-Queen's University Press.

Pantham, T. 1983. "Thinking with Mahatma Gandhi: Beyond Liberal Democracy." *Political Theory* 11(2): 165–88. https://doi.org/10.1177/0090591783011002002

Parker, J. 2017. *Democracy beyond the Modern State: Practicing Equality*. Abingdon: Routledge.

Pasha, M.K. 2013. "Return to the Source: Gramsci, Culture, and International Relations." In *International Relations Theory: Modern Princes and Naked Emperors*. Edited by Alison J. Ayers, 199–216. London: Palgrave Macmillan.

Pastor, J. 1991. "Movimientos sociales y nuevas demandas políticas: El movimiento por la paz." *Revista de derecho político* 34: 225–35.

Pateman, C. 2004. "Democratizing Citizenship: Some Advantages of a Basic Income." *Politics and Society* 32(1): 89–105. https://doi.org/10.1177/0032329203261100

– 2012. "APSA Presidential Address: Participatory Democracy Revisited." *Perspectives on Politics* 10(1): 7–19. https://doi.org/10.1017/S1537592711004877

Peirats, J. 2006. *Los Anarquistas en la crisis política española (1869–1939)*. Buenos Aires: Libros de Anarres.

Pereira-Zazo, O., and S.L. Torres. 2019. *Spain after the Indignados/15M Movement: Perspectivas críticas desde Europa y Estados Unidos.* Madrid: Traficantes de sueños.

Peruzzotti, E. 2008. "La democracia representativa como política mediada: Repensando los vínculos entre representación y participación." *Debates en Sociología* 33: 3–7.

Petit, S. 2012. "Desbordar las plazas: Una estrategia de objetivos." *Debate Feminista* 46: 86–90. https://doi.org/10.22201/cieg.2594066xe.2012.46.926

Pla, J. 2006. *La segunda República española. Crónicas parlamentarias 1931–1936*. Barcelona: Destino.
Polletta, F. 2004. *Freedom Is an Endless Meeting: Democracy in American Social Movements*. Chicago: University of Chicago Press.
Rebick, J. 2012. *Occupy This*. Toronto: Penguin Canada.
Reguillo, F. 1998. "El capitalismo catalán y Primo de Rivera: en torno a un golpe de Estado." *Hispania* 48(168): 289–308.
Reid, B. 1997. "Foreword." In Ulli Steltzer, *The Spirit of Haida Gwaii: Bill Reid's Masterpiece*. Vancouver: Douglas and McIntyre.
Requejo, F., and M. Sanjaume-Calvet. 2019. "Independence Referendums: Catalonia in Perspective." *Revista de Catalunya* 308: 77–101. doi:0.2436/20.3000.02.44
Rigby, A. 2000. "Amnesty and Amnesia in Spain." *Peace Review* 12(1): 73–9. https://doi.org/10.1080/104026500113845
Rivas, O., P. Gallego, F. Gándara, and K. Álvarez. 2011. *Nosotros, los indignados: Las voces comprometidas del# 15-M*. Barcelona: Destino.
Romanos, E. 2018. "Del 68 al 15M: continuidades y rupturas entre ciclos de protesta." *Arbor* 194(787): a430. https://doi.org/10.3989/arbor.2018.787n1003
Ruiz, D. 1988. *Insurrección defensiva y revolución obrera. El octubre español de 1934*. Barcelona: Labor.
Russell, B. 2004. *Sceptical Essays*. New York: Routledge Classics.
Russell, B. 2015. "Beyond Activism/Academia: Militant Research and the Radical Climate and Climate Justice Movement(s)." *Area* 47(3): 222–9. https://doi.org/10.1111/area.12086
Saward, M. 2009. "A Conversation with Benjamin Barber." *Contemporary Political Theory* 8(3): 317–50. http://dx.doi.org/10.1057/cpt.2009.1
Schiffrin, A. 2012. *From Cairo to Wall Street: Voices from the Global Spring*. New York: New Press.
Schumpeter, J. 2003. *Capitalism, Socialism, and Democracy*. New York: Routledge.
Sharp, G. 2005. *Waging Nonviolent Struggle*. Boston: Porter Sargent.
Shiffman, R., et al. 2012. *Beyond Zuccotti Park: Freedom of Assembly and the Occupation of Public Space*. New York: NYU Press.
Shiva, V. 2005. *Earth Democracy: Justice, Sustainability and Peace*. Cambridge, MA: South End Press.
Sitrin, M. 2006. *Horizontalism: Voices of Popular Power in Argentina*. Chico: AK Press.
– 2007. "Horizontalidad: Where Everyone Leads." *Yes! Magazine*, https://www.yesmagazine.org/issue/latin-america/2007/05/12/horizontalidad-where-everyone-leads.

– 2018. "Horizontalism and Territory: From Argentina and Occupy to Nuit Debout and Beyond." In *Against Capital in the Twenty-First Century: A Reader of Radical Undercurrents*. Edited by J. Asimakopoulos and R. Gilman-Opalsky. Philadelphia: Temple University Press.

Smith, A. 2007. "The Catalan Counter-Revolutionary Coalition and the Primo de Rivera Coup, 1917–23." *European History Quarterly* 37(1): 7–34. https://doi.org/10.1177/0265691407071800

Soríano Díaz, R.L. 2000. "Insumisión y desmilitarización." *Derechos y libertades: Revista del Instituto Bartolomé de las Casas* 8: 519–40.

Sourice, B. 2017. *La démocratie des places: Des Indignados à Nuit debout, vers un nouvel horizon politique*. Paris: ECLM.

Sousa Santos, B. 2006. *The Rise of the Global Left: The World Social Forum and Beyond*. London: Zed Books.

Suárez Navaz, L. 2007. *Las luchas de los sin papeles y la extension de la ciudadanía. Perspectivas críticas desde Europa y Estados Unidos*. Madrid: Traficantes de sueños.

Taibo, C., ed. 2011. *La rebelión de los indignados: Movimiento 15M: Democracia Real ¡Ya!* Madrid: Editorial Popular.

Tamames, R. 1974. *Historia de España Alfaguara VII. La República. La Era de Franco.* Madrid: Alianza Editorial.

Taylor, C. (Forthcoming). "Some Crises of Democracy." In *Civic Freedom in an Age of Diversity: The Public Philosophy of James Tully*. Edited by D. Karmis and J. Maclure. Montreal and Kingston: McGill-Queen's University Press.

Temelini, M. 2015. *Wittgenstein and the Study of Politics*. Toronto: University of Toronto Press.

– 2017. "Learning Politics by Means of Examples." In *A Companion to Wittgenstein on Education: Pedagogical Investigations*. Edited by M.A. Peters and J. Stickney, 287–304. Singapore: Springer.

Thomas, H. 1976. *La Guerra Civil Española*, Barcelona: Editorial Grijalbo.

Toret Medina, J., ed. 2015. *Tecnopolítica y 15M: la potencia de las multitudes conectadas: un estudio sobre la gestación y explosión del 15M*. Barcelona: Editorial UOC.

Tully, J. 1995. *Strange Multiplicity: Constitutionalism in an Age of Diversity*. Cambridge: Cambridge University Press.

– 2008a. *Public Philosophy in a New Key*, vol. 1: *Democracy and Civic Freedom*. Cambridge: Cambridge University Press.

– 2008b. *Public Philosophy in a New Key* , vol. 2: *Imperialism and Civic Freedom*. Cambridge: Cambridge University Press. https://doi.org/10.1163/18763375-00403004

– 2012. "Middle Eastern Legal and Governmental Pluralism: A View of the Field from the Demos.' *Middle East Law and Governance* 4: 225–63.

– 2014a. "On Global Citizenship: Reply to Interlocutors." In *On Global Citizenship: James Tully in Dialogue*, 269–328. London: Bloomsbury Academic.

– 2014b. "Responses." In *Freedom and Democracy in an Imperial Context: Dialogues with James Tully*. Edited by R. Nichols and J. Singh. London: Routledge.

– 2014c. "The Crisis of Global Citizenship: Civil and Civic Responses." In *On Global Citizenship: James Tully in Dialogue*, 84–100. London: Bloomsbury Academic.

– 2016. "Deparochializing Political Theory and Beyond: A Dialogue Approach to Comparative Political Thought." *Journal of World Philosophies* 1(1): 51–74.

– 2018. "Reconciliation Here on Earth." In *Resurgence and Reconciliation: Indigenous–Settler Relations and Earth Teachings*. Edited by M. Asch, J. Borrows, and J. Tully, 83–129. Toronto: University of Toronto Press.

– 2019a. "Trust, Mistrust, and Distrust in Diverse Societies." In *Trust and Distrust in Political Theory and Practice: The Case of Diverse Societies*. Edited by F. Rocher. Montreal and Kingston: McGill-Queen's University Press.

– 2019b. "Reciprocal Elucidation." In *Civic Freedom in an Age of Diversity: The Public Philosophy of James Tully*. Edited by D. Karmis and J. Maclure. Montreal and Kingston: McGill-Queen's University Press.

Valenzuela-Fuentes, K. 2019. "Militant Ethnography and Autonomous Politics Latin America." *Qualitative Research* 19(6): 718–34. https://doi.org/10.1177/1468794118787712

Velasco, P. 2011. *No nos representan: el manifiesto de los indignados en 25 propuestas*. Madrid: Temas de Hoy.

Wampler, B. 2018. "Developing Political Strategies across a New Democratic and State Architecture." *Latin American Research Review* 53(4): 708–25. https://doi.org/10.25222/larr.356

Werbner, P. 2014. *Political Aesthetics of Global Protest: The Arab Spring and Beyond*. Edinburgh: Edinburgh University Press.

Wiener, A. 2014. *A Theory of Contestation*. New York: Springer.

Williams, M.S. 2012. *Democracy's Global Future*. Unpublished manuscript.

Wittgenstein, L. 2001. *Philosophical Investigations*. Oxford: Blackwell.

Wolin, S. 1993. "Democracy: Electoral and Athenian." *PS: Political Science and Politics* 26(3): 475–7. https://doi.org/10.2307/419985

– 1994. "Fugitive Democracy." *Constellations* 1: 11–25. https://doi.org/10.1111/j.1467-8675.1994.tb00002.x

Zazo Ó., and S. Torres, eds. *Spain after the Indignados/15M Movement*. New York: Palgrave Macmillan.

Zibechi, R. 2005. "Subterranean Echos: Resistance and Politics 'desde el Sótano.'" *Socialism and Democracy* 19(3): 13–39. https://doi.org/10.1080/08854300500257922

Zinn, H. 2005. *A People's History of the United States*. New York: HarperCollins.

Index